FOAL

ALSO BY ANDREW ROSS

Under Conditions Not of Our Choosing

Stone Men: The Palestinians Who Built Israel

Creditocracy and the Case for Debt Refusal

The Exorcist and the Machines

Bird on Fire: Lessons from the World's Least Sustainable City

Nice Work If You Can Get It: Life and Labor in Precarious Times

*Fast Boat to China: Corporate Flight and the
Consequences of Free Trade—Lessons from Shanghai*

Low Pay, High Profile: The Global Push for Fair Labor

No-Collar: The Humane Workplace and Its Hidden Costs

*The Celebration Chronicles: Life, Liberty, and the
Pursuit of Property Value in Disney's New Town*

Real Love: In Pursuit of Cultural Justice

The Chicago Gangster Theory of Life: Nature's Debt to Society

Strange Weather: Culture, Science, and Technology in the Age of Limits

No Respect: Intellectuals and Popular Culture

The Failure of Modernism: Symptoms of American Poetry

SUNBELT BLUES

SUNBELT BLUES

The Failure of American Housing

ANDREW ROSS

METROPOLITAN BOOKS

HENRY HOLT AND COMPANY   NEW YORK

Metropolitan Books
Henry Holt and Company
Publishers since 1866
120 Broadway
New York, New York 10271
www.henryholt.com

Metropolitan Books® and ▥® are registered trademarks of
Macmillan Publishing Group, LLC.

Library of Congress Cataloging-in-Publication Data

Names: Ross, Andrew, 1956– author.
Title: Sunbelt blues : the failure of American housing / Andrew Ross.
Description: First edition. | New York : Metropolitan Books, 2021. | Includes
  bibliographical references and index.
Identifiers: LCCN 2021021699 (print) | LCCN 2021021700 (ebook) |
  ISBN 9781250804228 (hardcover) | ISBN 9781250804235 (ebook)
Subjects: LCSH: Housing—Florida—Osceola County. | Working poor—Florida—
  Osceola County. | Low-income housing—Florida—Osceola County. | Real estate
  investment—Florida—Osceola County. | Housing policy—Florida—Osceola County. |
  Osceola County (Fla.)—Economic conditions—21st century. | Osceola County
  (Fla.)—Social conditions—21st century.
Classification: LCC HD7303.F6 R67 2021 (print) | LCC HD7303.F6 (ebook) |
  DDC 363.5/10975925—dc23
LC record available at https://lccn.loc.gov/2021021699
LC ebook record available at https://lccn.loc.gov/2021021700

Our books may be purchased in bulk for promotional, educational, or business use. Please contact
your local bookseller or the Macmillan Corporate and Premium Sales Department at (800) 221-7945,
extension 5442, or by e-mail at MacmillanSpecialMarkets@macmillan.com.

First Edition 2021

Maps by Jeffrey L. Ward
Designed by Kelly S. Too

Printed in the United States of America

1 3 5 7 9 10 8 6 4 2

CONTENTS

AUTHOR'S NOTE

Most of this book is based on interviews I conducted in Central Florida from 2016 through 2020. The interviewees who spoke to me in an official or business capacity are typically referred to by their last names. Most of the others, especially those whom I spent more time with and got to know personally, are referred to by their first names. In some cases, I have changed the names of businesses and people quoted in these pages to protect their identities.

In Florida, the term most often used to refer to people of Latin American descent is "Hispanic," so I have followed that usage in this book. Likewise, while I occasionally speak of people who are "unhoused" or "unsheltered," I mainly use the term "homeless," since that is how most people living on the streets and in the woods (and even many of those living in motels) refer to themselves.

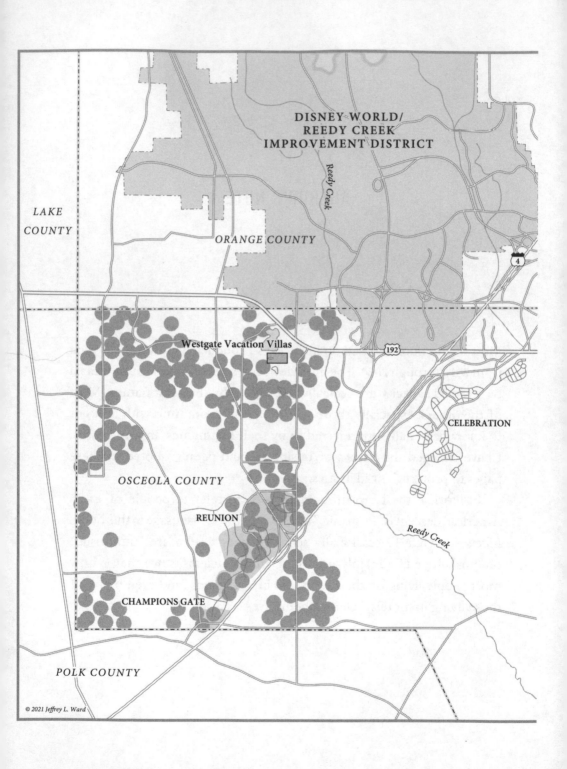

DISNEY WORLD/
REEDY CREEK
IMPROVEMENT DISTRICT

Reedy Creek

LAKE
COUNTY

ORANGE COUNTY

4

192

Westgate Vacation Villas

CELEBRATION

OSCEOLA COUNTY

REUNION

Reedy Creek

CHAMPIONS GATE

POLK COUNTY

© 2021 Jeffrey L. Ward

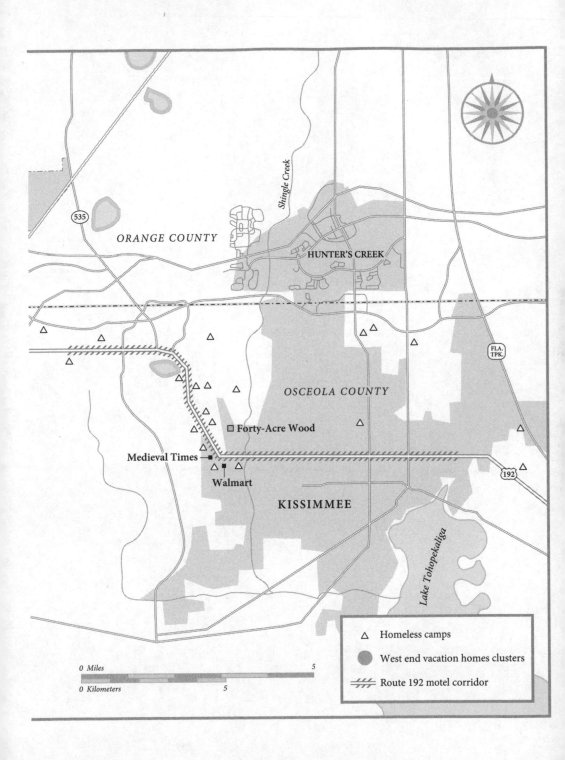

ORANGE COUNTY

Shingle Creek

535

HUNTER'S CREEK

OSCEOLA COUNTY

FLA.
TPK.

Forty-Acre Wood

Medieval Times

192

Walmart

KISSIMMEE

Lake Tohopekaliga

△   Homeless camps

●   West end vacation homes clusters

⫝⫝⫝   Route 192 motel corridor

0 Miles   5
0 Kilometers   5

SUNBELT BLUES

Introduction

CELEBRATION'S MAIN STREET is tailor-made for a Fourth of July parade. A redbrick road terminating in a dainty lakefront esplanade, lined with colonnaded storefronts topped by white balconies, it is a compact showpiece for small-town America, the perfect stage set for spectacles like this one. Kissimmee, the seat of Osceola County, fifteen miles to the east, has its share of old-town charm, but it cannot compete, and with its rapidly shifting demographic is more likely these days to attract a crowd for its annual Puerto Rican Day parade in September. Indeed, in 2019, I noticed that Kissimmee's mayor, Jose Alvarez, chose to march in Celebration on the Fourth of July—though the decision was no doubt swayed by the prospect of votes for his upcoming bid to be an Osceola County commissioner. The town's military veterans and Daughters of the American Revolution led the parade, but the biggest crowd pleaser was a *Star Wars* float flanked by Stormtroopers—a reminder that Galaxy's Edge, a massive *Star Wars*–themed attraction, was set to open in Disney World in just a few weeks.

Twenty-one years earlier, the Independence Day parade had been my swan song for a year spent in an apartment at the epicenter of this much-scrutinized town in Central Florida. I had come to write a book, *The Celebration Chronicles*, about the trials and tribulations of its pioneer residents.[1] Back then, in Celebration's fledgling years, the parade was more of an improvised affair, and I was cajoled by neighbors into playing the role of George Washington at the head of the procession. They also made me promise to return to Celebration, but only when it had grown up. Like children, new towns surely have the right to mature before their character is judged.

I kept my promise. A quarter century after Disney sculpted this New Urbanist experiment out of Central Florida's scrub and swamp and launched a thousand newspaper articles about the audacity (or folly) of building a planned utopia, I found that Celebration has some new lessons to teach us. But to see why, you had to lift your gaze above street level, to the upper floors of the downtown buildings. There, above the cheering throngs with their starred-and-striped socks and bandannas, were telltale signs of neglect and disrepair: patched and stained walls, rotting columns, bubbling stucco, broken tiles, cracked gutters. Many of the pastel surfaces were covered in layers of grime. And the distress signs on the exterior were nothing compared to the damage on the inside. The condo residents in these buildings have horror stories to tell about the ruination of their units: water intrusion that takes the form of small waterfalls during a storm, blooms of mold growth, vast termite colonies, sagging floors, and wobbly stairways.

In a town where aesthetics reign supreme, these centerpiece buildings had been designed with a deliberately dated, prewar look in mind, but they were meant to appear as if they had been carefully preserved through decades of weathering. Without *real* maintenance, of course, the look failed. Florida's climate can be unforgiving to wooden buildings, especially those faced with stucco, and most homeowners should know that diligent upkeep is required to stave off rot and decay. In this most iconic of places, someone was clearly falling down on the job. If this had been a Disney fairy-tale melodrama, the blight would be the result of a spell cast by some fiendish impostor, while the return of the rightful royal owner would restore health and vitality to all. But who was the culprit here, and what were the prospects for a happy ending?

Unlike almost anywhere else, Celebration's downtown did not grow organically along with the rest of the community. Its tidy retail core, with rental apartments perched on top of the stores (Osceola's first mixed-use arrangement in decades), was hastily erected in the mid-1990s, in advance of the arrival of residents. Disney's deep pockets allowed it to initially subsidize the carefully chosen retailers so that they could flout the standard rules of commercial development and open their businesses to visitors long before the town's population could support any of them. Without doubt, some of the blame for the current grunginess of these buildings is a consequence of that rush job, or what residents used to refer to as "Mickey Mouse construction"—that is, maximum focus on the facade and minimal attention to what lies behind it. And it was no surprise when other, wholly residential sections of the town also saw their share of construction flaws, as builders with undertrained work crews scrambled to meet the ravenous market demand for a Celebration address.

But expedited building with slipshod results is hardly unusual in Florida's real estate landscape, where entire subdivisions often sprout overnight, carved out of cow pasture. Nor is the problem wholly a legacy of Celebration's original construction. It is also the upshot of Disney's reckless 2004 sale of the entire downtown complex to a private equity investor who had no record of managing town centers nor any vested interest in keeping up the high maintenance standards set by the brand-conscious developer. From his Madison Avenue office, a thousand miles away, he followed the Wall Street playbook of squeezing revenue from his new asset by hiking rents, selling off land parcels for condo development, and refinancing his loans in order to drain off equity for his investors. Hardly any of the proceeds went back into the upkeep of the buildings, and the value of the downtown units plummeted.

The full scope of this trauma, and the dogged efforts of a group of downtown condo owners to fight it, became clear during my regular visits over the next few years. But I also quickly learned that housing distress was by no means confined to the upmarket precincts of Celebration. Variants of this affliction had spread all across working-class Osceola County, soon to be pinpointed as the place with the least amount of affordable low-income housing per capita in the entire

United States. And they were equally familiar to tenants and home-owners struggling with housing security throughout the country.

There is no single cause of America's housing crisis, either in Osce-ola or nationally, but the shift to out-of-town ownership is a big factor, and it can take many forms. More and more houses are falling into the hands of Wall Street firms and global investors looking to extract rents, fees, and other income streams from every square foot. The big-gest transfer of this property wealth has occurred in Sunbelt states whose economies are fueled by an unwholesome cocktail of breakneck growth, hands-off regulation, depressed wages, and real estate specu-lation. Adding to the money drain is the boom in short-term renting: Airbnb's "sharing economy" has turned a sizable chunk of the nation's housing stock into ad hoc hotels, while the surging number of vaca-tion rental homes with faraway owners has also claimed its share. Like other regions dependent on tourism, the nation's fifth-largest industry, Central Florida lends itself particularly well to this kind of prospect-ing. With seventy-five million annual visitors opening their wallets to vacation there, the giants of the travel and hospitality sectors are laser focused on funneling dollars out of the local economy of the Orlando-Kissimmee tourism corridor.

In the meantime, their underpaid service employees are hard-pressed to find a stable place to live, and more than a few are teetering on the verge of homelessness—or are technically over the line, accord-ing to some official definitions. Many reside within the attendance zone for Celebration's schools. When I discovered that Celebration High was enrolling the most homeless students of any school in Flor-ida, I decided to follow them past the town's white boundary fences and onto the Route 192 strip that runs the length of the county's devel-oped portions. That stretch would become this book's focal landscape. There, I found the children's families shacked up in dilapidated motel rooms, unable to find apartments priced within their reach.[2] Even before employers cut many of them loose during the pandemic, such households were only a paycheck away from being discharged into the streets and woods to join the ranks of those whom the federal govern-ment officially labels the "literally homeless."

Alongside the underpaid service industry workers, I found other casualties of America's low-road economy: "families in transition" who had lost their homes to foreclosure, disabled and elderly people struggling to subsist on thin government checks, economic fugitives carrying debt burdens from Frostbelt states, climate refugees from the Caribbean, and dealers pushing relief from the pain. Documenting their hardship and their aspirations took me further and further into Osceola's version of the tollbooth life, where rent is only the largest of a multitude of monthly fees—healthcare premiums, tuition and child-care bills, traffic fines, data charges, sales taxes, administrative fees, processing costs, property assessments, and debt service payments—that are extracted from wages hovering around the federal poverty line.

So what I had originally intended as a dutiful check-in on Celebration's progress turned into a much longer and different kind of report on the national housing crisis, as seen through the lens of challenges faced by one of the fastest-growing counties in the United States. How did this corner of the Sunbelt become such a tightly confining economic trap? Why is it so difficult to find a reasonably priced apartment or house in a part of the world where jobs are plentiful ("Disney is always hiring"), and where the promise of cheap and easy living in a frost-free climate attracts scads of new arrivals? More than sixty thousand people move to the region every year. When so many end up without adequate housing, what does that tell us about the warped workings of the real estate market? What can we learn from their downward mobility about the waning of the homeownership ideal that used to anchor the American dream, and the corresponding rise of a "rentership society" that has spread across the nation?[3] And what urgent steps are needed to secure decent housing as a basic guarantee for all, and not just as an object of speculation for the few?

FROM CRISIS TO EMERGENCY

To begin to answer questions like these, we first need to briefly revisit the aftermath of the 2008 housing crash. That calamity occurred because Wall Street cooked up more ways of spinning lucre from financing

homes than from almost any other kind of investment. Predatory lending and the Ponzi-style sale of bad debt were the root cause of the
market collapse in the US, and the outcome was a series of hammer
blows to households and economies all over the world. But in the years
following the crash, another mess unfolded, and once again the wolfish
financialization of housing was front and center.

Even as US government officials were infamously bailing out large
banks, they declined to offer relief to homeowners facing ruin. Instead,
they auctioned off hundreds of thousands of foreclosed homes to Wall
Street's private equity firms.[4] Sunbelt regions—including the metro
areas of Phoenix, Las Vegas, Sacramento, Charlotte, Memphis, and
Atlanta—were selectively targeted for large acquisitions of units, and
much of Central Florida's housing stock was bargain-picked in this way.
After 2008, major banks largely stopped lending to would-be home
buyers, but they eagerly provided capital for private equity firms and
real estate investment trusts (REITs) to assemble bulging portfolios of
homes.[5] By 2019, an estimated $220 billion of housing value had been
transferred from former homeowners to large companies and financial funds.[6] At the same time, the ownership of commercial real estate,
including mixed-use complexes like Celebration's town center, became
increasingly concentrated in the hands of a small group of corporate
giants.

While home prices fell during the Great Recession, rents did not,
and so the new corporate owners rented out their new assets to casualties of the foreclosures and to young adult households shut out of the
real estate market by student debt and the government's austerity policies. As their profits soared, single-family rentals became the fastest-
growing segment of the housing market; by 2018 they accounted for
35 percent of all rented housing units in the United States.[7] Notoriously, Wall Street's single-family rentals tend to be poorly maintained
by graceless managers who are hard-nosed about extracting all kinds
of ancillary fees, ordering evictions, neglecting promised repairs, and
failing to return deposits.[8]

Today, Wall Street's housing assets are often bought unseen by "automated landlords"; they are selected not by humans but by algorithms.

These computer programs don't see tenants as humans either, so the rental rates they set are decoupled from affordability as defined by local wage scales and are tied instead to the companies' national profit models.[9] Tenants who have no alternative but to pay the jacked-up prices are simply vehicles for whisking cash resources out of communities and into offshore investors' accounts or international financial markets where the asset managers play. Nor is there any way of knowing exactly who profits from the properties, since private equity firms and private or non-traded REITs draw on undisclosed investor pools.[10] In addition, as many as three million homes and apartments have been snapped up by anonymous LLCs, LLPs, LPs, and shell companies through loopholes that facilitate money laundering and hide the identity of actual owners.[11]

This ownership shift has led to land and rent inflation both in the US and abroad, closing off access to housing tenure and rights in numerous countries. Globally, the distress has spread into rural areas as well as cities: both have seen a steady rise in homelessness, mass eviction, and displacement, along with heightened cost pressure on those who are still clinging to their homes and landholdings. As early as 2014, McKinsey, the world's premier management consultancy, declared a "global affordable housing crisis."[12] In 2015, Miloon Kothari, the first UN special rapporteur for adequate housing, estimated that "1.6 billion people are considered to be inadequately housed, while one hundred million are homeless and another sixty million have been displaced from their homes."[13] In 2019, two other UN rapporteurs condemned Stephen Schwarzman, CEO of Blackstone, the private equity group with the largest portfolio of rental homes, for pursuing a business model at odds with international human rights law.[14]

By 2016, homeownership rates in the US had dropped to the lowest levels in sixty years—and the decline in Central Florida (from a historical average of 66 percent to 55 percent in the course of a decade)—was among the steepest.[15] The National Association of Realtors worried out loud that the American dream cornerstone of its industry was crumbling. The African American–led National Association of Real Estate Brokers lamented that reduced access to housing equity was

widening, not closing, the racial wealth gap. Largely due to foreclosures from subprime lending, Black homeownership had fallen to levels
last seen *before* the Fair Housing Act of 1968 prohibited all forms of
racial discrimination.[16] The African American ownership rate was now
more than thirty percentage points lower than that of non-Hispanic
whites, a stunning refutation of the policy consensus, shared by Democratic and Republican administrations alike, that greater inclusion in
the private housing market would increase the wealth and security of
minority households.[17]

In the 1980s, the American industrial economy was hollowed out
when manufacturers moved their plants to foreign lands in search
of cheaper labor and to escape environmental regulation. Over the
last decade, a different kind of asset stripper raided the nation's housing inventory, but the outcome has been similar; local resources and
income are being transferred offshore, and minority groups are disproportionately affected. For generations, national moralists preached the
sanctity of the owner-occupied private home as an engine of economic
prosperity, and then repackaged the promise for minorities who had
long been shut out of the deal. But as it comes under renewed assault
from corporate raiders, the formula for building family wealth from
real estate is running out of steam, especially for working-class and
middle-class households. Increasingly, no median-priced home is off-
limits to becoming a rental property, every quarter-acre lot has a distant
investor's dollar value on it, and the proceeds are flowing out of host
communities and into international finance markets.

Between 2010 and 2019, the number of renters in the country grew
twice as fast as the homeowner population.[18] Renters now make up the
majority of residents in most large American cities; in Orlando, just
north of Osceola, two-thirds of residents are renters.[19] Meanwhile, the
overall cost of housing, but especially rents, is eating up an ever-larger
share of most household budgets, rising much faster than incomes.[20] A
2020 study showed that almost half of US renters were cost burdened,
officially defined as spending more than 30 percent of their pretax
income on housing, while almost a quarter were spending more than

50 percent. The worst hit were minority renters: 55 percent of Black and 53 percent of Hispanic renter households were cost burdened, compared to 45 percent of Asian and 43 percent of white households.[21] New private housing supply (constrained by restrictive zoning, anti-density NIMBYists, and developers reluctant to diversify beyond their standard product of single-family homes) could not meet the needs of lower- and middle-income households, not even in the Sunbelt boom-burgs.[22] By the end of the decade, the inability to find housing at tolerable prices was a full-blown national condition, affecting every region and location.

Arguably the most telling figures are provided by the National Low Income Housing Coalition. As its 2020 report shows, there is not a single American county where a worker earning the local minimum wage and working forty hours a week—a standard full-time job—can afford a two-bedroom apartment without becoming cost burdened. Indeed, out of the 3,143 counties in the US, there are only 145 where a full-time minimum-wage worker can afford a one-bedroom apartment.[23] Even in states like Massachusetts, California, and Washington, with minimum wages much higher than the federal rate of $7.25 per hour, rents are still out of reach. In Florida, where the minimum hourly wage is $8.56, a worker would need to labor 114 hours every week to afford a two-bedroom dwelling, or 92 hours a week for a one-bedroom. The pathbreaking Fight for $15 campaign, launched in 2012 by fast-food workers, has won raises for tens of millions of low-income employees nationwide, but $15 an hour still won't make the rent in most parts of the country.

The majority of the nation's 3,143 counties are not urban, of course; they are rural or low-density suburban. Yet in the public mind, the housing crisis is still a distinctly urban phenomenon, a predicament especially of top-tier cities where so many aspire to live. This perception is shaped by countless articles about tech bros, investment bankers, or gentrifying hipsters displacing working people of color from New York and San Francisco neighborhoods, and by images of sprawling homeless encampments on downtown streets in Los Angeles and Seattle.

We know that "the rent is too damn high" for big-city dwellers because the lion's share of media commentary focuses on their plight, typically framed as a story about the runaway cost of living in the superstar metropolises.

But in many ways the crisis is more acute in rural areas and provincial cities and in suburban rings where lower- and middle-class households seek relief from the exorbitant prices in the metro cores but where poverty rates have steadily increased over the last two decades.[24] The map of upstate New York, for example, is peppered with counties where the percentage of cost-burdened households is as high, or almost as high, as in the better-off precincts of the metro region. And in those places, urban services and public resources are much thinner, getting from A to B is more costly, and jobs paying a living wage are few and far between. Most of their residents are ill-paid workers in retail, hospitals, restaurants, childcare, housecleaning, or construction, not financial or tech employees with stock options. So, too, as inner-city public housing complexes succumb to the bulldozer, and rooming houses and SRO (single-room occupancy) buildings fall prey to gentrification, more and more low-income families are living in hotels, motels, and inns on the urban fringe or beyond it. Motels in particular, whether or not they are designated as "extended stay," have become the default residence for a significant mass of Americans priced out of the rental and homeownership markets.[25] Countless others are doubled up, reliant on the goodwill of relatives or friends with a room or sofa to spare, and who may be in need of extra cash to pay their own bills. In the Sunbelt states, where right-to-work laws ensure paltry wages, budget motels are a convenient stopgap for the meager availability of affordable housing.

The COVID-19 pandemic amplified the preexisting conditions of economic stress. Converting the chronic housing crisis into an acute emergency, it threatened a massive wave of foreclosures and evictions, routinely anticipated in the media as a "tsunami." To stem the tide, federal and local governments issued temporary bans on evictions, but even before these ran out, the ranks of unhoused began to swell. In September 2020, a large Orlando homeless shelter reported that more than 40 percent of those who had sought admittance over the previous two months were experiencing homelessness for the first time.[26] The federal moratoriums lasted longer but did not bring foreclosures and evictions to a halt because they only covered mortgage holders with government-backed loans or renters who could prove hardship directly caused by COVID-19.[27] By January 2021, the nation's delinquent renters—as many as ten million people—owed a whopping $57 billion in back rent, utilities, and late fees.[28]

As small landlords faced ruin, market predators circled overhead, waiting to swoop, for the second time in a decade. By June 2020, private equity groups had amassed almost $1.4 trillion of disposable capital in expectation of another fire sale of real estate. They referred to it as "dry powder."[29] As the CEO of Starwood, one of the leading firms, reminded his shareholders: "It's really ugly . . . but obviously when it's really ugly, it's a good time to invest."[30] Enriched for a decade by tax cuts, loopholes, and exemptions, and further fattened by giveaways embedded in the federal stimulus program, the large corporate landlords and institutional investors were itching to once again profit from the distress of others. This time, not just owner-occupied houses but also buildings owned and managed by mom-and-pop landlords were the likely targets. According to PIA Residential, a private equity real estate firm based in Miami, "This eviction moratorium will, unfortunately, create a lot of distressed properties for landlords that cannot pay their mortgages," but "for us, it will be an opportunity to buy more."[31]

ORANGE BLOSSOM BADLANDS

The tri-county region (Orange-Osceola-Seminole) of Central Florida that straddles the I-4 corridor—famous for its role as a key swing constituency in presidential elections—is in one of the deepest holes. By 2019, the nationwide crunch was at its most extreme in the four-thousand-square-mile sprawl of the Sanford-Orlando-Kissimmee metro area. With a combined population of 2.1 million, the region was ranked No. 1 for unaffordable housing that year by the National Low Income Housing Coalition, with only thirteen affordable rental homes for every hundred low-income households.[32] Osceola, the poorest of these three counties, and the eighth-fastest-growing county in the US, was in the worst shape. That year, 57 percent of its households were categorized by United Way as ALICE (asset limited, income constrained, employed)—that is, working families struggling to afford basic necessities. In United Way's 2020 report, reflecting pre-pandemic data, that number had increased to 64 percent.[33] There are many sorry indications of this hardship, but if I had to pick a single example it would be the grim statistic that one out of every hundred homeless children in the United States lives in the tri-county region, most of them growing up in cramped motel rooms.[34]

Geographically, Osceola lies within the original "concentration zone" reserved for the Seminole people by the white settlers' treacherous 1823 Treaty of Moultrie Creek. It is named, like several other counties across the country, in honor of the Seminole chief who led his people's resistance in the 1830s and was heavily romanticized by white Americans after the US Army shamefully captured him while under a flag of truce. By the 1870s, the Seminoles who resisted removal to the territories of modern Oklahoma had been chased down into the Everglades, during the last domestic war east of the Mississippi. Kissimmee was as far south as the railroads came, prompting one commentator to declare that "white civilization ends here," while lands to the south were "in the possession of a cowboy race known as Crackers . . . and a remnant of a race of Seminole Indians who hunt, fish, and raise crops in the Everglades."[35]

A century later, with the arrival of Disney World just across the county line, Osceola began its growth spurt and has barely let up since then. The county's population—only 20,000 in 1960, before the coming of Disney—now stands at 375,000. It has tripled since 1990, and is expected to triple again by 2060, accounting for the largest share of Central Florida's projected growth. Its spacious cattle ranches, which once earned Kissimmee the moniker of "Cowtown," are still being gobbled up by developers.[36]

The profile of this growth is highly uneven, however. Most of the county's population, a majority of them Hispanic (predominantly Puerto Rican in origin) lives along or just off the semi-urbanized corridor of Route 192. Housing is cheaper here than in neighboring Orange County, where more than half of Osceola's employed residents work. But while the majority live in straitened circumstances, they coexist with Osceola's colonies of affluence, where comfortable lifestyles are taken for granted. These preserves of well-heeled locals and seasonal visitors include communities like Celebration, Reunion, and Harmony, as well as dense clusters of sumptuous vacation homes that skew the housing market toward the demands of out-of-state tourists. Indeed, the county promotes itself to visitors as the "Vacation Home Capital of the World," even as it strains to house the army of cleaners, waiters, maids, short-order cooks, busboys, janitors, drivers, concierges, baggage handlers, trash haulers, landscapers, laundresses, and maintenance workers who attend to their every need.

After 2015, Central Florida regained its pre-crash status as one of the hottest real estate markets, with investor home flipping back in fashion. In 2018, it was ranked No. 2 in home value growth among all US metro areas, and it led the major regional markets in rising rents.[37] By 2020, just before the pandemic, the region's inventory of houses for sale hit a record low.[38] A year later, supply had tightened even more, and buyers with cash were outbidding all others.[39] The mismatch between its rising home prices and languishing household earnings has grown ever more pronounced, with the gap as wide as anywhere in the US. In fact, Central Florida has the lowest median wage of any major metro region in the nation. The majority of jobs in the region pay less than $30,000 a year, and a quarter of them pay less than $20,000. Osceola hosts by far the largest share of these struggling wage earners.[40]

When COVID-19 struck, Central Florida's tourist-heavy economy was especially vulnerable, and unemployment cut a deep swath through the region's workforce. The tourism industry accounted for 50 percent of all jobs lost in Florida during the shutdown, and almost half of those losses were concentrated in the region. By June, Osceola's jobless rate all but topped the nation's counties, at one point hitting 37 percent, more than three times the national average. A year after the onset of the pandemic, when most businesses had reopened, it was still Florida's worst. Even with the prospect of a steady improvement, much of the

tourism workforce will not see their livelihoods return for the foreseeable future.

In the 2008 housing crash, one out of every fifteen Central Floridians
lost their homes to foreclosure, and many of them never really recovered. The plight of residents who fell into that crater, and who appear
in these pages, has only intensified as they face down another, potentially even deeper recession. To dig them out, and millions like them,
we will have to rethink the provision of housing both here and in the
nation at large. We will have to cast off the ruinous habit of seeing
housing almost exclusively as real estate—a tradable commodity, governed by market supply and demand—and treat it instead as a basic
need and human right. This shift in mentality is long overdue. The pandemic has made it all the more urgent.

SIX SIDES OF THE DIE

Sunbelt Blues is a report from the front line. It documents a journey I
took over the course of several years along different sections of Route
192, Osceola County's main drag. Each stop revealed a distinct and different facet of the housing crisis. To write this book, I talked to a wide
variety of people, including motel dwellers and the "literally homeless," elected officials, business owners and corporate executives, union
leaders and community activists, planners and environmentalists, realtors, builders and property managers, and a variety of tourist industry workers. These conversations gave me many angles from which to
view Osceola's housing problems.

To get a firsthand look at the crisis, I moved into the tumbledown
motels sprinkled all along the 192 corridor, where "extended stay"
can turn into a more permanent address. I spent time in the homeless
camps that are scattered throughout the woods just behind the strip,
loosely organized according to their residents' substances of choice:
beer, meth, or heroin. I took testimony from employees of Disney
World (whose land empire stretches down to Route 192) about their
campaign for a living wage that would enable them to find adequate

housing and stay afloat during the mass pandemic layoffs. I went back to Celebration, where I once lived, and found residents enmeshed in a nasty legal fight with the absentee investor who had literally bought the town center. I paid visits with cleaning crews and property managers to the palatial vacation rental homes at the booming western end of Osceola. And I ventured to the undeveloped eastern end of 192, where a conflict between environmentalists, county commissioners, and the Mormon Church, the state's largest landowner, will determine the fate of a plan to build a vast new city for the well-to-do while ignoring the region's current housing needs.

Each of these six case studies on the 192 corridor highlights a sharp challenge facing both Osceola and many other counties located outside America's overheated metro cores. Taken together, they graphically illustrate the state of the nonurban housing crisis as we endure another deep recession and stare down the barrel of catastrophic climate change. In particular, the plight of 192's residents helps us understand why the supply and delivery of affordable homes can no longer be left in the hands of private developers.

No two areas are quite alike, of course; one of the Osceola County planners I interviewed insisted that "there's nowhere else like us, so we do not really look at other places, not even other jurisdictions in our region." There are few localities, for example, that have an employer like Disney World on their doorstep. Nonetheless, the county's fringe location, its swelling population, and its dependence on out-of-town finance makes it one of the best places to see why the cost of housing is too high for too many of us. Osceola is one of the most severely challenged places, to be sure, but its blend of rock-bottom wages, developer-friendly officials, low-tax policies, and an investor-driven real estate market is an all too familiar mix in the boom-to-bust Sunbelt. Anyone looking to meet America's dire housing needs should take a hard look at the woeful results of that formula in those parts of the country that were trumpeted, from the 1970s onward, as a new frontier of opportunity and growth.

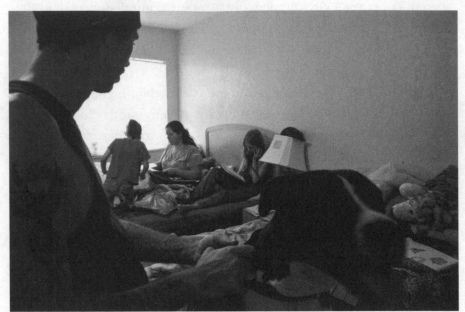

1

A Motel Is Not a Home

MELISSA WARREN IS carefully folding clothes on a bed in the motel room occupied by her family and their dog. One of two double beds in the 320-square-foot space, it is the only surface not heaped high with piles of packaged food and sundry belongings. As we talk, Brianna, one of her twin girls, skips into the room from the improvised school bus stop on the busy strip outside the motel. Reflecting on her family's plight, Melissa sums up their descent into motel living: "We went from the frying pan into the fire, and we're still in it."

Ten years before, just as their children were learning to walk, Melissa and her husband, Randy, secured a mortgage on a freshly built ranch home in Poinciana. Originally developed as a retirement community forty miles south of Orlando, the town got caught up in the frenzy of the mid-2000s housing boom. "We were suckered in by the teaser rate on the loan." She smiles wanly as she explains. "Everyone else had one, so we didn't worry too much about it." But after two years, the interest rate shot up, well beyond their reach. Soon, they were among the casualties of the foreclosure storm that barreled through the region in 2010. "It felt real good to be in our own place, a home sweet home and all of that, but it didn't last long, and then the bank just threw us out on the street."

After eighteen months doubling up with friends who owned a farm nearby, the Warrens moved into a rundown motel west of Kissimmee where I occasionally stayed. "It's been almost four years now," Melissa says, "and I can't see a way out of here. I don't want to think of us as homeless, but I suppose we are." She works part-time at Disney World, as do many of her motel-dwelling neighbors on the Route 192 corridor. But that does not provide much beyond the sprinkling of pixie dust bestowed by the name. "I can get a few shifts a week at the Animal Kingdom, but they make sure I don't get enough to qualify for benefits," she reports. "Disney is a company that gives its workers advice about how to apply for food stamps, so that has to tell you something." Unlike many of her fellow workers, Melissa is unsentimental about her employer. She is proud she is not one of "those Disney junkies," as she puts it, who stretch out a childhood fantasy by working in the theme parks. "They will do almost anything to get a job there, and I know some of them who end up sleeping in vans in the parking lots."

Melissa and her husband, a roofer who finds day labor whenever he can, are in a bind that is all too familiar to America's swelling population of motel dwellers. "We just can't raise the cash to cover first and last month's rent on an apartment, but that's not enough anyway," she explains. "Because obviously we have bad credit, so we're also talking about an additional two or three months' security." In spite of the odds stacked against them, "Randy is the optimist in this household," Melissa chuckles. "He says that construction is picking up." He was right about that: it was early 2017, and Sunbelt subdivisions were starting to sprout again. But even though rents and home prices were steadily rising, wages remained stagnant. And when I visited the motel again a month later, the Warrens were gone. "One of them got badly sick," reported the motel manager. A neighbor told me they had gone back to their friends' farm. Some folks manage to move up when they leave the motels; others, like the Warrens, are not so lucky. Their cramped room, with a hot plate and a mini-fridge for a kitchen, may have been the best hope for these former homeowners.

FROM TRAVELER'S RESPITE TO LAST RESORT

Motels (and motor courts, their predecessors) have been around for more than a hundred years, ever since they first sprouted along two-lane roads and numbered highways built to serve travelers at the wheel of the earliest automobiles. In the 1910s, the nation's first long-distance tourist routes were planned and created: the Lincoln Highway, running from New York City to San Francisco; the National Old Trails Road, from Baltimore to Los Angeles, incorporating Route 66; the Dixie Overland Highway, from Savannah to San Diego; Route 101 on the West Coast, running from northern Washington state down to Los Angeles; Route 1 on the East Coast, running all the way from Maine to Key West; the CanAm Highway, from El Paso to Saskatchewan; and the Dixie Highways, which ran along eastern and western routes from Chicago to Miami. Until the 1970s, when many of these storied roads were bypassed by interstate highways, budget motels with exterior corridors were the primary accommodations for motorists passing through or seeking overnight lodgings near tourist destinations. In the last few decades, most of those properties not physically stranded by freeways have been stylistically superseded by interior-corridor budget chain hotels.

Aside from handling the travel business, motels have always offered a housing option for people priced out of the market, in transition between domiciles and livelihoods, or simply down on their luck. But with the unforgiving increase in residential rents and the acute shortage of affordable housing units, they have become the default housing choice for a multitude of low-income households. Outside almost every American town or city connected by the old pre-interstate routes, and in the suburban peripheries around the newer edge cities, you can now find a wide range of occupants living indefinitely in motels that were not built for long stays. They are shacked up outside tourist destinations like Branson and Reno, in the inner-ring suburbs of Denver and Houston, in rural areas like Northeast Oregon and the Appalachian counties of western Kentucky, on the fringes of Kansas City and depressed

towns of upstate New York, and all across Southern California. The elim-
ination of budget urban accommodations—boarding and rooming
houses, welfare hotels, and SRO housing—and the steady increases in city
rents have pushed more and more low-income people out of the metro
cores and into sprawling suburbs, where poverty levels have risen dramatically since 2008. For some time now, poor people in these suburban
areas have outnumbered those living in cities. And that is also where the
motels are: according to the American Hotel and Lodging Association, 30
percent of hotels and motels are in suburban locations, and another 31
percent are on or near highways, usually at route intersections.

The new "extended-stay" service apartment is a growing sub-
market of the hotel industry, and much of the motel inventory that
survived the twentieth century is now the primary affordable housing option for families with limited income.[1] For those who live for
prolonged periods in these often rundown units—at risk from infestation, mold, harassment, and assaults—the motels are a last resort,
a stopgap, a place of refuge, or a trap.[2] But they also have had to
become something like homes, and their swelling occupancy rates
are an indictment of American housing policies that have failed to
provide the real thing.

One of the country's largest single concentrations of motel dwellers lies in the fifteen-mile section of Route 192 running from Kissimmee toward Four Corners, where Osceola meets three other counties
(Lake, Polk, and Orange). Aside from its motels and other low-rent
lodgings, this drag is jam-packed with kitschy attractions, novelty
architecture, mini-malls, gimcrack gift outlets, evangelical churches,
flea markets, factory outlets, chain restaurants, hookah lounges, tattoo
parlors, pawn shops, and ubiquitous dollar stores. Almost everything
on this unlovely strip owes its existence to Walt Disney's decision in the
1960s to locate his second theme park in an area where Florida's interstate highway and its turnpike intersect. As a result, the formerly ho-
hum Route 192 became the golden approach road to Disney World's
main gate for anyone traveling from the south or east. To handle the
traffic, it expanded into a four-to-six-lane divided highway. For much

of its length, it is officially named the Irlo Bronson Memorial Highway, after the county's most powerful cattle rancher and politician; its
eastern reach, leading to the Atlantic Coast, is also known as the Space
Coast Parkway. But as in most parts of the country, this lively thoroughfare is known to everyone by just its number.

Other than three resorts (Fort Wilderness, Polynesian, and Contem-
porary) that opened along with the Magic Kingdom in 1971, there were
no hotels in the early years on the Disney property, so the opportunity
to capture the lodgings market on the theme park's doorstep was wide
open. Immigrants and starter entrepreneurs flocked to Route 192 to
throw up motels on stretches of firm ground amid the swampy terrain.
Unprepared for the influx, Osceola County officials declined to build sewage lines along the route, and the largest setups that could be operated
off a well and septic tank were forty-room motels. With few amenities
beyond a dinky swimming pool, an ice machine, and a candy dispenser,
they were designed for get-up-and-go visitors. A multitude of small businesses set up shop on the strip to waylay motorists bound for Disney
World; the only principle behind the haphazard growth of garish signage
and wacky facades was grabbing attention by any means necessary.[3]

The original Disneyland, in Anaheim, California, was located on
a much smaller 250-acre plot and was quickly surrounded by two-bit
lodgings that were at odds with the company's hands-on aesthetic. With
his 30,000-acre Central Florida land grab, Walt Disney ensured there
was plenty of space to insulate Disney World from unsightly development outside its gates, and over time those ample acres started filling up
with the company's own vacation properties. In the 1990s, the company
embarked on a hotel-building spree, aiming to capture every last dollar
spent by its guests. As the profile of a Disney World vacation moved
into the upscale, multiday market, visitors were persuaded to expect
themed "experiences" from their living quarters, and so more and more
of them booked luxury on-site resorts. The motel occupancy rates on
the 192 corridor suffered as a result, and took another hit when Disney's
Good Neighbor hotel partnership program ensnared middle-market
franchises outside the park's boundaries. Finally, not content with the

middle and the top, the company took a big bite out of the "value category" market by building its own budget-priced All-Star Resorts.

Meanwhile, most motel owners on Route 192 had done nothing over the decades to upgrade their no-frills properties and had little to offer twenty-first-century tourists beyond a roof over their heads for forty or fifty dollars a night. During the Great Recession, even budget tourism was slack, so the owners turned to weekly and monthly rentals to fill their rooms. There was no shortage of takers: families like the Warrens, unable to fully recover from the foreclosure trauma; tourism employees scrambling to make ends meet on a poverty wage; hustlers working the informal economy; and homeless people with just enough income from government checks and panhandling to move themselves off the street.

THE SANDPIPER

The Sandpiper Inn offers cheap nightly rates, and not much else. Like some other budget motels on 192, it charges guests a small "resort fee" on top of their bill, but no one would mistake the Sandpiper for a resort. Set back a little from the road, bordering a tropical swamp, it has a tranquil air, but no amenities or advantages over any neighboring properties. Built in the 1980s with a well and septic system, it was eventually hooked up to the county's sewage lines, so it has the capacity to expand. But that is not in the cards anytime soon.

I stayed in a number of "fleabag" motels during my three years of reporting for this book, but the Sandpiper became my preferred base, and I got to know many of the regulars. Unlike them, I had no need to feel at home there, but I developed a loyalty to the place in spite of some off-putting incidents: at least one bout of bedbugs, significant roach traffic, a shooting in the room above, and many overheated altercations in the corridors and stairwells. The owners, an East Asian family who relocated from Brooklyn in 2015, were curious about my book, and we regularly exchanged insights and nuggets of information about the 192 business environment. Although I usually had to stay on the "vanilla" side of the hotel, where the nightly visitors are booked, the warm sociality of the other side, where the weeklies lived and hung out in the exterior corridors, became my workplace.

I did not expect to find much of a connection between the Sandpiper and my previous stint in Osceola County, when I was writing *The Celebration Chronicles*. But halfway through my time at the motel, I run into a couple who resided in Celebration at the same time I had been there. In 1998, Linda and Barney Hart briefly rented a downtown unit in Celebration before buying a garden apartment, the most affordable housing model in town. "Our street was considered ghetto by Celebration standards," Linda jokes to me. Still, she says, the apartment sold in 2007 for $390,000, "right before the economy went to hell in a handbasket." She had worked as a greeter in a builder's model home, and her husband owned and operated a landscaping company, but the housing crash decimated both livelihoods. "In a recession, the first people to get cut are the pool guys and the lawn guys," she explains. "We were left holding a huge bag of debt from another foreclosed property, in Poinciana, so we put everything in the storage locker, and our life has been a lot different since then." After a prolonged spell in Barney's hometown in the Indiana rust belt—where, she says, "everyone was on meth or opioids"—they were now back in Osceola, only ten miles but a universe away from the lawns they used to manicure in Celebration and the upscale community of Hunter's Creek.

Before checking into the Sandpiper, Linda, Barney, and their two children lived in the parking lot of a Walmart superstore on the 192 corridor. "Definitely the lowest point of my life," recalls their son, Brett. "Literally it would be burning hot, and, well, I'm sure you can imagine sleeping in a car with four people and a dog; you're batting heads all the time because you're all bunched up." Linda says she lost her birth certificate and currently lacks ID, so only Barney is working, earning $8.40 an hour as a day laborer. After they pay the Sandpiper's $280 weekly room rent, the cost of food, gas, and cigarettes easily consumes what is left over. Linda confesses how humbling it has been to nosedive from the gilded heights of Celebration ("I used to be so entitled") to "living hand to mouth on a patch of the county where my dog kicks up syringes all the time." At one time, she tells me, she was "making five hundred dollars a night working at Tony's Town Square Restaurant in Disney World, and now I would be picking up cigarette butts on the 192 sidewalk if I could for a wage." Still, she is upbeat: "I don't think we're stuck like a lot of people are stuck. We're just stuck for a minute, but it feels longer than a minute when you're stuck in it. We'll get back there again. It's just a matter of time." But when I next return to the Sandpiper, the neighbors report that Barney lost his job, and the Harts are again on the street somewhere.

For families like the Harts and the Warrens, a motel stay is like a game of chutes and ladders—it can be a step up or a slide down. At another inn, I met a family sideswiped by calamity: evacuated from Puerto Rico in the wake of Hurricane Maria, Isabel and Juan Romero were about to lose the FEMA vouchers that paid their rent for several months. Juan had found no stable income, and Isabel was working part-time in a laundry facility at another hotel. "Most of those who came from the island had relatives here they could live with," she tells me. "But we have no family, our home in Puerto Rico is destroyed, and we have nothing to go forward with our lives." Their fortunes would turn around in the following months, though. Thanks to assistance from the Hispanic Federation and a local church, the Romeros were able to put together the necessary funds—first and last month's rent plus a security deposit—required to move from the motel into an apartment complex in North Kissimmee.

The Romeros' next-door neighbors at the motel were in more or less the same boat. Brenda and Mike Mackie had been living there with their two children for almost three years. The Mackies both had casual work—Brenda in housekeeping, Mike in construction as a day laborer— but they made barely enough to cover the bills. "We can stay in place, but getting out of here and into an apartment is just not possible," Brenda explains. "We need a break, and not necessarily a big one." That break would come in 2018 when the Florida housing boom picked up steam, and Mike got better-paying work. Brenda found a two-bedroom apartment for them twenty miles to the south, in cheaper Polk County, and they were able to move up and out as well.

However, just as many motel dwellers are on their way down, on a path to the street, shelters, or tents in the woods. In the fall of 2020, I run into Melissa Warren in the parking lot of the Walmart on Route 192. It has been almost three years since our conversation in the motel, but she recognizes me. Remembering what I had been told about an illness in the family, I inquire after her husband's health. "Randy moved in with his brother in Jacksonville," she replies, "so we're on our own right now, just the girls and me. . . . For a while we were bled dry by his hospital bills," she adds, "and then we thought we had it together again, he had some work, and we had an apartment lined up in Kissimmee, but this virus has just knocked us out—no job, no apartment, no nothing right now, and so we can't even afford to get back into a motel." I ask whether they have anywhere to live. Melissa raises her hands, palms up and out, and screws up her face. "I'd have to say not really," she responds but declines to say more. However, she is pushing a supermarket cart with three five-gallon jugs of water—a telltale sign of the unhoused—and is headed out around the back of the superstore, where I know there are homeless encampments in the woods.

HOMELESS OR NOT?

The Sandpiper Inn has its share of occupants moving in the same direction. "I've been homeless before, and I'm not afraid to do it again," Ramon Perez, a fifty-year-old Cuban neighbor at the Sandpiper, tells me when he is served with an eviction notice after four months of residence. "This was supposed to be my best shot, and it hasn't gone the way I hoped." Ramon had found work on the strip as a dishwasher, but his heroin habit ate up his paycheck, and he fell behind on rent once too often. Some months later, when I'm visiting one of the homeless camps in the woods not far from the Sandpiper, I would be told he had been there until recently but was now in jail. Notably, like many of the extended-stay guests, he did not regard himself as a homeless person while he was at the Sandpiper. "I'm off the street, and you can't see me in here," he explained, as if his lack of public visibility gave him immunity from the stigma.

Ramon's comment was not entirely off the mark. The official government definitions of homelessness are complex and sometimes contradictory. The landmark McKinney-Vento Homeless Assistance Act of 1987 defined a homeless person as someone who "lacks a fixed, regular and adequate nighttime residence." The US Department of Housing and Urban Development (HUD) thus excluded from its services people who were doubled up in the homes of friends or family in addition to those living in motels. When the legislation was reauthorized in 2009, the category of homeless was extended to include persons who "will imminently lose their primary nighttime residence"—defined as those who only have housing for the next fourteen days or less, no subsequent place to go, and no resources to obtain permanent housing. If a government agency or a charity pays for a family's motel room, then that family also meets the HUD definition of homeless. But if the family pays for the room with their own income and has enough money to last more than two weeks, then it is not homeless as far as HUD is concerned.

When it comes to children, on the other hand, the classification is more expansive. Children who are living in motels or doubled up in others' housing *are* considered homeless under federal law, even though their parents may not be categorized as homeless by HUD. School districts often refer to these households as "families in transition." Osceola County has a large "families in transition" program, for example, which provides clothing, school supplies, some extra tutoring, and sixty-four school bus stops along the Route 192 motel corridor. Similar efforts can be found on commercial strips around the nation.

The plight of children growing up in motels has inspired a new wave of public awareness of homelessness, while the image of the unhoused has shifted away from the recognizable stereotype of the single male vagrant. Many of the "new homeless" look like Melissa Warren and her children—white middle-class families fallen on hard times after losing their jobs and houses.[4] Although this demographic adjustment has been occurring for some time, the Great Recession brought it into the open. And with Disney World next door, Osceola County's heavy concentration of motel families was almost guaranteed to attract media coverage. In 2011, *60 Minutes* aired a segment focusing on the plight of the Route 192 motel children, and local TV outlets further down the media food chain followed with their own stories.[5] By 2017, the population of Osceola County school-age children identified as homeless (most of them living in motels) had grown to 3,500, and that was before Hurricane Maria swelled those numbers.[6]

Of course, counting the homeless in any locality or in the nation at large is an imprecise undertaking. In 2019, HUD's much-criticized national point-in-time count found 567,715 people experiencing homelessness on a single January night.[7] But that number, as before, excludes people living in motels or doubled up with friends or relatives, so homeless advocates regard this "snapshot" as a wildly inaccurate undercount. The most reliable estimates of the motel-dwelling population come from school district surveys that collect self-reported data from enrolled students. Federal data shows that during the 2017–18 school year, more than 1.5 million kids in public schools experienced homelessness. In the three-year period from 2015 to 2018, sixteen states recorded increases of 10 percent or more in their homeless student population, and eight (including Florida, Connecticut, Pennsylvania, and Montana) saw increases of 20 percent or more; in Texas, the number of homeless students doubled in those three years alone. Over that same three-year period, the number of students living in motels jumped by 24 percent, offering a rough indication of the overall increase in the population of motel dwellers.[8]

Whatever the official definitions, self-perception among motel dwellers varies widely. Many of the motel residents I interviewed emphatically set themselves apart from those they regarded as *truly* homeless. "I pay my rent, I have a roof over my head, and I have a door I can close for privacy," declares Clancy Becker, a restaurant server who has been living for eighteen months with her ten-year-old daughter in one of the shabbier properties on the back stretch of 192. "I'm not pushing my stuff around in a supermarket cart," she adds, pointing to a woman who was doing just that, trudging with steady purpose across the parking lot. Previously, Clancy had spent a few weeks in Help

Now, a Kissimmee shelter for victims of domestic abuse. In the motel, although there are often fights among her drug-dealing neighbors, the environment is less threatening to her than the kind of violence she has fled. "I needed help then but not now," she tells me.

In a neighboring motel with a little more polish, Brianna Bond and her tween daughter are playing outside with their dog. "A motel is where you're supposed to be on vacation," she notes. "This is not a normal place to live, especially to raise a kid." Brianna's chief goal is to try to provide "a normal childhood" for her daughter: "I'm terrified that she would think of herself as homeless, and I don't want to feel judged as if I myself am homeless, so that's why we don't go to food pantries or clothes closets for the homeless, and also because that would take away from people who really need it." Brianna cobbles together her $280 weekly rent by working part-time in a hotel and as a substitute teacher, she says, because she is "too committed" to her daughter to work full-time. Three years before, she had juggled four jobs to try to stay in her Orlando apartment but ended up hospitalized for exhaustion, and her husband—"a very unsuitable man, when I think back on him"—ended up in prison. Her goal now is to negotiate a place where her daughter could have her own bedroom. "I'm not better than any others who live here, or over there," she muses, gesturing toward Clancy's motel, "but I keep apart from them out of self-respect."

Other motel dwellers openly embrace a homeless identity. Visiting a property on the other side of Brianna's motel, I run into Jackson McBain, the father of a Black family that had recently moved to Osceola from inner-city Baltimore. "It was too rough up there," he explains. "I have relatives who were killed on my block, and I just wanted my kids to grow up in a safer environment." After a spell living in their car in parking lots, he and his wife found part-time work at a KFC, giving them enough money to cram themselves, their three children, and two dogs into their small motel room. "We are definitely homeless," Jackson tells me, "and we will take any services that are available— food, clothes, clinic, food stamps, bus passes, you name it." He has a rap sheet and spends much of his day lobbying employers "who will give me a second chance," but "there are too many people like me in Osceola County hustling for crumbs." Warmly reminiscing about the rural Louisiana home of his childhood—"We had a spread and the living was easy"—Jackson dismisses any idea that the temporary roof over their heads is a home. "I know prison, and it's not exactly like that, but it still feels like we are trapped here, and every single day I hope for a miracle to get released."

Jackson is not alone in referring to motel life as a trap, or even in comparing it to detention. In Cameron Preserve, a hundred-unit complex that is the county's first (and so far only) effort at directly subsidizing the building of affordable housing, I spoke to John and Janine Clegg, a white couple who spent three years living, as they put it, "in the custody" of a nearby motel. "We moved in after we lost our home in Kissimmee and our jobs at Disney," Janine recalls. "At the time we thought, 'we are middle-class people, and motels are not for people like us, so this will only be for a month or two,' but after a year of trying to move on, it felt like the Hotel California—as in 'you can check out anytime you want, but you can never leave.'" Their motel saw evictions and visits from the county deputies on a regular basis, so the behavior of guests was closely monitored. "Everyone was being judged by the manager," Janine tells me, "really from the first time you ask for a room, to see if you are the ones who are likely to be behind on rent or stop paying, or if you will cause any trouble." John particularly resented the surveillance: "There were cameras everywhere for the manager to watch you, and for the police to review if there was an incident."

Once the Cleggs were in Cameron Preserve, where the monthly rental is well below market rates, they were able to breathe. "I can't tell you how much relief I feel from the stress of having to come up with rent every week or be turned out on the streets," Janine tells me. When they first moved into the motel, they were childless, so there was little county assistance available for them. "I guess we were just seen as poor, whereas if you are a family, you are seen as homeless and qualify for help." Having a child helped them get into the subsidized housing complex, she says, but "it's still a long way off from what we had in Kissimmee."

People used to sleeping rough are also likely to experience a motel room as a place of confinement. Captain Jack, a Vietnam vet who slept at a bus stop just to the east of the Sandpiper and had been homeless on and off for twenty years, prizes his freedom from the four-walled motel environment. "I couldn't live in a rat hole like that," he scoffs. "Every so often, I chip in with some others to rent a room, but I usually just take a shower, clean up, have a beer, and then come back out here. I don't sleep well there. I feel penned in, so I don't stay overnight." Jack is normally based in Southern California and wants to return there as soon as he has "located his VA check." With his flowing white beard and veteran's baseball cap, he is a dead ringer for the public image of Homeless Man, and he knows it. "It's my uniform for panhandling." He shrugs. Jack isn't sure whether motel residents "deserve" to be called homeless. "It's a reality, man, but it's also a state of mind," he muses, putting it better than anyone I'd encountered.

STABLE BUT INSECURE

Instead of putting themselves firmly on one side or another of the homelessness question, many motel people split the difference, declaring homeless status when dealing with service providers and other authorities but shunning the label in their personal lives.[9] Alicia, a short-term Sandpiper resident, who, like Clancy (and many other women in the motels), is a refugee from an abusive relationship, struggles with the label's stigma and shields her circumstances from relatives who live in Orlando. Like countless others, she was drawn to Central Florida by the lure of employment and a cheaper cost of living, but the personal challenges she brought with her from the Bronx did not sit well with family members. "My brother—my own kin—evicted me from his home and gave me some money to get into this motel, and I have my job at Marshalls to see me to the end of the month," she tells me. "To some people, I suppose I was homeless when I lived with him, and now even more. When I go for homeless services, I'm homeless, but I wouldn't use that term by myself. It's too embarrassing. I'm not a bum."

Behind that distinction lies a long history of how indigent people are viewed and labeled. From the time of the sixteenth-century English Poor Laws, programs of direct relief in the UK and US have differenti- ated between the "deserving poor," whose circumstances are viewed as beyond their control, and the "undeserving poor," who are held to be personally responsible for their misfortune. Versions of these judgmen- tal labels have persisted through successive eras, personified by popular types—pauper, vagrant, transient, hobo, tramp, dropout. We continue to hear that the blameless poor are only temporarily needy—with a little charitable or government help they will be back on their feet. By contrast, it is considered a wasteful use of resources to assist the less worthy poor—they will always be a burden.

The real problem of poor people is their poverty, just as the root cause of homelessness is their lack of housing. Yet the presumptuous distinctions and labels persist. The more noxious ones are never far from the lips of conservatives, who reserve the right to decide who merits a leg up, but vilify welfare as an irresponsible handout that rewards idle- ness and encourages dependency.[10] They are hardly alone, however. It's likely that the same kind of moral calculation flits through the mind of almost everyone who is petitioned on the street by a panhandler. Does this person deserve my dollar or not? The decision to give is based on many factors, but in deliberating whether to do so, we reproduce and reinforce this timeworn, more or less arbitrary separation of the des- titute into two different populations. The moralizing is so pervasive that it is easily internalized by those struggling with poverty, and it was clearly reflected in the comments I heard among people in and out of the motels.

The least likely to identify as homeless are elderly singles, living on Social Security, disability, or other forms of public assistance. Motel life to some extent makes economic sense for such people on a fixed income. Wayne, a grizzled, thrice-divorced septuagenarian who lives in a motel opposite the landmark turreted attraction of Medieval Times, explains the motel's appeal to him: "I have no utility bills, insurance, or other overheads, my room gets cleaned once a week, my light bulbs get replaced, and best of all I don't have a yard to mow." He is all too aware that his checks would not stretch to cover an apartment, especially with rents steadily on the rise. Some nights there is pandemonium on his side of the motel, but he is untroubled by it. "We have drugs and prostitution here, and yes, the deputies come around every few days, but these people know not to bother me. I got nothing they would want." As for his neighbors in the motel who are also receiving government assistance, Wayne, whose casual racism was shared by a great many of my white interviewees, is careful to distinguish himself from Hurricane Maria's climate refugees. "They are young and they're Puerto Rican, and so they don't want to work—why would they leave Florida if they get paid to stay here?"

Elderly women living alone in the motels are more difficult to find. Mary Decker, a longtime Michigan snowbird who migrated to Osceola full-time after her husband passed away, tells me that "it's true that men might be more comfortable in this kind of place, but I get treated with respect." She moved out of an apartment in the nearby town of St. Cloud when the rent increases outpaced her late husband's pension. "This works best for my budget," she reports, and "as long as I can walk or take my scooter to Walmart and the other places I need on 192, its better than being more secluded." Does she feel safe? I ask. "I did not grow up in Detroit," she replies, "but the crime never stopped me from visiting that city, and this is nothing compared to Detroit."

Occasionally, I ran into younger long-term occupants who had well-paying employment and simply preferred a motel room to being bound by an apartment lease. In fact, the Sandpiper's most longtime resident, an urbane, single, white transplant from Tennessee who has been occupying the same room for seven years, could easily afford to live elsewhere. A diehard Beastie Boys fan with eclectic tastes and talents, Wesley holds down a managerial day job in sales at a successful time-share firm. He also makes money doing freelance writing for software companies and uses various pen names to indulge his passion for the written word, blogging absurdist stories that he calls "short O. Henrys." Feeding another of his passions, he writes a column for the magazine of the Society of American Magicians. "I like being semi-transient," he tells me. "Maybe it's a fear of commitment, but originally I thought this would be an easy exit if I wanted to move on." However, he acknowledges that "it is probably complacency or familiarity that has kept me here for so long, and to me the rent is just like hush money."

Wesley recalls earlier incarnations of the Sandpiper through his own culture lens: "When I first moved here, it was pretty much untouched, and the lobby was like a set from a Wes Anderson film, with papers and letters stacked up, and nothing electronic." Even after two rounds of renovations, he notes, "it's still a bit of a money pit—look at the low nightly rates." I ask him about the rowdy neighbors. "Yeah, they can be a pain, and some of them are a real headache, especially if they are next door, but these people usually move along or are asked to leave." Every so often, he meets "mystical fellow wanderers" who feed his curiosity. "You find them out on the walkway, they have deep knowledge of their fields, and you can have amazing late-night conversations leaning on the balcony."

Wesley deliberately keeps a little commuting distance from his daytime job, but there are many residents on 192 whose workplace is in the motel where they live. Indeed, the vast majority of motel maintenance and cleaning is done by long-term occupants in return for discounts on their weekly rent. For owners, it is a great advantage to have cheap, off-the-books labor performed in-house, and these informal employees are akin to live-in domestic workers. They are also more familiar with the situations of their neighbors than the managers are, and so they are often leaned on to act as informants when owners want to weed out and evict "troublemakers." The flip side is that the tenant-employees often have inside knowledge about the exploitative operations of their landlord bosses.

Jonny Rivera has lived and worked as the maintenance guy in almost a dozen properties on Route 192, from some of the more shipshape brand-name chains to the most ramshackle motels. He has seen his share of reckless conduct from residents ("one of them ran a meth lab that blew up and caused a big fire") and shady behavior from owners ("they will rob you blind if they can, and they never pay the taxes they should"). Jonny specializes in fixing up infrastructure, which often means dealing with pest infestations and especially with bedbugs, the scourge of 192. "You have to seal up all the cracks with caulking," he explains, "but there are catwalks between the walls here for piping. Not enough room for a squirrel, but these are the bedbug highways." At one hotel with a notorious bug problem, which rendered most of the rooms unrentable at one point, he had to take a class to better understand the enemy:

> They're not like roaches. They are red because they suck your blood, and when they bite, they insert an enzyme that numbs the spot, like an anesthetic, and they leave tracks . . . just like dope addicts. There are two steps to killing them: freeze them and dry them up with tremendous heat. You come in with the chemicals and you spray, then you freeze the room, the coldest you can get it, so they stay there and absorb the liquids. Then you seal everything off, put all the furniture in the middle of the room, and bring in a hose hooked up to a machine outside that heats the room to almost two hundred degrees. That won't light a fire, but it will kill any insect in there.

Jonny's wife, Jane, has also done housekeeping at hotels along the strip. "They would give you maybe twenty rooms a day," she recounts, "and about thirty minutes to clean each, for eight twenty-five an hour. Really, you're being asked to work a miracle because there's a lot of details to take care of. Many times I couldn't take lunch, and by the time I got out of there I could hardly walk." At their current motel, they have an agreement with the owner. "Basically, we're working for our room," Jonny says, and "he will also give us a little cash sometimes, like it's pocket money." There's no contract; every arrangement they make is informal and subject to the manager's will.

As with so many others on 192, the domiciles and livelihoods of Jonny and Jane are temporarily stable but constantly insecure. Large numbers of US workers are in the same boat, scraping to hold on to jobs and apartments that could slip out of their grasp on short notice. What the motels offer is a particularly vivid demonstration of this national predicament. Built for the leisure of people on the go, they are now serving the basic needs of people who can go nowhere else.

ANDREW ROSS

Reluctant Landlords

BECAUSE THE NATIONWIDE upsurge of motel dwellers has escaped official documentation, accurate estimates of their numbers are hard to come by.[1] But their rapid increase has hardly gone unnoticed. Partly due to its shock value, their quandary has been the focus of news articles in almost every region of the country. Photographers drawn to the plight of these "invisible homeless" have also compiled high-profile portfolios. A 2020 *New Yorker* feature, "The People Staying, and Living, in America's Motels," included Danna Singer's shots from Texas, Wyoming, Nevada, and Arizona, while Elizabeth Lloyd Fladung's 2012 photo project, "The Hidden Homeless," featured images from New Jersey, California, Alabama, and Pennsylvania.[2] Florida has its own photo-documentarian of motel life in Melissa Lyttle, former president of the National Press Photographers Association.[3]

At least two filmmakers have stepped up to chronicle the experience of children growing up in motel rooms. In 2012, Alexandra Pelosi made an HBO documentary, *Homeless: The Motel Kids of Orange County*, focusing on the California county that hosts Disneyland. With the 2017 release of *The Florida Project*, Sean Baker's acclaimed indie film about the bittersweet life of motel children, Route 192 found its own place in celluloid history. For those familiar with motel life, the movie gets a lot of things right: the manager with the big heart (played by Willem Dafoe), tenants scraping to make the weekly rent, bedbugs in the rooms, children hopped up from a fast-food regimen, and police officers regularly in the picture. The film revolves around mischievous six-year-old Moonee and her friends, who spend the summer turning the strip into their playground—a makeshift wonderland of adventures and japes, more suited to their needs and budgets than any high-priced attraction or theme park.

Moonee's mother, Halley, a single parent who hustles to survive, is herself little more than a child at heart, and a wayward one at that. Viewers have found it easy to moralize about her poor parenting. But Mary Downey, director of the Community Hope Center for homeless services—who aided the film's producers with Route 192 locations and casting—asks people "to remove their judgment hat for her because you can't just do things that nobody's ever taught you how to do." At the end of *The Florida Project*, Moonee evades the agents from child protective services and tears off with a friend into the Magic Kingdom.[4] That journey is not logistically viable (Baker calls it "their headspace"); the scene is a fantasy about a place where they might be safe, without their parents. Although they live only a few miles from Disney World and can see the glow from the nightly firework display, they could never afford the entrance fee.

Not surprisingly, the film has many detractors in Osceola County, not least among the motel owners. Most hoteliers try to cash in on any kind of association with a high-profile film, but not in this case. Linking motels to homelessness, prostitution, pedophilia, and other kinds of criminal activity is especially toxic for the tourist industry. One prominent motel owner, who had never seen the film, insisted to me that it had single-handedly resulted in falling occupancy rates at his property. Several other owners whom I interviewed demanded to know whether my book was going to be like *The Florida Project*. They deplore any publicity about the struggling families occupying their rooms, even though they willingly reap the benefit from the extended-stay rents.

A notable exception is Debbie Buxton, the owner of the purple-walled

Magic Castle, the film's most recognizable location, which has seen a bump in traffic from niche visitors on a pilgrimage. "The people who come by are infatuated," she says, "and want to take pictures of everywhere the kids go in the movie, and then some of them end up booking a room." Like many owners I interviewed, Buxton insists that she no longer caters to the kind of weekly renters who resemble the film's main characters.[5] She and her husband bought the property in the mid-2000s, and then struggled to recover from the devastating post-crash slump in tourism. "You could throw a bowling ball down 192 and not hit a thing," she recalls. Having previously run an extended-stay hotel in Miami, they decided this time to focus more exclusively on budget tourist bookings and forgo the headaches of long-term renting. According to Buxton, "the locals want the most and to pay the least . . . plus they cause damage and, of course, there are the lifestyle issues."

Buxton's disapproving sentiments about the weeklies are widely shared among her peers, even though these occupants have become their bread and butter. The small proprietors on 192 went into the hospitality business to service nightly guests and ended up as reluctant landlords, hosting long-term residents whose rights as tenants are unclear. It is by no means a wholly local predicament. Despite their original aspirations, moteliers across the country have become providers of affordable housing for the working poor and are unofficially joining the ranks of small landlords, who own almost half of the rental buildings in the US. The housing crisis has presented an opportunity for them to generate steady income from a new supply of customers. But the responsibilities of landlordship are quite different from the task of catering to nightly guests. It is a new and often unsought role.

Unlike the Wall Street financiers who have bought up large numbers of single-family rentals, these mom-and-pop owners have close personal contact and relationships with the families who fill their rooms. Their residents do not show up as numbers on a spreadsheet to be manipulated by a corporate algorithm; the owners are more aware of the uphill battle to make the rent, and the rough consequences of an eviction. It is more difficult for moteliers to ignore the hardship, even though the rooms they rent out are as shoddy (and just as expensive) as the properties of slumlords who establish a predatory business model at the bottom of the market. The hospitality profession is built around customers' comfort and well-being. How much of that ethos carries over into the treatment of the less welcome guests whose stays can extend for years?

There are also moral and legal implications of their new landlord-like functions. Moteliers are in a position to take advantage of their long-term guests' plight. They set weekly rates of between $250 and $300 that are comparable to market rents for apartments (minus utilities), so they are profiting from the inflation at the root of the housing crisis. Yet the uncertainty of their guests' status typically allows them to pay less tax than regular landlords. How should they be better regulated to reflect those advantages, and how can their residents be better protected?

THE MOTELIERS

Traditionally, and before the takeover by corporate-owned hotels and chain restaurants, tourism in Florida was the preserve of small family-owned businesses. Running your own motel was as much an expression of the Florida dream as owning a five-acre orange grove. It was also an immigrant dream: most of the original motel proprietors were from the Indian subcontinent or from East and South Africa's Indian communities.[6] By the 1990s, more than 50 percent of the motel owners in the United States were of Indian origin, and up to 70 percent of those were Patels, a surname associated with landowning families from Gujarat.[7] The Central Florida contingent made up the southeastern colony of the so-called "motel-Patel" empire.

For most of the nation's small-motel proprietors, the exact location of their property determines where it falls on the distribution curve between catering only to transient guests and wholly to the non-transient. On Route 192, the only moteliers who can fully hold on to their hope of subsisting entirely on nightly tourist bookings are located on the westerly sector of the corridor, nearer to the Magic Kingdom's main gate. They do not mince words about their privilege. "I won't rent to the riffraff," sniffs one stately Indian owner, fortunate to be operating in this golden zone. "They only bring trouble and filth, and besides, we don't need them in order to break even." Gary Rumford, a West Indian manager at a nearby Howard Johnson franchise plagued by bedbug problems, tells me he has recently issued eviction notices to all of his remaining weekly renters. "Because they move all their belongings from their house into one hotel room, my housekeepers cannot get in there to clean," he complains. "That's how the infestation begins." Cleanup, he reports, costs as much as $650 per room.

"In general, the further away from Disney, the more locals you will have in your rooms," explains Vimal Kapoor, one of the original Indian proprietors. His motel is on the back stretch of 192, east of Route 535, the corridor's main feeder route to the three other Disney World gates. "Over here," he laments, "we live off Disney's crumbs." Some owners insist that they would rather keep rooms empty and lose revenue than fill them with locals. But in most motels on that back stretch—which is where I usually stayed—managers try to maintain a balance between nightlies and weeklies, segregating the two populations on either side of their property and adjusting the mix for high and low season. As one approaches the Kissimmee city line, beyond the ramparts of the Medieval Times attraction, the occupancy mix, like a river meeting the salty ocean, turns over to all locals. At some extended-stay motels, known to be family-friendly, there are waiting lists to get in. Others, known for drug traffic and shootings, employ seasoned managers who will turn a blind eye to the mayhem in exchange for some kickback.

With the first generation of Indian owners on the wane, life is only getting harder for motel dwellers. Few of the original owners' sons and daughters are attracted to the family business, and those who do go into it have a more hardheaded attitude, bemoaning their parents' soft hearts for occupants who cannot always make the rent. One of these is KJ Nana, an urbane entrepreneur whose family came to the area from apartheid-era South Africa in the 1980s. He successfully converted a one-hundred-room motel close to Kissimmee into the Staymore, a set of studio efficiency units with a proper kitchen for extended-stay occupants. He has unsparing words for others in the Indian motelier community who have failed to "diversify" their business by renovating their properties. "My honest opinion," he says, "is that a lot of these hotels need to be torn down. Their time has gone, and the budget market is no longer there."

Indeed, many of the longtime moteliers are looking for an exit. Mohamed El-Alfy, for example, a retired agricultural engineer and long-running owner of the Gator Motel, is ready to pack it in. His motel used to share a parking lot with one of 192's great roadside attractions, a 126-foot-long, open-jawed alligator drawing visitors to the Jungleland Zoo at its back.[8] But the zoo, with a long history of failed inspections, was forced to close in 2002, and its main building is still unoccupied. The abandoned feel of the site does not help El-Alfy's business. "These days my only walk-ins are homeless people from the strip," he grumbles, "and while I have real pity for them, my blood pressure has only gone up. The business is dying out here, we are selling up, and others, mostly South Americans, are taking over." Indeed, in my own door-to-door survey along the corridor, I found a good deal of turnover among the motel owners. Many have been bought up by foreign investors—from Vancouver, São Paulo, Hong Kong—with no hands-on relationship to the properties. Managers and staff that I quizzed in these places never saw the owners. The number of motels transferred to non-US owners increased by 110 percent over the last decade, while those registered to Osceola County addresses decreased by 380 percent.[9] This trend parallels absentee ownership in the national home rental market, where tenants increasingly deal remotely with corporate property managers.

Other moteliers have retained ownership of their properties but turned over their bookings to corporate franchisers. The owners of the Sandpiper, desperate to upgrade its rooms and attract more tourists, entered into a contract—the first in Florida—with Oyo Hotels and Homes, the mammoth Indian hospitality chain. The company started out as a room aggregator, linking customers to hotel rooms much like Uber links passengers to drivers. Over time, as it built a brand, Oyo shifted to a franchise model; at its peak, just before the pandemic, it was the world's second-largest hotel chain. In return for exclusive control over Sandpiper operations, including the all-important booking process, Oyo paid for a slapdash makeover of several rooms and pressure cleaning of the facade. But it also took a 7 percent cut from each booking and drove down the rates to as low as thirty-five dollars per night, seeking to outbid competitors at the bottom of the local motel market. Because it was the region's first Oyo franchise, the Sandpiper owners actually got a sizable discount on the pricing: at other properties, Oyo takes as much as a 20 percent cut. Ultimately, however, the motel owners were unhappy with the outcome, and the contract was not renewed after a frustrating year.

Like small business owners everywhere, the moteliers have lots to complain about, and so they formed the 192 Hotel/Motel Association to promote their common interests. The longtime president is Jitu Patel, owner of a Knights Inn franchise and head of the local Hindu temple. Patel takes a dim view of the economic development decisions made by a succession of county commissioners, and especially their periodic efforts to improve the business profile of the 192 corridor. He is still bitter about the county's $30 million beautification project in the early 2000s, which brought some visual order to 192's wild signage, expanded the long-neglected sidewalks, and set up elaborate mile markers that few people ever use for orientation purposes. "We suffered during the reconstruction of the highway for two years," he recalls. "My rooms were empty, and all of us had to pay a special assessment to fund it." He also bemoans the commissioners' failure to bring a convention center to the county, an initiative that moteliers hoped would restore the corridor's glory days. Orange County's convention center, the second-largest in the US, has served as a dynamic anchor for International Drive, Orlando's own highly successful tourist corridor. A tastefully landscaped thoroughfare, International Drive has added enough attractions over the years to become its own brand destination, competing with Disney and Universal for tourist time and dollars, and it is now the envy of its Osceola County neighbors.[10]

Patel struggles to maintain a 60 percent break-even occupancy rate at his hotel, partly because he accepts only nightly rentals. He is not the only owner to exclude locals in search of housing, even when that policy hurts the bottom line. Peter Sharma, who moved from Australia in 2010 to pursue his Florida motel dream, has made the same decision. Sharma's purchase and makeover of the Oasis, well known to Osceola deputies as a drug haven, into the Seasons Resort Hotel was praised by county officials, who even helped him install an advanced security system. When he found out how expensive bedbug cleanups can be, and how difficult it was to evict local tenants, he cleared them all out. "I love homeless people, but I won't rent to them," he tells me. After the makeover, which included the renovation of a grungy bar into the popular Capone's Dinner and Show, featuring a "Prohibition-era speakeasy and cabaret," Sharma began to advertise heavily to South Americans. Weekends were good business, but overall his occupancy rates were flatter than anticipated. "Right now," he blithely informs me on my first visit, "there are only fifty-five rooms out of a hundred and twenty booked for tomorrow, and I am selling rooms at cost, just to pay the staff's wages." The previous year, he says, he made only $28,000 in profit.

The Seasons Resort Hotel was one of the Route 192 motels that closed down during the pandemic, shuttering in April 2020. Sharma tried to interest a corporate franchiser in the property and was looking for a buyer in advance of moving back to Australia. When I dropped by several months later, he was allowing a crew of Disney union members (from UNITE HERE and the Teamsters) to use the motel's expansive parking lot as a food bank for those in need. People slept overnight in cars to save a spot and were queued up in droves by the time trucks unloaded Farmers to Families food boxes from an Atlanta distributor. Among those waiting in line was Cristina Gomez, with three young children in tow. She was staying in a motel half a mile to the east along 192 and had just been served with an eviction notice. "The owner has been good to me in the past," she says, "but this time, I don't think so."

EVICT OR NOT?

Among moteliers across the country who do allow their guests to stay for long periods, the biggest headache is the gray area around their right to evict. The owners enjoy the dependable revenue, as any land-lord would. But they do not want their long-term guests to enjoy any legal rights pertaining to tenants, so they fiercely defend the preroga-tive to remove them at will. In Osceola, as properties fill up with locals desperate for housing of any kind, the right to evict has become a flash-point.

Historically, motel owners have relied on sheriffs' deputies to promptly evict residents for nonpayment or for being a "nuisance," and they are quick to detect any shifts in enforcement policy. As the 192 corridor struggled to pull out of the Great Recession, the Osceola sheriff was increasingly reluctant to evict anyone who might add to the unhoused population on the streets. The language of Florida's statute 509, which regulates residency in public lodgings, leaves some leeway for counties to interpret. According to the law, "nontransient occupancy" is defined as "occupancy when it is the intention of the parties that the occupancy will not be temporary." At the same time, the statute says, the default assumption is that "when the dwelling unit occupied is the sole residence of the guest, the occupancy is nontransient."[11] In Osceo-la's interpretation of this language, motel operators cannot summarily ask nontransient guests to leave, but, like any landlord, must file a court action to evict them—a lengthy and costly process.

The 192 corridor is full of guests for whom the motel room is their sole residence: they use the address on their hotel receipts to secure driv-er's licenses and to register children for school. So how should officers respond to owners who want to evict them promptly? According to the Osceola sheriff's general counsel, Robert Holborn, "our officers will ask 'Do you have another place to go?' and if they say no, then we cannot evict." What would he say to the owners who believe this policy is unfair? "Our position is that you are supposed to be operating a motel, but this is an apartment setup, and you are not paying a landlord's taxes." Even so, Holborn concedes that the statute 509 language should be amended to provide some clarity, and more fairness on both sides.

In 2013, Dianna Chane, owner of HomeSuiteHome, a large property on 192 with many long-term guests, sued the county sheriff for not complying with her eviction requests, claiming that this was a violation of her constitutionally protected rights. "I have been denied the right to manage my own property," she said. "I feel like we have been taken hostage."[12] The hotel/motel association mobilized to support her and filed a suit of their own. But in 2015, a federal judge in the US Middle District Court sided with the sheriff, upholding his discretion not to evict guests who have nowhere else to go and dismissing the owners' claims that they have a "right" to evict or that officers have a "duty to arrest" at their request.

The moteliers' hopes of tipping the policy in their favor suffered another blow the following year with the election of a new sheriff who ran as a progressive, promising "community-oriented" policing. This included leniency around street homelessness. "Our jails are too full to be used as shelters," Holborn explains, "and so we don't arrest anyone for panhandling, unless it's a dangerous situation." Nor, he adds, "do we like the county's nuisance laws, like the ordinances against loitering or camping in public spaces, and so we exercise discretion on these." He shows little sympathy for the moteliers' exasperation.

Among the owners, any mention of the sheriff's position is guaranteed to ignite resentment. The Gator Motel's El-Alfy is a mild-mannered conversant until the topic comes up. "Where are my rights? Why do they allow someone to stay at my house for free?" he fumes. "I am not in business to provide a charity, and I cannot eat at a restaurant for free." Several others recount "worst offender" stories about guests who took advantage of the federal court ruling to stop paying after a few weeks, enjoying a month or two of free rent while the evictions court process plays out. Jitu Patel, at the Knights Inn, tells me about a current case at another hotel: "He wears Armani clothes, drives a BMW, and sends his children to a good school." During our conversation, he makes a point of calling the other hotel's manager to ask if the guest is still there. "He has managed to stay for six months," Patel reports, "and has only paid for two weeks." All in all, his profile of this motel cheat sounds uncomfortably like the Reagan-era stereotype of the Black "welfare queen," who was caricatured as driving a Cadillac in furs and paying for T-bone steaks with food stamps.

Rene Sandoval is among the moteliers who decided to get out of the business entirely after the court's decision—though not before he and his daughter, Peggy Choudhry, were featured in an infamous segment of the Travel Channel's hotel improvement show, *Hotel Impossible*. Sandoval's Sevilla Inn proved quite a challenge for the show's host, Anthony Melchiorri, whose role is to advise owners on how to transform their properties. After finding swarms of bedbugs in many of the rooms, a swimming pool in serious decline, a bodega in the registration lobby, and rates too low to even attract tourists, Melchiorri advised Sandoval to hand over management of the property to his daughter for cleanup and upgrades. Though the episode could have been very damaging, Choudhry (who made the initial call to bring in the TV show) rode the local publicity wave to raise her profile as an advocate for small businesses. Backed by Disney, she ran successfully for a county commissioner's seat.

A supporter of the hotel/motel association's lawsuit against the sheriff, Choudhry acknowledges that her experience as a motelier has shaped her political agenda. She, too, has some worst-offender stories involving troublesome tenants:

> Someone rents a room, and decides: "I'm not paying, so you will have to kick me out. I know my rights and you have to take me to court, which will take at least a month." And then they rent the room to their friend, and make thirty bucks a day. And when these people come with drugs or party guests, we literally can't get them out of the hotel.

"That felt very unjust to me," she says. "The small hotels were being used, and also judged, as the scapegoats of the county, because Osceola doesn't have a place for the families to go."

Once in office, Choudhry claimed for herself the moniker of "the People's Commissioner" and successfully negotiated with the Salvation Army to launch an emergency resource center (not a shelter) for the unhoused. But she remained a firm advocate for the motel owners. "We don't yet have a secure way of running a business on 192," she says, "because the squatter issue is still there." Often on the losing end of 4–1 votes on the board, she confirms that changing or clarifying the state law, which she has tried to do, is "not a priority" among her fellow commissioners.

For many other moteliers, the "squatter issue" is a moral dilemma. Akash Parekh, owner of the Red Carpet Inn and the Ambassador Inn, sums up the ethical quandary: "Human nature says 'Take pity,' but we have no obligation to the homeless. If they have nowhere to go, you feel for them, but your business head says, 'No, don't be nice.'" Like Choudhry, he affirms that the county's approach to nontransient guests is the biggest headache that Osceola motel owners face.

That said, there is always a way to make a profit from balancing the risks against the benefits, especially when market rents are so high and occupants have no alternatives. As El-Alfy puts it, "If you have a hundred rooms, and you have to deal with the cost of two evictions every month, that is sustainable, but it's more difficult to do that with thirty rooms." Yet even the smaller thirty-room motel could find long-term renters profitable: by operating at near-full occupancy with nontransient guests, it could collect much more revenue than a place that is only half-full of tourists. With that balance sheet in mind, some owners have decided to switch over entirely and run their properties like an apartment building. Mary Jensen operated her Palm Motel on a mixed-occupancy basis—with nightlies, weeklies, and snowbirds—until she went all in by offering six-month leases. "They pay weekly and are on probation for the first month," she explains. "Some stay for five or more years, in one case seventeen years." Jensen is known for her big heart, so she ends up carrying some tenants who are in arrears. But the Palm has near-full occupancy and there is a wait list. "I don't have to worry about May or September," she says, referring to the low tourist seasons.

For those who do not sign a lease, Jensen imposes a "28-day rule," requiring them to check out after four weeks. This house rule stems from the fact that many states regulate the stays of nontransient guests in order to require establishments to collect taxes from them. Depending on the state, "legal residency" might be conveyed after 30 days, 70 days, or 90 days, after which these new residents are expected to begin paying state and local income taxes. In addition, there are often regulations bestowing tenants' rights on occupants who stay beyond a legally prescribed minimum period. The most common residency requirement is for 30 days, which has resulted in the custom of obliging guests to move every 28 days.

In Osceola, this widely observed practice is particularly fraught because of the legal imbroglio about the owners' right to evict. Holborn, the Osceola sheriff's general counsel, firmly dismisses the 28-day move-out requirement as a fiction: "It is simply not codified in Florida law." Moteliers, he says, take advantage of the "false pretense" of the rule, moving occupants from one room to another to "restart the clock" or forcing them to sign statements attesting to their transience. But under the federal court ruling, guests for whom the motel room is their sole residence are protected even after only one day of occupancy, so hosts are required to go through the standard legal process to evict them. Of course, moteliers are not the only ones who might be hazy on the legal details. Low-income guests are even less likely to know the law is on their side, and they typically lack the resources for legal representation. Fearing a visit from the deputies, they often just move out after owners tape an official-looking three-day eviction notice to their door. Most of them also acquiesce when told to vacate temporarily after 28 days in the belief that this precludes them from exercising their tenants' rights. All along the 192 corridor, families go through this sorry routine every four weeks, dragging the contents of their rooms to another property for a couple of days before checking back into their regular location.[13]

This rigmarole of "musical rooms" plays out all across the country. In Los Angeles, an epicenter of homelessness, it is known as the "28 day

shuffle," and is widely practiced by hotel owners despite being illegal under state law. Of course, long-term guests of motels are not the only residents for whom evictions are a source of anguish and torment. After the housing crash, expelling people from the only place they could call home became a national scourge. Even before the COVID-19 pandemic set off alarms about a new eviction wave, around 3.6 million eviction cases were being filed annually in the US, resulting in 1.5 million judgments giving landlords the legal authority to remove a tenant.[14] When home foreclosure is the initial cause, the evicted household tends to enter a cycle of displacement, moving from one substandard unit to another.[15] This high turnover is not a money-loser for landlords. They are usually able to profit from insecurity and vulnerability at the bottom of the market, and every slumlord knows how to balance "hard" and "soft" treatment of tenants in order to extract maximum income from substandard dwellings.

When the pandemic struck, many parts of the country saw a spike in extrajudicial evictions from extended-stay motels. With the courts closed, unscrupulous owners and landlords took advantage of the legal confusion, using intimidation, lockouts, utility turnoffs, and a host of other unlawful tactics to force out residents who were unable to pay. Once the courts reopened toward the end of the summer, eviction cases from motels and other transient lodgings that had not been covered by the state moratorium were among the first to be dealt with. As of this writing, a federal moratorium (under legal assault from landlord and realtor associations across the land) is keeping apartment and house renters from being evicted until June 30, 2021, but housing advocates await its expiration with dread.

The only really surprising feature of Osceola's occupancy wars is that government power has not come down on the side of the property owners. The right not to be displaced is a moral principle seldom recognized by the courts or law enforcement officers. Usually, lawmakers and officials back the right of owners to set unaffordable rent rates, while enforcers are instructed to respond promptly when landlords want tenants forcibly removed. Moteliers who have properties both in

Osceola and in neighboring Orange County, for instance, told me that though the deputies in both counties are bound by the same regulations, the ones in Orange County are more inclined to comply with operators who want guests of any kind removed.

Notably, Orange County's hotel industry is dominated by large corporate owners with substantial influence over officials. Osceola's mom-and-pop owners have less political leverage. And the interpretation of the law adopted by the Osceola sheriff aligns with the county's economic priorities. The motels have become a convenient way of warehousing the working poor with just enough income to stay off the streets and out of the woods. After all, the visibly homeless population who panhandle on 192 or who rest or sleep on its benches and sidewalks are considered a grave threat to the county's economic backbone: the tourist industry.

In the absence of alternatives, motels across the United States have become an all-purpose solution, serving at one and the same time as welfare housing, workforce housing, and transitional housing. As long as the burden of these needs can be borne profitably by private-sector providers like the moteliers, then there is no requirement for all that much public action. That is why officials have not taken a harder regulatory line with owners. Treating them more like private landlords would upset this arrangement. To some, the motels might be a blighted eyesore or an offbeat relic from a bygone era of hospitality, but they are indispensable to local economies for reasons that go far beyond the taxes they generate. This vital role was on display during the COVID-19 economic crash, when the motels once again helped to keep some people off the street. Hotels emptied out by the tourism slump were happy to have any kind of revenue from their rooms. In some cities around the country, hotels were asked to take in unhoused people at public expense.[16] Some struggling mom-and-pops also saw an influx of new tenants when nursing homes dumped their less profitable residents in motels to make room for COVID patients.[17]

But the motels are not a housing guarantee, of course. In October 2020, a manager at one property told me that he had been averaging four evictions a month. "It's not something I'm proud of," he admits. "I'm told what to do by the owner, who lives far away, in Asia, and she doesn't understand why people should live here for almost free." The manager of a neighboring motel had started limiting guests to stays of seven days. "I don't want them to have squatters' rights," he explains, referring to the legal misapprehension that has become a fixture on 192. While the federal and state moratoriums barred landlords from evicting most kinds of tenants, they had placed no such restraints on motel proprietors whose guests are hit by the same rent payment crunch.

HOPE ON 192?

In most cities, people who find themselves on the streets after an eviction from their motel rooms or apartments can seek refuge in a shelter. Orange County hosts several homeless shelters, but Osceola has none, and that is largely due to strong public opposition. The county is already considered the region's poor cousin, and it is feared that a shelter would be a magnet for unhoused people from elsewhere. However, Osceola does have the region's most noteworthy provider of homeless services: the Community Hope Center.

The center was founded as a project of the women's ministry of Celebration's Community Presbyterian Church. Responding to the high number of homeless children in the town's schools, the ministry persuaded the pastor to use a member's bequest to launch a local mission for the homeless. Mary Downey, a charismatic advocate for the homeless who was undergoing ordination as a United Methodist deacon at the time, was approached to head up the project. She pitched her dream of the Hope Center as a "one-stop shop in the middle of 192 to provide holistic services," a logistics point for the dozens of nonprofits, faith groups, and agencies offering services to the county's swelling homeless population.[18] She was given the startup funding almost immediately and took over a building that formerly hosted a Mexican restaurant, complete with a giant sombrero on its roof. Over the next six years, the Hope Center would go on to serve almost 45,000 clients, most of them living in motels on 192.

When we first met, Downey wanted to make it very clear that Hope does not provide emergency services, let alone temporary shelter. "It's not a crisis center," she says firmly. "We don't want to change moments; we want to change lives. Everyone wants a quick fix, but that doesn't work. Offering long-term assistance and advocacy is what provides people with a life." The center's philosophy is that simply helping poor people with their urgent needs can actually hurt them because it only addresses symptoms rather than underlying conditions. By contrast, the Hope model aims at building a pathway of support toward self-sufficiency.[19]

The center has a "no wrong door" policy: no matter what problem its clients first come in with, they can receive help from any of the agencies under the Hope umbrella. But they have to make their own choices about stabilizing their lives: the Hope employees they meet and form relationships with are called advocates, not case managers. "We are not saviors, and we never make decisions for others," Downey insists. "Our role is to empower them in ways they are already gifted. The people we serve tell us what success might be for them, and through 'motivational interviewing' we encourage them to do more than what they have set themselves up for." The advocates ask questions that go far beyond their client's immediate needs. "What are your hopes and dreams? Where do you want to go? What do you want to do? Where do you see yourself in the future?"

The Hope Center reaches far beyond the typical soup-kitchen profile of a mercy ministry offering food and clothing. It even ventures into the realm of justice work, challenging the social structures that keep people down and out, incapable of claiming their rights. Downey sums up the difference: "The mercy tradition says, 'I'll give you the shirt off my back,' while a justice ministry insists that 'I have a shirt and you deserve to have your own shirt.'" Originally trained as a journalist, Downey does not shy away from what she calls "oppression" language, nor does she hold back from using the center's political leverage. In

2017, when FEMA was planning to end its housing voucher program for Hurricane Maria's climate refugees, she lobbied federal lawmakers for an extension. "Based on our trauma-informed care work, we advocated that turning families out of the motels would re-traumatize them, and so we were able to re-house fifty households because the extension was approved." So, too, she pushed back when opponents of a living-wage measure in Osceola asked her to testify about the burdensome impact it would have on nonprofits. "Everybody on my team earns a living wage," she says. "If I was paying poverty-level wages, I would be contributing to the same oppression that the people we serve are struggling with."

The center opened at a time when the approach to homelessness nationwide was being turned upside down by the new paradigm of "Housing First." Before then, homeless service providers had subscribed to the model of "Treatment First": clients were presumed to be "broken" and had to be prepared for housing through a lengthy, multistep rehabilitation process that often involved a high degree of behavior modification. But evidence-based research showed that it is more effective (and far cheaper) to house people first and then offer services once they have a roof over their heads.[20] However, the new paradigm depends on ready supplies of permanent, supportive housing. As the affordable housing crisis deepened, that has become an ever-heavier lift.

In the chronic absence of available housing units, Downey is taking steps to provide them herself—a notable expansion of Hope's mission. In 2018, she began devising plans for Hope Village, an apartment complex to be constructed just off the 192 corridor, providing 225 units of permanent rentals built out of stacked shipping containers. The United Methodist Church donated five acres of land, and county authorities made it easier to build the complex by waiving impact fees. It was supposed to be a showcase project for Osceola, though Downey would be the first to acknowledge that the county needs a hundred more like it. However, the funding drive for Hope Village faltered during the pandemic crunch, as more urgent humanitarian needs came to the fore, and the project was put on hold. In its place, Downey started looking at an unanticipated solution: to buy a motel of her own and convert it into livable apartment units. The goal is to offer regular leases so that residents can build a rental record for themselves.[21] Having spent six years trying to move her clients out of motels, the prospect of operating one, even in renovated form, is a hard pill for Downey to swallow.[22] She herself does not perceive this pivot as a form of "mission drift," since no one could have imagined what people's emergency needs would be during a pandemic. Nonetheless, it looks as if the Hope Center might become a motel landlord, though for reasons and goals quite different from the other owners on the strip. With several properties on 192 for sale at discount prices, and thousands more across the country likely to be shuttered due to the prolonged impact of the pandemic, retrofitted motels are turning into an increasingly viable option for supplying the homes so urgently needed by the Housing First model.

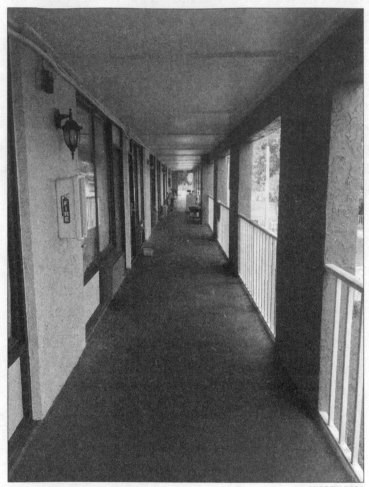

ANDREW ROSS

3

Dopesick and Homesick

HECTOR TORRES WAS not the first person I met at the Sandpiper Inn, but he is the main reason I kept returning. On my second day there, he noticed me writing in a notebook by the poolside. Because it is his business to know what is happening on his "block," he hollered down from the second-floor walkway to ask if I was a journalist. He wanted me to know that he was a writer too, and he invited me to a barbecue that evening with his family and some neighbors. I had to miss the cookout but caught up with him the following afternoon. It turned out that Hector had two writing projects underway: a film script of a sequel to *Scarface,* and a memoir about his ten years of hustling on 192. They were both efforts, he later told me, to divert him from his illicit livelihood, which he was trying—with little success—to walk away from. Though an accomplished storyteller, he was finding it difficult to steer his anecdotes onto the page. "I thought it was going to be easy," he admitted. "I figured I already got the stories, so I could just write them down." I gave him some writing tips and encouraged him to go with his flow.

The son of a pastor, Hector had been reared in stable Puerto Rican communities in the Bronx ("in the same project as Sonia Sotomayor") and then out on Long Island. But he broke away early: "I was born in a church, raised in a church, and if you look at my family as a pizza pie, there's eight slices—seven slices were Christian people, and the other was pure street, and that's the side I wanted to be with always." He sold his first bag of marijuana at nine years old and was first arrested at twelve. Advised, eventually, to flee New York state before he was detained on more serious charges, he landed in Central Florida and "tried to go legit" with a series of jobs—running a fishing operation for disabled clients in Tarpon Springs, training as a short-order chef and working in some restaurants in Tampa Bay. He drifted back into the game to support a growing number of dependents (by his estimate he has ten children by seven different women) and hit rock bottom in a homeless shelter in Ocala, north of Orlando, just after the financial crash. When he arrived on the 192 corridor in 2010, with a new family in tow, he methodically sized up the business opportunities that would carry him in the years to come, figuring out how best to sell to customers in the motels while scamming tourists on the strip. "Once I had seen it all," he recalls, "it was like clockwork."

Like most successful hustlers, Hector exudes charisma and menace by turns and is a persuasive raconteur. After several conversations, I ask him to give me a drive-by tour of the motels he knows best. These days he doesn't often leave his corner of 192, but he warms to the idea of reliving some of his exploits. It is a late spring afternoon, just before rush hour clogs up the flow, and it's not long before cars are tailgating and honking at us because we are cruising too slowly along the corridor, especially the long stretches between lights where the three-lane strip becomes a racetrack. Hector keeps up a running commentary.

> "There's one of the cheapest places, the Central, but every time I go over there something bad happens. My child opened the drawer one time and found two bags of heroin and syringes."
>
> "That one, the Saffron, is a child-molester hotel. Eighty percent are all sex offenders, they have nowhere else to live, and the county pays the owners of the hotels for them to stay there."

"The Star, yeah, is mostly locals. They just found a dead body here a month ago, son of a big-time drug dealer; they duct-taped his face shut and he suffocated. Now they got a hit team up here from Puerto Rico looking for the guys that did it—I tell you, these people won't give up till they find them."

"That's the Magic Castle. I never really stayed there. It wasn't conducive for operations. The driveway was too long, and the owners were not, how you say, very understanding."

"This is where I used to run a Disney ticket scam until I got busted by the ticket task force. Disney would pay overtime to the narcotics squad of Osceola County police—they were on-duty, fully dressed cops, but they were working for Disney."

"This affordable housing complex used to be a motel, but the owner was strung out on crack. The dealers paid him in crack to be able to stay in the rooms and operate."

"That place used to be HomeSuiteHome. Man, it was infested and so badly maintained. But it was a good place to hustle. People made money there, but you'd be doing it amongst bedbugs and cockroaches."

"When I lived in that place over there, I got into it with the narcotics squad. They were covering their badge numbers with electric tape and then coming to my room and robbing me. Got to the point where one guy would just walk in with his hand out. I even tried calling internal affairs to complain. I'm from New York, and we got the dirtiest of the dirty up there. But these guys down here are their own special breed of good ole boy, and if you're not from Florida, you're a target automatically."

"I made a ton of money out here at Celebration Suites—five or six grand a week, easy. And we used to work the bars in Celebration itself—Mulligans, Celebration Tavern. We were all up in there. I provided the muscle and security, and I had a clean-cut partner who took care of the clients. He comes from money, so they weren't scared of him. And I knew all the security guards, so they looked out for him anyway."

"Here comes the Sienna. Fuck that place. The resident drug dealer who worked in the office called me and told me that I didn't fit the image they wanted to portray at the hotel. I said, 'Didn't I just see you selling a bag of weed a little while ago?' She's like, 'That's irrelevant.'"

"I got kicked out of that place over there. I had just moved in when the owner says, 'You got to leave, dude,' and I'm like, 'Why?' 'Because someone just walked up and congratulated me for having one of the biggest drug dealers in Kissimmee move in.'"

"I also had to leave this one. The owners set fire to the hotel to get us out. Then the health inspectors came in and condemned the building. They threw about seventy families into the street."

"That's it," he concludes, as we pull into the Dollar Tree for provisions. "Good ole 192. I can't wait to get the fuck out of here."

For residents like Hector, 192's motels aren't just places to sleep, play, and bring up a family—they are business outlets, full of potential clients with needs to meet. "I'm a master at finding out what you lack in life," he brags, "and then I put it right there." Over time, he has developed a stark fellow feeling for others trapped in the motel life and is often righteously wrathful about how they are labeled and treated. That day, as we drive around, his bittersweet memories make him burn. "The reality of it is—nobody cares about these people," he fumes. "They don't even call us homeless no more; we're squatters now. What kind of shit is that? They're basically dehumanizing us little by little until by the end we're not even human anymore; then they just throw us out, saying you're nobody, not worth anything."

Hector's 192 is not the domain of middle-class families tossed from their foreclosed homes. His turf is among the dwellers who have been damaged by trauma, abuse, addictions, incarceration, police brutality, and nihilism, and whose struggle to cope with the consequences is exploited by profiteers—including himself, as he would be the first to readily and regretfully admit. But he is not a class apart from his clients. He has suffered more than his share of contempt from the forces of respectable society—business owners, employers, lawmakers, and the law enforcement officers who protect property interests. These are the voices who speak loudly and publicly about "cleansing" Osceola County of the "low life" of its skid row, and he knows what they think of people like him.

The class divide even cuts through the Puerto Rican population of Osceola, the only US county where Puerto Ricans are the largest ancestral group. Those who, like Hector, migrated from northern states such as New York, New Jersey, and Illinois are poorer than those who have moved directly from the island since the 1980s. The latter are better educated, they mostly identify as white, and they are claiming an ever-greater role in the power structure, all the way to the Ninth Congressional District seat of Darren Soto, the first Floridian of Puerto Rican descent elected to Congress. Hector's people have not risen in the same way. Because they cannot be consigned to out-of-sight rental apartments off the strip or in North Kissimmee, they are an inconvenient reminder of poverty to their "social betters"—the elites with standing or influence on county committees and the chamber of commerce, or the free-spending visitors motoring along the strip and utilizing its restaurants and tourist attractions.

HECTOR'S PEOPLE

Running your own drug operation is entrepreneurial, but it is not like running most small businesses. It is an intensely social trade, dependent on often complex relationships with suppliers, associates, customers, family members, neighbors, security staff, and a sales crew. These connections need to be constantly managed and finessed to ensure trust, loyalty, and protection. In Hector's case, his trade was embedded within a larger network, the Ñeta Association, whose loose alliance with the Latin Kings made them a force to be reckoned with on the national gang scene. Originally formed in the 1970s by pro-independence detainees in Puerto Rico to protest prison conditions on the island, the Ñetas eventually expanded to the mainland and took

over parts of the regional drug trade. Alongside their involvement in
illegal enterprise, the Ñetas retain their political outlook—fiercely resis-
tant to federal authority—and their formative focus on prisoner rights.
As Hector puts it, "Yeah, the Ñetas were born in prison, but the mission
is to get out and to make things better for the guys that are in. Once we
get you onto the streets, we expect you to stay there. If you keep going
in, you're defeating the purpose."

Hector played a role in establishing the Ñetas' presence in Florida, and he enjoyed a high rank in the group for the best part of two
decades. But though it served him well, he is now "one hundred percent retired and looking for a way out," he says. He claims that he has
"stopped selling the harder drugs and stepped away from all the people
I was dealing with during those times." But, he adds, "if the old lady
down at the end of the block needs a bag, I get it for her." And like
many semiretired professionals, he finds it difficult to resist the lure of
consulting work. "I have a talent," he concedes, "for seeing how your
business is lacking and how we can make it better. I restructure drug
businesses. I know that sounds fucked up, but I can take a look and say
exactly where you need more workers, more cars, and it will take the
pressure off of you. If they take my advice, it all works out."

His retirement notwithstanding, he is still a well-known anchor figure in the underground economy of the 192 strip, and the social life of
the Sandpiper revolves around his family's room. "Every hotel's got a
person," he points out. "You can go to any hotel and you'll find someone who can get you whatever—that's the way it is here; these are the
projects of Florida." There is always a steady stream of people at his
door, which is usually open from noon onward. Goods flow in and out.
"It's not all take, take, take," he notes. "I got boxes of clothes and food
in there; folks have needs, and we look after them." Though he cau-
tions: "I do it because it's the kind of people we are, but don't mistake
our kindness for weakness."

Scratching together a living from those mutual relationships is what
keeps Hector and his family off the street. But the street itself is a main-
stay of his trade, just as it is a workplace for many motel people. After

dark, sections of the 192 corridor are dotted with women from the motels selling sex to passing motorists. Hector was a single parent for several years, and he harbors "a deep respect for single mothers who get themselves in crazy situations where they have to go fuck this old man just to get the rent paid. I had to do it once myself," he confesses, adding, in case I got the wrong impression, that "it was with a fat girl."

Even after ten years of occasionally very profitable activity, Hector is still trapped with his family in their single motel room. His wife and daughter clean the rooms or run the reception desk in the Sandpiper to get discounts on the rent and stave off their third eviction—the last one put them out on the strip for a few days. Like many of the motel dwellers, he spends each day grinding out the money he and his family need to make it through. "I wake up without a dollar in my pocket," he explains, "and the minute I walk out of my door, four people come up to me asking for things they need. I charge them for this. I go over there and get it for them. I come back and give them their shit. Now I've got fifty dollars in my pocket. And this happens to me four or five times a day." The world-weariness shows in Hector's face and in the way he carries his still-trim body. "I'm like a Corvette with no engine," he sighs. "It's beautiful, but you can't go nowhere with it, and I feel it's got a time limit."

Try as he might to step away from his primary business, circumstances usually intervene. At one point, his brother, Angel—a major narcotics dealer—is arrested and held on serious charges. His supplier is willing to pay for an attorney but wants Hector to step back in to run the operation and keep the money flowing while Angel is inside. Hector has no choice but tells himself that he will earn enough on top to finally make the transition to an apartment off the strip. "After this is over," he vows, "I really need to not be so available." Meanwhile, he and a Sandpiper neighbor make plans to move into an RV camper, but they cannot find a park nearby that will lease them a lot. "They are all owned by crackers who don't want dark-skinned Hispanics in their space," he scoffs.

Still, he dreams about new livelihoods. One plan is to revive a catering business he started with his brother. Another is to set up a business selling water purifiers. But a bigger passion is to educate street kids about staying out of prison. "I want to get there before the guns are in their hands, when they're at most risk," he says. "Early middle school—sixth, seventh grade. I'll be bringing people to the table that have been there, that have just spent the last thirty years of their life in prison, who were tricked and fooled by the rap videos they watched on BET and MTV." His advice will be to "learn the trades that have put people through college, have built homes, taken care of people, taken them on vacations. How many drug dealers do you know can say they've got their own house? One percent maybe."

Hector sometimes speaks about the force field that keeps people in the motels. "Any ambition they have is just gone. They'll go from a 200K home to the street, or to prison, then they take a room here, and that's their life now. I can see it in their faces. This isn't where they belong—they come from somewhere else, and they think they can get back to that life. But every time they come into that room someone's putting a magnet inside them." There is nothing mysterious about this inertia. Some of it has to do with addiction, trauma, and fear of even more insecurity. But the more powerful forces are economic ones. The motel people are in the sticky spot on the Venn diagram where the bad sides of the housing market and the labor market overlap in the form of inflated rents, lousy wages, ruined credit, and often a prison record. As for the motel owners, long-term residents are a stabilizer for their business, and they provide a vital service by showing new guests the ropes—where to find food, clothes, and employment, and who to go to for other needs. In Hector's case, his presence is also a guarantee of security: when he was temporarily evicted, other guests complained to the owner about not feeling safe.

Despite this staying power, Hector and his family were evicted again at the end of the pandemic summer of 2020. This time, it seemed for real: their rent was several thousand dollars in arrears. I found them doubling up with friends in an apartment just off 192. Hector had secured a job doing landscaping. "Look at the calluses on these hands!"

he tells me. It's steady work, and a world away from the heady flux of his Sandpiper life. "I miss not knowing what the day will bring to my door," he confesses. As for the eviction, he claims that his wife's work cleaning the motel rooms had not been accurately discounted from their rent and that his role as stabilizer was not recognized. "After we left," he points out," there were three overdoses and one death."

As in many states, the Florida governor's temporary moratorium on evictions during the pandemic did not cover hotel residents, and so the Sandpiper owners had filed eviction papers, over time, on all of those who had not paid since March. On my last visit, just before the November 2020 election, the motel is almost deserted. Wesley is one of the few left, and he seems to have become even more metaphysical. He has taken up bird-watching and has excited tales to recount about his observations of red-shouldered hawks, sandhill cranes, and penduline tits from his vantage point overlooking the adjacent swampland. Over the course of the summer, the drug traffic on his side of the motel had gotten quite hairy, and now Wesley is making the most of the new-found tranquility. "But it's not the same without Hector," he concedes. "He kept this place alive, and he made me feel safe."

I had heard many such tributes before. For a few months earlier that year, Hector's neighbors were Gary and Maria Loughlin, Gary's parents, and two service dogs. They had been renting a large family home in Orange County but fell behind on rent by $200—"the first time in my life," says Gary—and were ruthlessly evicted. Motel life beckoned, but they made a poor choice and ended up getting sick from the unsanitary conditions in the first place they chose. "Roaches were crawling over me as I slept at night," recalls Maria with a shudder. Both are employed—Maria at a 7-Eleven, Gary in construction—but their medical bills stand in the way of an apartment rental. Like everyone else, Gary has a plan to escape. "When Universal breaks ground on their new theme park, I am a shoo-in, and that will get us out of here," he vows. Until then, moving into the Sandpiper has helped them heal. "It's a warm and welcoming place," Maria assures me, "and Hector and his family are a big part of it." Gary agrees. "This whole block is like a cozy neighborhood where everyone gets along, and Hector keeps it good."

Depending on the guest turnover, and the volume of drug use and trafficking, the block didn't always resemble Sesame Street. Hector says that the most valuable service he offered to the manager, Jake, was to broker his relationships with guests by explaining their troubles to him:

> When Jake took over, he was only twenty-two and probably thought: "We'll buy this cute hotel in Florida; all you have to do is check on the rooms and it's gravy." I said to him, "In one year you're going to look in the mirror, and you won't recognize your-self because this place is going to change who you are. Every room here is a different problem. All of a sudden, a door will open and someone is calling you for help, and when you walk in, there's a person lying on the floor from a heroin overdose. You will be forced to help people, whether you want to or not, and find out whether you're kind of the person that can't throw people out on the streets just because they are a week behind on their rent."

One of Hector's insider tips was how to resuscitate someone who had stopped breathing from an overdose: "You have to slap the soles of their feet real hard; there's a lot of nerves there, and that sends the stimulation to get them going again."

Jake readily acknowledges the steep learning curve, though he is less inclined to credit Hector. "I've seen every kind of human situa-tion here," he says. "I've seen all the hookers and the pushers, and I know the police—but I've also learned that helping people can often hurt them, and they lie all the time anyway, so you cannot really know what's going on, and you can't always make the right decision." He gestures toward the strip: "I can also see what's happening out there—the arrests begin with the high season, and then the police drop off the homeless again when things get slow. Like the jails, the motels are used as containers; that's really turned into our role." Jake and his mother were always hoping to tip the balance of tourist and locals in favor of their nightly, or transient, guests. But fiercer competition at the bottom of the budget market shaved the family's profit margin on nightly bookings and ended up making them even more reliant on locals.

Jake sees the drugs economy as an unpleasant fact of life, and an occupational hazard for any motelier on the corridor. Hector is more philosophical on the topic. "Addiction is a problem," he concedes. "It can be a functional problem, but at some point it turns into something else." Having seen it so often, he is fascinated by this tipping point. "Guys will still be with the family, do things with the kids, work, et cetera, et cetera. Maybe they'll slip up here and there, but they can get by. Then at some point it breaks, and they turn their back on family, children, their hygiene, everything, and end up sleeping in the woods because nothing matters anymore except that twenty-dollar rock."

"THE PAIN THEY ALL SEEM SO SCARED OF"

The kind of addiction that Hector and Jake see on a daily basis is a staple of motel living across the country, especially in semirural areas hit hard by the opioid crisis. Florida is particularly implicated in the country's opioid problems. In the first decade of the twenty-first century, its largely unregulated "pill mills" were the primary supplier of oxycodone products to the East Coast and Great Lakes states.[1] "Doctor shoppers" drove down and back up Interstate 75 all the way into New England, picking up and delivering pills on a route known as the "Oxy Express." Between 2006 and 2012, pharmaceutical firms sent 5.6 billion pills to Florida's pharmacies and drugstores.[2] By 2010, ninety of the top hundred opioid prescribers in the country were Florida doctors, and 85 percent of the nation's oxycodone flowed from the state. After the crackdown came in 2011, users turned almost overnight to heroin. Overseas suppliers had found a way to evade the post-9/11 security blanket and could now offer a cheaper opioid product than the pills. Processed from opium poppies, heroin has a similar molecular structure to oxycodone and produces the same kind of high.[3] The overdose statistics flipped from one opioid to the other, as heroin-related deaths shot up.

Greg and Linda Murrin, Sandpiper residents for a month in the winter of 2018, told me how the pain pills were a gateway to the needle for them and many others they knew. After work dried up in their South Carolina town, they rode the Oxy Express down to Broward County in 2009. "We just cut out the middleman by moving to where the clinics actually were," Greg explains. "And then they shut down. At first, we used a little of both, but by the time we moved up to Orlando three years later, we had switched over to heroin." Now they were motel hopping in Osceola and working on and off in fast-food restaurants, in the semi-functional mode Hector had described. "There's a lot of pain on either end of our journey," Linda says. "It all got started as a way to forget the pain, but now it's all about the fear of stopping." For many addicts, the ordeal of withdrawal is the thing they most fear, and dopesickness is the condition that reminds them of that pain. As Hector puts it, "The worst ones have already been through withdrawal, and so they have felt the pain they all seem so scared of." In any event, the state offers very little help: only twenty-six of Florida's sixty-seven counties have a methadone clinic. Even as the opioid crisis deepened, the Department of Children and Families issued only two licenses for new clinics over the course of five years.[4]

The economy of peninsular Florida is driven by tourism but also depends on a steady flow of retirees, so it is inseparable from the business of pain care. Medicare and Medicaid are the lifeblood of a state often known as "heaven's waiting room." Florida's elder poverty rates are among the nation's highest, and, outside of well-heeled retirement and "active adult" communities, the less fortunate elderly suffer from social isolation, depression, multiple chronic conditions, and alcoholism. In Central Florida, meanwhile, the median age has been falling; it now hovers around thirty-three, nine years younger than in the state overall. This younger demographic subsists on the depressed wages of the leisure, hospitality, and tourism industries, and the poverty level in that workforce produces its own varieties of sickness. Substance use, especially of opioids, is a readily available way of dealing with the pain.

Housing insecurity is a major, though often neglected, factor in the breakdown of health. It is easy to understand why physically or mentally unhealthy people end up in precarious housing. But the opposite is also true: the lack of a stable dwelling can trigger illness in its own right. High stress and depression are common afflictions of people struggling to make rental payments and avoid eviction—or, in the case of the motel dwellers, those who may feel trapped in an alienating and demeaning arrangement.

A home, of course, is much more than just a stable dwelling. It is supposed to be the familiar place where we feel nurtured and sustained. That is why "homesickness" typically refers to our distress about being cut off from a support system or a place with which we have a strong emotional connection. But a home can literally make us sick when it offers none of that support, nor any proper measure of constancy, privacy, comfort, or dignity. Motel rooms are almost by definition designed and built for customer needs that are the opposite of homefulness, so they are badly equipped to function as semipermanent homes. They are also likely to be unwholesome, with poor air quality, bad hygiene practices, and toxic contaminants.

In an environment where narcotics are readily available and consumed by neighbors, people will turn to them to cope with morbid motel living. For seasoned users, the motel is often just a shift in scenery, but for many of Hector's people, their addictions are a direct offshoot of employment and housing options stacked against them. Shut out of permanent lodging and starved of adequate income, they cannot lift themselves out of the motel trap. So why hold back on the vices, small or large, that would lift their mood instead?

ANDREW ROSS

Forty-Acre Wood

WHAT HAPPENS TO those who fall through the underside of the motel trap? If you are evicted from a place as dilapidated as the Sandpiper, it's quite likely your next neighbors will include possums and alligators, alongside the people that HUD labels the "literally homeless." Most of Osceola's unsheltered lie well out of public sight, under blue tents and tarps in thickets of scrub woodland just off the 192 corridor. The homeless camps in the woods are an open secret. They provide sufficient privacy to ward off unwelcome visitors but are close enough to sources of income, food, and medical assistance. Sporadic traffic, by foot or bicycle, runs between the strip and the dirt trails leading to the tent clusters. The denizens of these woods are part of a large population nationwide, swelling from year to year, in warm- and cold-weather locations alike.

Because they are more visible than the woodland denizens, the unhoused living on the streets of LA's Skid Row and dozens of other US cities have become the trademark symbols of the nation's housing crisis. After 2008, as homelessness spiked, urban tent cities sprang up all across the country. Compared to homeless shelters, which only accept individuals and impose tight and often authoritarian restrictions over movement and conduct, the tent clusters offered more community, autonomy, and even security. Reminiscent of the tramp colonies and hobo "jungles" of the late nineteenth and early twentieth centuries, or the Hooverville shantytowns of the 1930s, the tents migrated from the margins of cities to more central neighborhoods and downtowns during the Great Recession.

Most were makeshift and temporary, but by 2014, several tent cities—in Washington, Oregon, Massachusetts, California, Florida, and Texas—were legalized as self-organized villages by municipal authorities who had no alternatives to offer the down-and-out.[1] Some even had waste disposal services, running water for showers and sanitation, needle disposal, and food provision. Others, in states as diverse as Alabama, Georgia, Indiana, Nevada, New Mexico, North Carolina, and Maryland, were semi-sanctioned. However, the majority of the encampments generated a public outcry and were promptly shut down. Occupants were evicted and even arrested in response to the coldhearted sentiment that rough sleeping should be regarded as a nuisance crime.

Only New York City, Massachusetts, and Washington, DC, have codified a legal right to shelter, and recent legislative efforts to establish a "right to survive" or a "right to rest" in public places have mostly failed. In 2017, however, the San Francisco–based US Court of Appeals for the Ninth Circuit ruled that fining or jailing rough sleepers violates the constitutional bar on cruel and unusual punishment. Numerous cities backed an appeal to the Supreme Court seeking to overturn this decision, but the court declined to hear the case, leaving the Ninth Circuit ruling intact.[2]

In response to this legal development, and also to the recognition that urban encampments are here to stay at least for the foreseeable future, several municipal authorities have tried meeting the challenge of Housing First by building or approving communities of "tiny homes," mostly in the form of wooden cabins. Pioneered in Portland (as "Dignity Village") and in other Oregon cities, versions of these communities have cropped up in Madison, Austin, Ithaca, Nashville, Syracuse, Detroit, Tacoma, Los Angeles, and Dallas. The communities are often supplied with basic services, including on-site counseling; some of the more solid and well-designed micro homes are set up as rent-to-own arrangements for low-income tenants.[3] In October 2020, with the pandemic winter closing in and no solutions to the affordable housing crisis in sight, Minneapolis went one step further by approving an *indoor* micro-home village for the homeless, situated inside an abandoned Kmart.[4]

Unlike these highly conspicuous, and often controversial, urban developments, homeless camps in the woods have grown more quietly, on the fringes of small towns and suburban sprawl where poverty levels have risen most rapidly. In many cases there is a clear link between sharp job losses and the surge in woodland living. In Hickory, North Carolina, for example, a small city in the western Piedmont that used to be considered the "furniture capital" of the world, the offshoring of that industry saw encampments take root rapidly all over the wooded hinterlands.[5] Escalating urban rents and home foreclosures are the most immediate cause in many other locations, where the impact of housing loss is magnified by the triple scourge of heroin, meth, and opioid pills. Unhoused populations in rural areas of the country, where poverty rates (especially among children) are higher than in cities, are the most neglected of all. Rural communities have fewer services to begin with, and then they routinely get passed over by HUD's annual point-in-time homeless counts that form the basis for federal allocations of funds. When I participated in the Osceola County count in 2020, the territory for volunteers to cover did not extend far beyond the semi-urbanized 192 corridor and the Kissimmee city limits.

The HUD survey, widely recognized as unreliable and inadequate, is conducted on only one January night to determine the numbers of those sleeping "in places not meant for human habitation." The Osceola count took place on the rebound from subzero temperatures, and the organizers warned us that it might not be easy to find people in the open air. But by then I had spent enough time with the woods people to know that cool weather is often favored over the unforgiving heat and humidity of Central Florida's summer, fall, and late spring. Though it is widely believed that homeless people gravitate toward warm climates, evidence shows that most of them remain close to where they lose their housing. A recent study, for example, found that more than 81 percent of homeless adults in Oakland had lost their homes in the Bay Area itself, while only 10 percent had done so outside California.[6] States where the housing crisis is most chronic also have higher rates of unsheltered homeless. The 2019 HUD count showed that 44 percent of the homeless in Florida and 72 percent of those in California were unsheltered, for example, well above the national average of 35 percent.[7]

During the time I spent in Osceola's woods, I found that the camps accommodate a wide range of people—most of them working in some aspect of the informal economy, though some are employed in full-time regular jobs. A goodly number have been woods dwellers for a decade or more. Others are more recent casualties of the low-road economy—shunted out of stable employment, starved of income, and fallen prey to the drug addictions and mental health problems that chase poverty. By far the majority would be thriving with a proper roof over their heads, rather than a leafy canopy of live oaks and sand pines.

INTO THE WOODS

Moving into the woods adjacent to 192 is for those who are out of options, but they do have a choice about where to pitch their tents and how to set up their new domicile. Joining an existing tent cluster is the most sensible pick. Many of these camps are overseen by self-elected leaders and are often populated according to the primary addiction of their residents—beer, meth, or heroin. They offer conviviality and a degree of protection against unfriendly visitors. A more risky alternative is to live at a distance from the established camps.

Charlie Green is one of the loners, and I have been advised not to approach him cold. "He's a real redneck," Billy, a panhandler outside Burger King, tells me. "You should let him know well in advance if you are coming by." Others who live in the western parts of this wood also mention Charlie's name with careful expressions of respect, so I build up a forbidding picture of him. As it happens, I come across him by accident. One day, I follow a trail that leads through the live oaks and bitter orange trees past a knee-high Honeywell Security sign and opens out into a level clearing with several tents, tarpaulin canopy structures, and a large inflatable swimming pool. A pit bull rouses itself and drags on its rope leash as I come into sight. Charlie is at the back of the compound and does not hear me announce my presence above the low grumble of the generator, but he soon ambles up to see what is troubling the dog.

Woods people have every reason to be wary of strangers. I have heard of camps where the entrance is booby-trapped with trip wire, and I have come across watchdogs with a keen understanding of their purpose. But Charlie—in his fifties, compactly built, and wearing a "Defending Freedom Since 1776" cutoff T-shirt—turns out to be a courteous host. After I tell him why I am here, he shows me around with some pride. His five-hundred-gallon swimming pool is fed by rainwater channeled down from the tarps. He has a separate guest tent, rabbit cages, and a nice gas grill; his open-air living room hosts a fridge, sofa set, and a medium-sized flat-screen TV. Off to one side of the compound is a collection of bicycles in various states of assembly. "I put them together to sell to pawnshops," he explains, "and I sure like building things." Pointing to a recently motorized model, he declares: "I'll be keeping that one for myself. It has a fifty-mile range."

Compared to others I have seen, Charlie's setup is superior in construction and maintenance. "I got almost everything I need," he says, "though I just bought a bigger pool, and I am hearing about a wedding tent on sale at Walmart that might be useful." No doubt there is some neighbor envy involved in that recent purchase. Thirty-five yards further into the wood is John's compound, which boasts a much larger pool from which he can view his seventy-inch TV screen, along with an additional pool for washing his clothes. However, these conveniences are exclusively for him to enjoy. "John don't like anyone," Charlie warns, which I am able to confirm when his neighbor sends me packing later that week. In another wood I heard about an even more elaborate spread whose owner has contrived a surround-sound media system, but I was unable to locate it. Among the woods people, vital information about accessing resources, locating better camping or panhandling sites, and evading police surveillance travels fast and effectively through the grapevine, but so do dubious rumors.

The forty-acre wood where Charlie lives hosts between ten and fifteen camps. Tents within the camps are typically pitched fifteen or twenty feet apart, but the social ties between occupants can be quite complex. Even spatial outliers like Charlie and John still rely on each other for neighborly help or protection, and trash talk is useful for ostracizing those regarded as highly unsociable or even a potential threat. Charlie hears all of the wood's stories when people drop by to chat and watch TV. "Yes," he admits, "there's a lot of drama, and some folks don't want any of it, but I don't mind too much." On my second visit, though, Charlie is sore about the latest news. His girlfriend, who lives on the other side of the wood, has gone off with another man. He wants to know if I have met or seen her, and if I do, will I mention that I have visited him. It is that easy to get drawn into the drama.

In the meantime, he has other concerns on his mind. "I had a little party here two nights ago," he reports, "and we smoked some weed, so now I need to test clean for a job." He is currently unemployed while recovering from being hit by a car, a common occurrence for homeless people on the 192 corridor. (He would get hit again later in the year while on his bike.) His leg cast is about to come off, and he is looking to start up again as a dishwasher at a hotel close to Disney World. "You need to drink a lot of this cocktail of vinegar and cranberry juice to get the THC out of your system," he explains, mixing up the concoction, "and it really burns your throat." Unlike some others in the wood, Charlie has no government income aside from food stamps and does not have the best profile or personality for panhandling. So when the disability checks from his accident run out, he depends on scavenging things to trade. "The hurricane was a good time," he recalls. "There was tons of scrap that you could sell."

"I've been homeless pretty much for twenty-one years now," Charlie tells me. "I've been in jail for meth and tried living in the motels, but being hemmed in by four walls is just too claustrophobic for me." Like many of the predominantly white tent dwellers, he has a rural background, and living in the outdoors is well within his comfort zone. He grew up in a Tennessee country town and spent weeks outside as a kid, hunting deer, rabbit, turkey, quail, and pheasant. Unfortunately, there is not much edible game in his vicinity now: "The deer around here are full of worms," he mutters. Charlie ignores the bobcats that come around occasionally, but he sets a trap for particularly intrusive raccoons and has his own effective methods for killing snakes. Everyone in the woods is intimate with the copious wildlife—snakes, otters, key deer, fox squirrels, armadillos, raccoons, wild boar, and turkeys—and some of the regular critters are regarded with affection, as friendly familiars. In Florida it is considered unwise to pitch a tent near a channel or body of water. But in camps that seemed, at least to my eye, to be perilously close to water, occupants told me they had cordial relations with alligators to whom they assigned names, or knew by reputation.

Animals are not the main source of danger for the woods people. A Florida summer downpour can wash out a tent if it is pitched on a site with poor drainage or if a tarp is not hung properly. During the summer of 2019, when I was regularly in the woods, the rains were uncommonly harsh on people sleeping rough, and the storm season began early, culminating in the mayhem of Hurricane Dorian on Labor Day. Other threats include the county deputies who pay frequent visits in search of drug pushers or people with outstanding warrants or are looking to break up and disperse especially rowdy camp clusters. Landowners can also bring down the law to evict. Because most sites are just off 192, the land is so valuable that owners are always selling off parcels to developers and pushing out the squatters.

But the biggest risk is from other homeless people—who raid tents for supplies and valuables, steal bikes, or are just overly aggressive in their conduct. Desperation, bad drugs, and mental instability are the most likely catalysts. Charlie tells me about his own fear of a charismatic individual known as the Professor, who has attracted a cluster of thirty or more companions in a tent city in the southern sector of the wood. "He uses a cane when he's panhandling even though he's not disabled," he reports, with a classic burst of trash talk, "and he's also a pedophile." By the time I locate the Professor's camp, deputies have broken it up and arrested him for some misdemeanor. Still, Charlie clearly fears his return and confesses that he picked up Coco, his pit bull puppy, to guard against the Professor and his followers. Coco reacts badly to people who smell strongly, and the odor of meth, according to Charlie, really sets her off.

OLD SHINGLE CREEK

Charlie's camp is on land bordering Shingle Creek, the uppermost headwaters of the Everglades watershed. Just to the north of him, the Shingle Creek Regional Park features a Pioneer Village that showcases buildings from Osceola's settler past, including a wood-frame Cracker house, a blacksmith's shop, a schoolhouse, and a railroad depot. It also contains a traditional Seminole village composed of *chickee* houses, supported by log stilts and with roofs thatched with palmetto leaves. The Seminoles originated as a fusion tribe of runaway Black slaves and Oconee Creek, Miccosukee, Yamasee, and Yuchi migrants from Georgia, Carolina, and North Florida. They were refugees from slavers, settlers, and, eventually, the US Army. Their bold quest to fashion a freedom state out of Florida's lands foundered in the course of a long frontier conflict that is broken up by military historians into the three Seminole Wars.

As the Seminoles were pushed further south, they improvised the art of living in Florida's woods, especially in the dry islands of hardwood trees known as hammocks, situated in swampy terrain that soldiers could not penetrate easily. Though Seminole communities had long-standing livelihoods as cattle herders (and still do), settler aggression made them into a guerrilla people, and then dragooned many of them onto ships bound for west of the Mississippi as part of Andrew Jackson's removal policies. Notwithstanding this forced nomadism, Seminole habitation in the Shingle Creek area is long documented.

Locals remember Seminole families running airboat businesses on the creek as recently as the 1950s.[8]

Though far removed from the plight of the nineteenth-century Seminoles, the homeless in the woods off 192 have some things in common with them. For example, their innovative shelters—especially the open canopies—are evocative of traditional Seminole dwellings. Many of the tents I visited are erected on a base of wooden pallets and have raised platforms, like the Seminole chickees, for sleeping and storing food supplies. The occupants have also been made into refugees, pushed out of sight and into the woods, harried and occasionally imprisoned by armed government officers and forced to migrate from one site to another. Like the Seminoles of the past, they are wholly unwanted by the latest wave of settlers and are encouraged in one way or another to self-deport to other counties and states. Unlike the Seminole chief Osceola and his warrior cadre, they cannot or do not fight back, but there is no dearth of fierce resentment at their treatment by police and by authorities unwilling to offer adequate services or housing.

The entrance to most camps is marked by telltale signs at the wood's edge—a shopping cart, discarded clothing, backpacks, or other detritus—and the trails that lead into the interior are often lined with clumps of castoff items, beer cans, rotted furniture, and charred remnants of garbage fires. Abandoned campsites by the side of the trails await new occupants, and smaller trails branch off into dense thickets of trees and shrub that obscure the signature blue presence of the tents and tarps with their foliage. Some recurring landmarks pique my surveyor's curiosity, like the armchairs or sofas that often stand alone in clearings, and whose occupants must have once lounged, in repose or in a stupor, contemplating the peace of the forest. Paintings, ornaments, colorful patches of decor, and broken kitchenware are strewn around, deserted by owners who once brought their sense of taste, along with touches of homeliness, to a woodsy shelter. Cultural archeologists, I am sure, would have a field day.

Some of the camps I visit are garbage-free, but for most of the woods people, the task of cleaning up their refuse, even in their immediate backyard, is not a priority. It might require a coordinated effort and also some means of transport to carry it all off-site. Besides, many know they will be moving on anyway. "Most of us live in a disgusting landfill," admits Danielle Graeber, who keeps a tidy tent compound in the western end of the wood. She is sweeping leaves and dirt out of her open-air living room—with its own sofa set, carpet, and coffee table—to the perimeter, around which she has woven branches and twigs into a makeshift trellis. I compliment her on the setup, which includes some paintings propped up against the entrance gate. "I was trained as an artist, you know . . . by Disney," she mentions matter-of-factly. "I wore a colonial costume and sketched portraits of families outside the Haunted Mansion for seven dollars an hour." Looking around, she sighs. "I would like some new furniture—like a hypoallergenic mattress—and maybe a new box spring, and that leaky tarp needs replacing. I don't really belong here in the woods," she muses, "but this is my home, after all. I have to take some pride in it." Danielle winces as she sweeps, and I realize she is trying to distract herself from the painful fire-ant bites all over her legs and arms. I offer to take her to lunch at the McDonald's nearby, which I often do when interviewees drop hints about their needs. "Homelessness is a real test of people," she says, as we get in my car. "They either sink quickly, or they struggle to get back on land."

On the way, we slow down to greet her boyfriend, Rob, a wiry, agitated forty-year-old who is biking along the 192 sidewalk. He joins us at the McDonald's and proceeds to order large combo meals, with triple-thick milkshakes on the side, for both of them. The electrical outlets in the restaurant are covered over, Rob points out, to stop homeless people from dropping by to charge their phones. Queens-born and -bred, he has worked on and off in construction for many years, but admits that his heroin habit has made him increasingly unreliable. "I'm malnourished," he explains, "and always tired because we often can't sleep until three in the morning when the heat breaks, so I just wouldn't be able to hold down a regular job." He has also learned that he doesn't have the best profile for panhandling. "So I hustle a little, I get people what they need, and my brother sends a check every so often." Danielle, by contrast, has been cut off by her well-heeled Orlando family. "I was spoiled and never learned how to be responsible, and so I always had too much money to spend on the wrong things," she tells me. She rode her addictions through a marriage with three children, but when she started stealing from her grandparents, and worse, they threw her out and took custody of the kids. "My sons always ask where I'm going after a visit, but I can't tell them where I live," she says. "It's better to disappoint them once rather than over and over."

Like most of the homeless users I interviewed, Rob and Danielle are quite up front about their addictions. "It feels so good to wake up in the morning and not be dopesick," declares Rob. Weeks later, I run into them at the Hope Center. Rob tells me they had checked into a motel for several days and tried to detox on their own. "It really was the worst experience that I could ever imagine," he says. He also takes pains to bad-mouth the meth-head couple who live further up the trail. "These are violent people that you must stay away from," he advises. "I'm pretty sure they stole our bikes and other shit." Danielle chimes in: "You can hear them fighting all night long, and so we are considering moving away from this side of the woods."

Rob and Danielle's camp was more populous when I first visited, but it has been losing occupants to the county jail all summer. Before they were arrested, Sandy and her boyfriend, Nick (who told me he had written a book manuscript called "Memoir of a Civilized Hustler"), kept their elementary-school-age children there for a while, though it is very rare to see kids in the woods. Also detained around the same time was Javier, a Cuban Marielito, who had slept rough in dozens of counties in the South but insisted that the local sheriffs—especially in Kissimmee and St. Cloud—were the toughest of them all: "They don't like how many Hispanics are around here now." In November 2020, voters elected the county's first Hispanic sheriff, who pledged to diversify a majority-white agency that no longer reflects Osceola's demographics, though once in office, he selected a less diverse command staff than his predecessor.[9]

Danielle herself is about to return to detention. In a week, she will
be on trial for a drug-related violation, and she expects a sentence of
between sixty and ninety days. "I did fifteen months before, in Orange
County, so I'm not worried," she tells me. She wants to know the title
of my book, and I ask her to suggest one. "Don't Ever Ask Me to Go
Camping Again," she replies and laughs loudly, surprised and amused
by her own merriment as it echoes through the woods. When I return
a few weeks later, all that remains of her scrupulously kept compound
is a rolled-up carpet and a bag of trash.

Later in the week, I take Gary and Julie, the youngish couple whom
Rob described as "dangerous meth heads," to eat at the Perkins restaurant on Poinciana Road. Gary, who was gruff to me earlier that morning, apologized when I caught up with them later in the day. "I was
dopesick, and my job is to protect her," he explains, gesturing toward
his girlfriend, a striking, tall blond woman who avoids all eye contact.
"We are both very empathetic people, we feed off each other's emotions, and she is quite sick right now," Gary says, as he makes a show of
attending to her. Julie has AIDS, I will later learn. "She relies on me—
who is a poor example of a man—to get by, and I've done what I can to
keep her healthy, but being an addict just makes it very difficult to help
others." Gary himself has made the transition from opioids to heroin,
though he still makes a little money selling the pills. He also relies on
some financial help from his mother, a Kissimmee high school teacher,
who pays for a motel room every so often. "I'm essentially an addictive
person," he admits, "and beyond my addiction, I have no ambitions for
myself. People in our situation have no interest in housing or getting a
job. If it's not a service or handout, I'm not interested."

Once Julie had eaten something—they often go for days without
food—she solicits my concern by explaining her own predicament,
albeit not very convincingly. "I went overnight from being a soccer
mom in Peoria, Illinois, to this poor homeless person in the middle
of nowhere after my car broke down on a Florida vacation," she says.
"And now I'm just stranded." As she takes a phone call outside from
one of her teenage daughters in Illinois, Gary quizzes me about my

book. Like Charlie, he advises me to steer clear of the Professor and his pedophile camp. When Julie returns, she adds a warning that the eastern side of the woods has "bad energy, connected to its Indian history" and that I should not go over there. I run into Gary and Julie a couple of times later in the year before they disappear from the site, and, contrary to Rob's opinion of them, they are always polite and helpful. Not for the first time, it is difficult to square my experience of someone in the woods with how others describe them.

The only other resident of that camp to make it through the entire summer on-site is Big John, a gentle soul from Gainesville with a long swimmer's body, who tells me he suffers from PTSD as a result of childhood sexual abuse. John is also hooked on opioids he took to soften the pain of a spinal injury. We converse quite a bit whenever I meet him in the woods, but he courteously declines to sit down for a longer interview. "I have to avoid violent people," he relates, "which is sometimes difficult here, and so unfortunately that means I just avoid most people." John is highly articulate, like some others I encounter, and considers himself to be "a man of intellect." He was spoiled by his family, like Danielle, and dropped out of college. In his case, being homeless has confirmed what he regards as his natural inclination to "live as a free man," explaining, "I don't care to have my life scheduled, and being someone else's employee would not work well for me. I prefer to go by my clock. I was in jail once for stealing a chicken from Walmart, and being confined was utter hell to me." John's flow of thought can take a philosophical turn. "I don't consider myself to be an anarchist," he declares to me, unprompted, on one occasion, "though I have no liking for government, especially this current one." Forced to hustle or panhandle to get through the day, he considers any thoughts about his future to be a "luxury I cannot afford." He reflects, "How much time do I have? Who decides that? I welcome death, but I'm not in a hurry."

As with many woods people, it is not easy to detach John's professed love of freedom from his circumstances. No one, not even Charlie or other old-timers with decades of camp life under their belt, is likely to be in the woods because they actually want to live full-time in a tent, exposed to a variety of threats and harms, and at the mercy of Florida's storms, hurricanes, and pitiless summer heat. They are driven out there by their addictions, trauma, mental illness, economic deprivation, or rejection by their families, while the county's chronic lack of support- ive or affordable housing keeps them homeless. They make the most of their situation by developing views and beliefs that make it seem more voluntary—"life inside four walls is too claustrophobic for me"—but in most cases, they also admit that they would take a more comfortable or stable haven if it came their way.[10] Even Charlie, who appears to savor his lifestyle, tells me he is ready to move out if his girlfriend comes back to him and he can find the right apartment or RV.

Among the exceptions are those with terminal illnesses, for whom the woods are a one-way ticket. One evening at Charlie's compound we are joined by Veronica, an elderly hippie wreathed in bracelets and necklaces, whom I had met in passing in another part of the wood. Thinner than she should be, Veronica has comments to make about the nutritional value of the grocery items she is carrying with her: "I got some twelve-grain bread, that's the healthy stuff, and some beef- steak tomatoes that are fresh and juicy." When she steps away to feed her dog, Charlie, who is unfailingly direct about other people, tells me that Veronica has cancer and has probably come out here to end her days. She is one of several people with cancer I encounter in the Florida woods over the course of the summer. None of them are looking for further medical care, or else they have exhausted what little resources they had on inadequate treatment. The woods are a sanctuary for them, where everyone is in some kind of pain, and where no one will moralize about the narcotics, pills, and alcohol used to ease it.

Originally from Levittown, on Long Island, Veronica was living in an Orlando apartment until two months before, when she fell out with her roommate. After she landed on 192, a police officer directed her toward this patch of woods. "He warned me away from the meth heads over there," she says, gesturing to the west. It has not been an easy tran- sition. Though she has a good barking dog, her tent has already been robbed twice. And because she has a car, her new acquaintances are taking advantage of her to run errands or ferry them to meetings with clinicians and case workers.

Newbies in the woods, especially single women, are easily manipulated, exploited, and worse. Most of the women are in flight from domestic abuse; faced with their new circumstances, they often quickly attach themselves to "boyfriends" for protection, even when these men are themselves abusive. Veronica seems to have different reasons for being here, however. "I get $530 a month from my widow's pension," she tells me, "and $147 every two weeks for disability, and food stamps is another $190. That's better than most people around here, but it's not quite enough for a motel, and the shelter [in Orlando] doesn't take dogs." On the other hand, she says, "Living out here is more expensive than I thought because without a fridge or freezer you have to shop by the day and cannot buy in bulk."

Along with her bag of groceries, Veronica brings some news: a mutual friend has been detained by Walmart security for making a scene, and another one broke her foot that same day in a bike accident. Just then, Todd, a grizzled buddy of Charlie's with biker looks, blows in from the south side of the wood with some beer. Like two retirees sitting around the community pool, he and Charlie share some tips about blood thinners and skincare products and trade appraisals of the squirrel they grilled for their recent Fourth of July dinner. Hearing about Veronica's misfortunes, Todd offers to help relocate her tent and advises her on the best place to sell blood. The two men reminisce about the good times in another wood they used to share further to the west along 192. "Everyone looked out for each other, even though we lived apart," Charlie relates, "but that was before the Puerto Ricans and Mexicans came." Todd warms to the slur: "Yeah, now we have homeless people attacking and stealing from each other. Imagine that!" Racist comments like this are common enough among the almost exclusively white occupants of camps. This one is entirely gratuitous, since it is rare to find Black and Hispanic people in the woods, except in the most remote areas. In any event, minorities are much more vulnerable to aggression from white campers than the other way around.

Long after the summer's end, I run across Charlie's now ex-girlfriend, Louise, a genteel Englishwoman with her own Gothic relationship to the maladies of the woods. "Have you heard about the oak fever?" she politely inquires, as if we are having afternoon tea in the garden of a country house. "I don't know if it's entirely true, but it's well known, and everyone, including the older generation of locals, says it drives Shingle Creek people crazy." I tell her I am aware that certain species of scrub oak have allergens and toxins poisonous to some animals. But she has something more eccentric in mind. The fever, she explains, is caused by "the combination of the decaying oaks that the colonials brought and the native species of scrub and vine." Could she distinguish between woods people who were already mentally unstable and those who are deranged by the trees? "It's difficult to say, but people who leave this area seem to get better, and I know there is a higher percentage of crazies here," she says, adding almost as an afterthought, "I may be one of them."

The forty-acre wood is more than a little enchanted for Louise, and it seems to be protected, in her mind, by the benevolent intervention of those who eliminate threats. She tells me that peregrine falcons released from the nearby Medieval Times attraction have picked off "all the nasty critters," leaving only the lovable and charismatic animals. Likewise, she says, the previous owner, who was "pro-homeless," shot all the troublesome feral hogs. The tranquility of the forest is a battery recharger for her, where she returns to get her "balance" after periodic bouts of employment in Orlando as a live-in caregiver for disabled people.

In her case, the romance of the woods dates to her childhood. Born in Trinidad, Louise was raised in North Wales and the British Midlands. Her grandparents came to vacation in Shingle Creek every year, a tradition continued by her parents (who remembered the Seminole airboat operators). So Louise has been coming to the area all her life, back to the days when the area hosted an orange grove supplying Tropicana, before the great freezes of the 1980s. Over time, her attachment to the wood has turned into a sense of stewardship. "I am worried about the aquifer as well as the trees," she tells me, "because I suppose that

I think of Shingle Creek as a kind of Radiator Springs"—the town in Disney's *Cars* that got bypassed by the highway. This warm sentiment also extends to Osceola County itself. Though the 192 corridor is quite built up, Louise speaks of it still as a "marsh," routinely describing it as a part of the Everglades in need of restoration. Her affection for the place is real, even if her references to its history play loose with the factual record. "Everything is rumor and hearsay in the forty-acre wood," she reminds me.

As it turns out, Louise has also lived in Celebration. Injured in a skating accident in 2013, she moved into the only multifamily unit in the Celebration core that had an elevator, raising her son for a few years there "as a Disney kid." The transition from the prosperous town to the woods was not a tragic descent for her. As much as she enjoyed Celebration living, she had no desire to reside in a multiunit building. "I don't like the density," she confesses, sounding for all the world like a suburbanite with a quarter-acre lot. "I'd rather live in my tent here, surrounded by all this beauty." Ironically, her enchanted wood is now advertised for sale as a lot zoned for multifamily apartments. She hopes it will be saved because the ground is prone to flooding, and so any developer would be required to "fill and build"—a costly prospect. "If you dig a firepit," Louise points out, "you'll hit water pretty quickly here."

By the end of the pandemic summer of 2020, the camps were filling out again with returnees, new arrivals from a wave of motel evictions, and a sprinkling of COVID refugees. During the coronavirus crisis, concentrations of unhoused people in cities around the country were seen as public health threats, and some widely ridiculed alternatives to shelters were introduced by authorities. As most hotel rooms nearby lay empty, San Francisco opened a "safe sleeping village" for socially distanced homeless in the Civic Center Plaza, just yards from City Hall. Las Vegas officials, more notoriously, converted a parking lot into a quarantine area for rough sleepers. In Los Angeles, a thriving self-organized encampment in Echo Park was forcibly uprooted and its members relocated to motel and hotel environments where their behavior was managed as if they were detainees.[11] In Orlando, the shelters were so overcrowded that authorities elected to move some occupants into vacant hotels, but the woods emerged as a better option for distancing and self-isolation. (Camping destinations around the country also saw their busiest season ever.) Even so, the supply of services was stretched thin. Churches shut down operations, and charities lost donors and outreach volunteers, heavily denting the provision of hand sanitizer, masks, and healthcare information. Camp occupants had to rely on their own networks of mutual care.

In the fall, when I visit for the last time, Charlie confirms that no one in the wood has contracted the virus. As Louise points out, "There's nowhere safer from COVID than here in a tent in the great outdoors—we don't go anywhere, and we hardly see anyone." In the interim, a for-profit affordable housing developer from Minneapolis has submitted plans for the forty-acre lot, to build an assisted-living facility for seniors who earn less than 60 percent of area median income.[12] But to Louise's delight, the surveyors found that in some places the water table was higher than they had bargained for. Her charmed wood might be saved after all.

Charlie's leg has not healed properly, but he has acquired a solar panel to run his TV and to charge the batteries he uses for other devices. He is still trying to keep pace with the camp upgrades made by his neighbor John, but his plans for moving out of the woods are more elaborate now. He's thinking of going back to Tennessee: "I found a double-wide with four bedrooms, and it's on twenty acres. I like the idea of some land. I aim to rent it out and build a container house on the property for myself." There might also be someone else in the picture. "I also found me a girlfriend online who is a registered nurse in Nashville," he reports. As with almost everyone I meet in the woods, his escape plan sounds to my ears both practical and improbable at the same time.

HOUSING IS HEALTHCARE

Some of the woods people qualify for services from the Orlando-based Health Care Center for the Homeless (HCCH). This means that they can use the organization's Orange Blossom Family Health clinic, which shares a building with the Hope Center. Raul Salas, the HCCH's outreach coordinator, spends his days ferrying patients to the clinic or to other health facilities to pick up medications, and on occasion I ride shotgun with him. A gentle Bronx-born giant, Raul is passionate about his work, though, due to rural neglect, he faces the challenge of serving the entire 1,500 square miles of Osceola County almost on his own. He knows the camps better than anyone and can expound at length on the difference between "rules of the street," which govern the interactions of urban homeless people, and the camp culture of the woods, where home sites are relatively stable, and camp leaders exercise some say over occupancy and conduct. He is also up on the latest consumption trends—the escalation of heroin use, the explosion of K-2 (synthetic cannabis), and the battle for market dominance between cheap malt beers like Hurricane, Steel Reserve, Icehouse, Four Loko, and Edge. Familiar with the more diverse demographic of New York City's homeless population, Raul is impressed by the resilience of the mostly white campers in 192's woods. "The older ones with rural backgrounds really know how to survive out there," he observes. "And anyway the woods are much more dangerous for minorities, so you generally find them in Orlando or Kissimmee, on the streets."

Meeting with or checking in on clients where they actually live is key to HCHH's healthcare philosophy. For a field worker like Raul, the direct contact allows him to earn trust, pick up on useful gossip, and help stave off calamities before they develop. That said, HCCH, like most homeless service providers, has been transformed by the Housing First paradigm, which prioritizes housing before treatment. According to Dewey Wooden, the clinic's director of behavioral health, the organization's initial aim was "to keep people as healthy as they could while they were in the tents." But now it is committed to transferring them into permanent supportive housing whenever it becomes available through their participation in Central Florida's Homeless Services Network, following the new mantra, "Housing Is Healthcare."

A 2013 survey found Orlando to be the worst midsize metro area for homelessness, and several highly publicized deaths occurred on the streets while people were waiting for housing. An economic impact study, commissioned the following year by the Central Florida Commission on Homelessness, showed that Orange County was spending as much as $31,000 annually on outreach, jail, emergency room, and hospitalization bills for each chronically homeless person.[13] By contrast, the cost of placing them in supportive housing, with case managers to supervise their health, was only $15,000 a year, less than half the cost. Skeptical taxpayers could now be informed that for every dollar spent on services to a homeless person on the street, a mere fifty cents would put them in housing and on the way to self-sufficiency. Advocates have found that citing this kind of proof of reduced costs and quantifiable benefits is more effective than appeals to human rights in persuading lawmakers, officials, and the general public to get behind the Housing First paradigm. In 2016, HCCH initiated a follow-up study, evaluating the effect of placing chronically homeless people in permanent supportive housing with minimal barriers to entry. The results showed significant stabilization and improvement in many areas, including income, incarcerations, and hospitalizations. At the end of the program's first year, every program participant was still housed.[14]

In theory, a combination of federal, state, and county money could be pieced together to cover most of the cost of supportive housing. It is not so easy, however, to find landlords willing to rent to employed homeless people, let alone to the chronically homeless who experience difficulty in holding down a job. In all of Osceola County, there is only one apartment complex—the Remington, a converted fifty-room motel east of Kissimmee—that caters to the latter, and it only accommodates clients fifty-five or older, most of them on disability. In scouting out permanent housing for their clients, Raul and his colleagues are also competing with the transitionally homeless, always looking to move on from their motel rooms. The result is a small trickle of placements, forty at most in Raul's recollection. It is all part of Osceola's poor response to the housing crisis on its doorstep.

"Society's blind eye to homelessness is bad enough," Raul snorts, but when there exists a proven remedy in the form of Housing First, "it is frustrating to have so few opportunities to apply it." Unlike the motel people, very few of the chronically homeless in the woods can be "diverted" to the homes of families or friends. In the meantime, Raul points out, while cheap housing is unavailable, it is all too easy to get your hands on cheap booze, cheap heroin, and cheap cigarettes (305s, made by a Miami firm)—and I find it is very rare to meet anyone in the woods who does not consume at least two of the three.

In Raul's opinion, a small tax on the seventy-five million tourists who visit the region, or those who profit from their visits, would make a big dent in getting Central Florida's unhoused off the streets and out of the woods. Suppliers of housing would still struggle to meet the demand, however. The soapy promise of jobs and easy living brings five thousand new residents to the region each month, among them batches of people who will end up experiencing homelessness. When they wind up in the woods, Raul notes, "they break down mentally before they break down physically." Eventually, he says, "the stigma and hurt and trauma makes it difficult for workers like me to reach them." Faced daily with these obstacles, Raul is scrupulous about reserving his judgment. "I never had your trauma," he tells himself when he meets clients. "I just chose my path in life, but I could easily have gone down your path."

Despite the mental disorientation of many of his clients, it is a mistake, Raul reminds me, to assume they are unaware of how the maldistribution of resources affects them. Later that day, I run into Brandy, another up-front addict, who proves the point by bending my ear. "Why is there county money to build new parks and police precincts and not one cent for a homeless shelter or a treatment center?" she demands. "And why will they only cover three days for detox when everyone knows it takes much longer for heroin withdrawal?" Brandy believes that "alcohol and not heroin should be regulated because heroin addicts don't drive and kill people." She is especially irate about being talked down to by health professionals. "No one will listen to us addicts," she complains, "though we are the ones who know most about substance use—for example, the connection between pain pills and heroin." Soon enough, however, the target of her anger shifts to the county's growing Hispanic population. "I'm American, born and raised here, and I can't get any help," she rages, "but racial favoritism means that the Spanish, who come from another country, get a free ride in the motels, and vouchers, and food stamps."

Brandy tells me that her boyfriend died from crack addiction, and she was evicted from their motel room. Though she had never been a user, she says, she got hooked on heroin from being around homeless addicts. As she puts it, "If you hang out in a barber's, you're gonna end up getting a haircut." Her tent compound, located in a wood to the east of Kissimmee, sports an unusual range of amenities—an outdoor chemical toilet, an array of ice boxes and storage containers for food, a small Christmas tree around the back. As we talk, she is dipping into her box of cleaning products to help remedy some flood damage from the night before. In a house-proud mood, she takes me to the adjacent camp to show off its elaborate outdoor bathtub setup. "At first, I thought: 'I cannot live like this,'" she says. "But I have made it more tolerable, we manage to keep out strangers, and I found that I really like eating in the open air." Still, she keeps returning to the injustices that trap her there. "I've been hearing about these European hostels where they let you have drugs," she muses, "yet here they only build more jails."

In a way that no longer surprises me, Brandy expresses scorn for the inhabitants of another part of the woods. "The alcoholics over there in Betty's camp are judgmental about us drug users," she says. "But they are just as addicted as us, and they are much more rowdy." True enough, when I visit her beer camp the next day, Betty and her companions are loud and jolly. It is late morning, and their drinking has not yet made them soporific. "We only drink beer; that's what we do all day 'cause we can't afford liquor," Betty explains. "We watch all the dealers come and go out there on the street. And we miseducate the po-po when they ask us to inform on them." But, she adds firmly, and with a frown, "no one who uses drugs is allowed in my camp." I decline

Betty's offer of beer and ask about her hospital bracelet. She has had a platelet transfusion for liver cancer, but her health does not seem to be improving. "My brother wants me to go to a hospice, but to me that's a prison. I'd rather be out here, with my freedom," she declares. "And my medication," she adds, tapping the beer can in her lap.

A shy young man, whom Betty calls her adopted son, drops by with some groceries. He chose to live alone deep in the woods after his grandmother died and the house was foreclosed, and now he and two other male companions are Betty's family, for all intents and purposes. "We don't have a dog in this camp," she tells me, "but a raccoon often comes to sleep with me in the tent, and I rub his belly even though I know he is nature's thief." The three men chip in to the conversation with comments about other animal sightings and the water supply (from a nearby warehouse spigot), but they visibly defer to Betty. "I am the physically weakest here, but I have all the authority," she crows. I am thrilled to find out that she also has a Celebration connection—she once had a job there laying sod for a landscaper.

Aside from Brandy's, there are two other heroin camps in the same woods. One of them is run by another cancer sufferer, Frankie, a sad, handsome man in his sixties who has decided to forgo further treatment. His camp has some distinctive features: a walkway of artificial lawn leading through the woods into the compound, an air-conditioning unit set up to blow cold air into his tent, and a wide assortment of butane, propane, and electric grills. Frankie had been a "dirty cop"—a police sergeant running a cocaine operation in New Jersey—and got away with a lighter sentence than he should have, he admits. He is fond of reminiscing about the cocaine scene in 1980s New York City and is able to pinpoint exactly where the drug is locally available, "at the more well-to-do end of 192." His camp is protected by an impressive tarp canopy but has poor ground drainage. At the edges the summer rains have delivered large pools, along with water moccasins, which he ruthlessly dispatches. He spares the even longer indigo snakes, though, because they are a protected species.

The camps of Frankie, Betty, and Brandy are in a good location:

there is a bus stop on the nearest road, a PeopleReady location (for casual labor) and a Wawa store on the corner of the strip, and several prime panhandling spots within a short walk. Frankie found work through PeopleReady for a while, until he was diagnosed. Now he restricts his income-generating activities to working the McDonald's exit—after work is the best time of day for panhandling, especially on Thursday paydays. He recently invited his friend Wendell to stay with him. With Wendell's VA checks, they share the costs of food and gas for the generator.

Older, more fastidious, and with a military bearing, Wendell shares with Frankie a rural upbringing and many of the same self-sufficiency skills. While Frankie's West Virginia family raised cows and pigs, Wendell was reared on a fifty-acre North Carolina farm, growing corn, watermelon, cotton, tobacco, wheat, and cantaloupes. "We were taught how to stretch a dollar," Wendell declares. "I was raised up very hard." Like many homeless people, both Frankie and Wendell are careful about what they eat—we have an informed discussion about mercury levels in fish—and although Frankie is a junkie, he goes along with the health consciousness of his abstemious boarder. Naturally, sharing a tent at their age leads to some friction. Wendell tells me that he "can't stand being dirty and hates smells." But he downplays the issue. "I understand Frankie's feelings, and he understands mine, so we don't argue about anything. We just talk things through."

After he left the army, Wendell had a varied employment history—taxi driver, restaurant sous-chef, security guard—but got swept up in a pill ring and served a two-year sentence. After that, his prospects went downhill. Although he has been homeless for fifteen years now, he says he would like an apartment, preferably near a good fishing spot. His felon record is a liability, however. In any case, he has decided that most of his VA check will go to a college fund for his grandchildren. "I won't need money for my funeral," he declares, "because I'm giving my body to science." Besides, he takes pains to inform me that "we are living in the end days, and it is obvious from the wars all over the world that the Antichrist is afoot." "I do not go to church," he adds, "because most preachers won't talk about Revelations, but I know the Bible real well, and I've reached my own conclusions."

It's unlikely that Frankie and Wendell would get along, let alone form a friendship, under other circumstances. In the extremity of the woods, improbable kinds of camaraderie form around acts of sharing and offers of hospitality. Some are alliances of convenience; others draw on long-standing relationships. Because mental illness is prevalent, wayward behavior and eccentric opinions are tolerated for the sake of companionship. The woods are a last resort for people who have been pushed out of the market but still participate in the economy—as consumers, occasional workers, recyclers, and panhandlers, redistributing commodities and wealth. However loosely the camps are organized, they mostly run on the principle of mutual aid, with services, goods, and information exchanged according to need—and so they offer lessons, surely, in how to make another kind of society, though not under conditions of anyone's choosing. As Frankie puts it, "If you need something, just ask around because someone here will have it or know where you can find it." Then he adds, with a junkie's knowing smile, "but there's only so much that you can actually get."

ANDREW ROSS

5

The Disney Price

THE EXACT ROUTE taken by Hernando de Soto in his foolhardy 1539 journey through the territory of modern-day Florida is much disputed. Some amateur historians propose that, on their trek north from Tampa Bay, de Soto and his companions passed through the Reedy Creek watershed, the location now occupied by Disney World.[1] Most scholars these days chart his path a good bit farther to the west.[2] But the Disney connection makes for a good allegory. After plundering the Inca civilization in the 1530s, de Soto was granted permission by the Spanish king to invade and colonize La Florida, the name given to the entire US Southeast at the time. His goal—to extract gold, found colonies, and exploit native labor—came to naught. There were no precious metals in Florida, and the value of the state's vast phosphate deposits was not recognized until the 1880s. But more than four centuries after de Soto's journey, that Reedy Creek location would become an inexhaustible treasure trove for the Walt Disney Company, pumping out revenues at a scale comparable to the world's great gold fields in South Africa's Witwatersrand Basin, Brazil's Minas Gerais, and Peru's Yanacocha.

Disney World's southern border runs along Route 192, bounded by I-4 and SR 429, which lies to the west of Reedy Creek, a headwater of the Everglades. The south side of Route 192 forms the northern border of Celebration, the iconic town that Disney built during the 1990s. Neither entity has buildings directly on Route 192, but Disney's ability to squeeze profits from these lands and those who labor on them is key to understanding many of the housing and homeless challenges associated with the corridor.

The Disney World enterprise (originally code-named "The Florida Project") has been the most successful capitalist land development in modern history. In 2019, Disney's theme parks and resorts generated more revenue ($26.23 billion) than its media networks ($24.83 billion), and more than twice as much as its studio entertainment division ($11.13 billion).[3] As for the material impact on populations, there is no comparison with the other divisions of the company's global empire. Of the seventy-five million people who come annually to Central Florida, most are drawn by Disney's four theme parks, two water parks, 24,000 hotel rooms, and 3,000 time-share units. This is a mass annual migration unmatched anywhere on the planet. By comparison, before the pandemic, New York City attracted about sixty-five million domestic and international visitors per year but has a much larger population, range of accommodations, and quality of public infrastructure to support them.

A visit to Disney World is the nearest thing to a compulsory secular pilgrimage for many American families. It is expected and demanded by generations of children, whose parents tailor their household budgets for several years to save for a trip, then repeat the cycle for second and third visits.[4] There is no comparable ritual in American life, except perhaps for obligatory school trips to the nation's capital. However "nationalized," the Disney ritual has also been successfully marketed to international visitors, enabled by mass air travel. It gets pitched, with particular attention, to populations in the orbit of the company's overseas locations. The establishment of Disney theme parks in France, Japan, Hong Kong, and China, far from satiating domestic tourist appetites, seems only to have stimulated the desire for a second visit, to sample the "real thing" in Florida or California.

Central Florida has only 2.5 million residents, so the ratio of guests to hosts in the area is thirty to one. The region's primary economic role is therefore to serve as a *destination*, primed to prioritize the accommodation, transportation, and recreational needs of visitors who spend several days at a time there. The well-being of locals plays second string to that of visitors. This is especially true of Central Florida's army of 280,000 leisure, hospitality, and tourism (LHT) workers, who represented a full 20 percent of the region's labor force before the pandemic. According to one study, LHT workers nationwide earn an average of $311 per week—less than half of the nationwide weekly average of $710 for all workers.[5] In Central Florida, their prominence within the workforce means that their paltry pay packets significantly depress the region's median wage, making it the very lowest among major tourism destinations and metro areas in the US.

Despite almost fifty years of continual expansion, Disney World still has lots of room to grow within its remaining land dominion of 24,700 acres. Over the years, the company has stepped up its efforts to corral and contain the movement of its customers, striving to capture their spending within its own property line by building thousands of hotel rooms and a full spectrum of eateries, micro-attractions, and shopping centers. But this has not slowed the rapid commercial development of land outside the line, transforming the entire region into a $75-billion-a-year tourist trap, and yielding the unsightly sprawl that urban planners and old-time Floridians regard with loathing.

Nor has the explosion of rival attractions—Universal Studios, Sea World, Discovery Cove, Gatorland, Holy Land, Legoland, Icon Park, Old Town, and dozens of others—eaten away at Disney's revenue stream. The price of entry to the company's Magic Kingdom, EPCOT, Animal Kingdom, and Hollywood Studios keeps rising, with no discernible impact on attendance figures. In one decade, between 2007 and 2017, ticket prices increased by 50 percent, despite complaints about overcrowding and laments about "leaving behind the middle class." In 1971, when the park opened, one-day admission for an adult cost $3.50, or $22.24 in 2019 dollars, whereas the equivalent 2019 ticket price was as much as $129.[6] Given the stagnation of average American wages over the last four decades, these numbers speak to the increasing gentrification of the theme park experience. At least one commentator has pointed out that Disney "doesn't really know the maximum price that a guest will pay for a ticket to their theme parks."[7] Nor do middlemen and hucksters know of a limit to how much prospective visitors will pay for "discounted" tickets; roadside signs advertising these kinds of dodgy deals pop up as soon as you cross the Florida state line from Georgia, hundreds of miles to the north.

Company profits aside, there are many other ways to talk about the impact of the "Disney price" on the land and livelihoods of Central Floridians. The environmental toll of tourist industry development on fragile ecosystems has been particularly devastating, and the region's economic landscape has been entirely remade as well. Almost every LHT business in the region is parasitical on the Mouse, vying for a bite of the spending budget that visitors bring with them. Many other sectors—retail, construction, professional and business services, and the convention business—are indirectly dependent on it. A single-industry economy is highly vulnerable to a downturn. And this is exactly what happened when the coronavirus struck, forcing families to sacrifice Florida vacations and decimating the industry workforce.

Disney's career in Central Florida is a well-known case study in how a private corporation managed to seize for itself expansive governmental powers. After buying up forty-three square miles of land through multiple shell companies, Disney petitioned Florida's legislature for the creation of a "special district," a governmental entity that can issue its own tax-exempt bonds instead of drawing on the local county budget. Most such districts are single-purpose, designed to pay for infrastructure improvements such as swamp drainage. Disney, however, unveiled a vision for a new city of twenty thousand inhabitants to be built on the property: EPCOT, the Experimental Prototype Community of Tomorrow. Dazzled by the proposal, state officials granted the new Reedy Creek Improvement District a wide-ranging charter. Not only could it issue bonds, but it could also write its own building codes, control its own utilities, policing, and fire service, and even build its own nuclear power plant. The district would be governed by a five-member board elected by a vote of the district's landowners, among whom Disney is by far the largest. It is effectively a puppet government.

Introduced to the public by Walt Disney in a 1966 short film, EPCOT was presented as an initiative for addressing urban challenges. As Walt himself put it, "There's nothing more important to people everywhere than finding solutions to the problems of our cities." The film's pitch was for high-quality planned urbanism focused on "public need." "There will be no slum areas because we won't let them develop," he proclaimed. "There will be no landowners and therefore no voting control. People will rent houses instead of buying them, and at modest rentals. There will be no retirees; everyone must be employed." In retrospect, it is ironic that EPCOT was envisaged as a town where workers could be housed "at modest rentals." Had this promise been carried out, it would at least have created a kind of company town, guaranteeing affordable housing for Disney World employees. But this was not to be. Within a few years, it became clear that this draft of EPCOT was little more than an expedient vehicle to extract planning permissions and self-governing powers for the fiefdom sometimes referred to as "Florida's 68th County."[8] Once the company got what it wanted from Florida's wide-eyed lawmakers, Walt's idealized rendering promptly vanished.

The resulting immunity from public scrutiny and regulation has always rankled locals, so Disney is under constant pressure to diplomatically present itself as a force for good in the region. In 2011, for example, in a bid to fight back against its reputation as an imperious, stingy neighbor, the company commissioned a study on Disney World's economic impact.[9] According to this report, prepared by a GOP consulting agency, the theme parks and resorts generated $18.2 billion in economic activity—2.5 percent of Florida's GDP—and were responsible for one of every fifty jobs in the state.[10]

Coming in the depths of the Great Recession, numbers like these painted a rosy picture and lent credence to the enduring belief that business is better for everyone when the Mouse is in your backyard. But the survey offered no accounting for how much money is siphoned out of the state by the company or by the other businesses dependent on the Disney World visitors' budgets. In fact, the *Orlando Sentinel* calculated in 2019 that a full 35 percent of the money that vacationers spend on a typical Disney trip ends up out of state.[11] Nor does the state collect its fair share of taxes on these extracted profits. Because Florida's tax laws allow income shifting between a company's divisions and do not require combined reporting of revenue, corporations are able to minimize their tax bills. Through the loophole of setting up "pass-through" businesses, profits can be hauled off tax-free. Only one in a hundred firms actually pays the state's 5.5 percent tax on corporate profits.[12]

Disney benefits from these loopholes, just as it has followed the corporate trend of parking profits in overseas subsidiaries and havens to avoid US taxation.[13] The corporation does generate significant revenue in sales and property taxes for the state and local counties, but it zealously lobbies to reduce its tax obligations wherever possible, and its influence over the state legislature is legendary. In 2018, for example, Disney spent a whopping $28.3 million on Florida elections, including a substantial amount targeted at tax-avoidance measures.[14]

While the company lavishes millions on politicians, most of the 78,000 workers in "The Happiest Place on Earth" are paid a poverty wage. It's a long-standing grievance that the company's much-vaunted employee benefits do not outweigh the deficit in their wages. Those benefits include passes to the parks, discounts at participating restaurants, discounted on-site child care, college tuition, and the opportunity to buy decommissioned company items at the "property control" store. But the perks do not make up for the often desperate financial circumstances that Disney workers find themselves in. Even as the cast members (as all employees are known) bring pixie dust into the lives of Disney's paying guests, most of them struggle to make the rent.

HEIGH-HO, HEIGH-HO?

In 2017, Occidental College analysts issued a devastating study of employee conditions at Disneyland, in Southern California. When adjusted for inflation, the report found that hourly wages at the resort had actually decreased by 15 percent since 2000. While the company was negotiating CEO Bob Iger's four-year compensation agreement for an estimated $423 million, almost three-quarters of the Anaheim workforce did not earn enough to cover basic expenses, two-thirds were food insecure, more than half had concerns about being evicted, and one out of ten reported being homeless in the previous two years. Since their workplace is located in one of the nation's most expensive housing markets, at least a third of them were undertaking hour-long commutes.[15] In the wake of the report, stories emerged of workers living in their cars; almost inevitably, news circulated that one of them had died in her vehicle, undetected for several days.[16]

Bernie Sanders and other high-profile politicians jumped on the report, excoriating Disney for paying starvation wages as it was raking in more than $12 billion in annual profits and rewarding executives with stratospheric salaries. Worker testimony was heartbreaking. "Since I started working for Disney, because my wages are so low, I had to move my 16-year-old daughter out of the house," an employee at Disney's Grand California Hotel recounted. "I can no longer afford to take care of her, so my family members have taken her in and are supporting her. I currently don't make enough to eat three times a day. I eat cans of tuna or celery sticks and carrots because that's what I can afford. I typically eat once, sometimes twice, a day because I can't afford three meals a day."[17]

In the environs of Disney World, conditions are just as dire. Gabby Alcantara-Anderson, a shop steward at UNITE HERE Local 362, which represents many of the lowest-paid cast members, tells me that "for many years, the wage hikes were minimal or none at all, and our bene-fits were being cut." Gabby, whose household includes an ailing mother she is committed to nursing, is no stranger to hardship. She commutes sixty miles each way to reduce her housing costs. "There have defi-nitely been times in my household," she confides, "when it's like, 'okay, kids, there's rice for tonight, then rice tomorrow, but there will be dif-ferent sides with the rice; you can have soy sauce or duck sauce, and

whichever white rice you like.'" But despite her own struggles, Gabby—
a much-loved supervisor at Frontierland attractions like Thunder
Mountain and Tom Sawyer Island—is good for twenty dollars when
one of the cast members in her team has nothing to eat. "Eight or nine
of them live in a two-bedroom apartment, with air mattresses and
sleeping bags and a couch, and they rotate through who gets the bed on
certain nights," she tells me. "They only have one bathroom, so they
have to ration shower time, and their clothes are all in trash bags."

These grim living conditions make for a stark contrast with the
cheery emotional labor required from cast members. Much of their
work lies in producing a "magical" customer experience, even when
dealing with guests frustrated by long lines and the rigid rules of conduct on rides. The anger of visitors has to be absorbed or redirected by
the protective shield of the employee's Disney smile and upbeat persona. Guests are quick to detect cracks in the shield, Gabby says, and, as
an area supervisor, she often has to field the complaints. "A typical kind
of low-energy comment might be, 'That cast member doesn't look too
happy,' or 'That's not very Disney,' or 'What's wrong with her magic
today?'" Meanwhile, cast members are an easy target for overheated,
dehydrated, and often inebriated visitors (hard alcohol is available in
almost all sections of Disney theme parks). Employee tales of physical
and verbal abuse, sexual assault, and race-baiting are legion.[18]

Deflecting or turning around customer anger is an occupational
challenge for almost every service worker coached in the credo that
"the customer is always right." But Disney managers take it to another
level, striving to uphold the company's reputation as the gold standard
for customer satisfaction. While the ability to project an animated,
welcoming presence is a minimum requirement of the job, more is
demanded. Cast members must learn how to communicate their
perkiness as "authentic" because visitors are always on the lookout
for fake emotions. They have paid through the nose to visit an artificial landscape, but they want real responses from the greeters, guides,
and attendants. As Gabby puts it, "Disney ideally wants the guests to
believe theme park employees are happy-go-lucky kids doing this job

for fun," so the company takes pains to conceal the fact that "most of us are career employees who have pensions, at least if we are union, at the end of our work lives."

In a much-cited study of Delta flight attendants in the early 1980s, Arlie Hochschild found that the workers spoke of their obligatory workplace smile as being "on them" but not "of them."[19] The requirement to keep a happy face for hours on end (which has become much less widely observed in today's airline industry) has significant health consequences. Some attendants developed smile lines; others found that the constant pressure to simulate warmth and friendliness with customers harmed their social lives when they were off duty. Not surprisingly, I found that this kind of forced geniality is also an occupational hazard in "The Happiest Place on Earth."

In one of my meetings with a group of Disney World employees, several individuals let off steam about the emotional gap between their onstage and offstage personalities. Brian, a Magic Kingdom ride operator, admits he became "dangerously skinny" from "not eating enough" during his time in Disney's college program. Now in a regular payroll position at Splash Mountain, he confesses that he "has trouble finding the real me" after dropping his happy workplace face. "My wife wonders which Brian she is getting when I get home." His coworker Laura forewarns her husband "to give me twenty minutes, to deal with when I am screaming inside from the hurt and anger." Stella, a Frontierland guide who says her "face often hurts from smiling," resents that she has to make herself frown when she is offstage to snap out of it. Gabby points out that "it takes lots of mental fortitude to maintain that persona," especially when you do not have a sunny disposition, or "when there are personal troubles in your life." Of course, an effective servicesector smile also depends on having healthy teeth, and it is therefore ironic that in a 2018 survey of Disneyland workers, 43 percent reported that they could not afford adequate dental care.

Despite the high performance standards expected of them, the guest-facing cast members I interviewed were not cynical about the workplace pressure to be perky. In the boot camp environment of

Disney University, they receive instruction on how to "create happiness." They learn that their personalities are the key ingredient in the theme park experience, so their own pleasure must be made noticeable to visitors. Critics quite reasonably see this as a form of indoctrination, a sinister aspect of the "cult of the Mouse" from which the company harvests its profits. But the employees I interviewed were not dupes of the training modules. They were fully aware of their employer's self-interest in providing this attitudinal training, but many of them still spoke about their own passion for the workplace and the pride they took in their paid roles as cast members.

"No one cares that much about the rides," observes Gemma Danes, who has worked for thirteen years in the Magic Kingdom and EPCOT. "Everyone knows that we are the magic. We are the ones who make the memories for guests." She does not consider herself to be a "super-happy person in real life" and is impressed that some of her coworkers "just seem to wake up covered in blissed-out pixie dust at six a.m." But she has found it difficult to "resist the fun that is all around us in the parks." When I ask her to elaborate, she says, "The fun is not just infectious, like coming from the kids and families. It is something that we create by being there, and it's just not anywhere else in our own lives. No one works here for the money," she assures me. "We get our kicks in other ways, giving the guests what we got when we came here as kids."

This is a reference to Disney's doctrine of intergenerational continuity: the company wants young visitors to return when they have children of their own, and then again later with grandchildren. Cast members are trained to work hard to turn a child's positive experience into a "memory" that Disney will try to reactivate and re-create later in their life through marketing and outreach. For cast members, likewise, gratitude for their own memories feeds their appetite for delivering the magic to a new generation of visitors. Gabby, the Frontierland supervisor, recalls the joy she felt "the first time I moved a guest to tears," and also "the first time that I made a truly magical moment for a family": "I was playing checkers with a little boy, and I let him win, of course, and then made him 'Checkers Champion of the West' so I could give him a Fast Pass. That's how I was able to directly improve that family's day."

For Gemma, as for many others, the time she spent in the Disney College Program is key to her workplace commitment. "Having anything Disney on your résumé is a big advantage, and that's partly why so many students do it," she acknowledges. "But it's also where I learned that work did not have to be soul-destroying, which had been my experience up until then. It was a lot of fun, and I wanted more of it." At the same time, Disney critics have rightly portrayed the college program as a convenient source of cheap labor—and, as in any company town, the employer recoups most of the wages in the student's housing fees, with much of the rest captured by their patronage of in-house eateries or groceries.

In a similar vein, the workplace joy described by Gemma and others is a good example of how "passionate labor" is now routinely exploited by employers.[20] This is how the trade-off works: because love of performing, crafting, teaching, or problem-solving in a creative field delivers personal gratification, employees are then implicitly offered this emotional reward as compensation for underwhelming pay. Sometimes termed "self-exploitation" because the concession (or sacrifice) is voluntary, it is a staple feature of "interesting" or fulfilling workplaces. Employers are able to take advantage of the personal buy-in to extract longer hours, extra effort, and commitment to delivering a polished product or fun service. The Disney employees I interviewed fully acknowledged their affection for the pixie dust. But they seemed perfectly capable of separating that emotional allegiance from their indignation about the mismatch between their low wages and area rents—which often leads to workers living in cars or in overcrowded apartments where beds are shared by cast members assigned to different shifts.

Compared to those arrangements, a room in one of the extended-stay motels on Route 192 could seem like a relatively stable option. When Ramona Gutiérrez, a short-order cook from Georgia, got a promotion to one of the Magic Kingdom's biggest restaurants, she

opted, like many other cast members, to stay in the poorly maintained motel known as HomeSuiteHome. (Its owner, Dianna Chane,
is the one who sued the Osceola County sheriff for not carrying out
evictions she wanted.) "I lived off ramen noodles and the McDonald's
Dollar Menu in an apartment with four others until I checked into that
motel," Ramona recalls. "There was more privacy there, but I still felt
homeless—technically I guess I was—and was too embarrassed to tell
any of my family or friends. I never felt safe, it was crawling with bedbugs, and then the ceiling collapsed on me. All this time I was working
at the happiest place in the world and felt fulfilled in my job."

FIGHT FOR FIFTEEN

The master contract negotiated periodically between Disney and the
company's unions was due for renewal in 2018, and the plight of pre-
cariously housed company employees inevitably became part of the
unions' PR campaign in the run-up to the negotiations. "I was one of
those motel cast members," says Mike Beaver, who, like Gabby, is a
shop steward for Local 362. A Disney employee for fifteen years, Mike
started out sharing a house owned by a fellow cast member, but the
struggle to make the monthly payments proved too much. Motel life
beckoned, and Mike wound up taking a room share with a friend at
the Star Motel, long notorious as a drug hot spot that attracted almost
daily visits from Osceola deputies. "It's not the greatest motel," Mike
concedes, "but you don't want to be out on the streets or be in a car."
He keeps to himself and tries to block out the often messy lives of his
neighbors. "My roommate and I pay $127 a week each," he tells me. "It
would be cheaper if we could pay the monthly rate of $900"—but that
would require more money up front than they can spare at any given
moment.

In 2017, Mike was profiled in an *Orlando Sentinel* story that contrasted his economic challenges with his upbeat personality. Unable
to afford a car, he commutes from his motel to the Magic Kingdom
by public bus and is known for the Donald Duck impersonations he

provides for his fellow passengers. "I love putting smiles on people's faces," he tells me at our first meeting. "I can get on the bus and if someone is having a rough day, they'll look around and smile." Since he works in the Magic Kingdom interactive comedy attraction called Monsters, Inc. Laugh Floor, mirth making is part of his job; his own laugh is an explosive discharge. But his true passion seems to be his role in the union. "God called me to be a shop steward, and so now God has me in this motel for a reason," he assures me. "I got to see, firsthand, how the families in there are struggling. Even if I move to an apartment, what I have experienced in this motel is a life-changing experience I'll never forget, and I'll fight for the people that can't do so for themselves."

The stakes of the union fight were particularly high in Central Florida, which has a much less diverse economy than Southern California and has had a hard time attracting industries with higher-wage jobs. This gives Disney World an outsize local role: the Mouse is in a position to dictate the wage floor in the tri-county region. During the previous master contract negotiation, in 2014, Disney World's service unions had negotiated a rise in minimum hourly pay from $8 to $10. In a tightening labor market, other big employers in the area had followed suit. Now the unions wanted to get to $15 per hour—a 50 percent raise. Eric Clinton, president of Local 362, summarized the challenge: "Could Disney afford to pay a decent wage like that? No question. But how could we make them do it?"

Fortunately, the negotiations came at a time of widespread public anger about deepening economic inequality, particularly the yawning gulf between top executive pay and the wages of workers at the bottom. What's more, by 2017 the campaign for a $15 minimum wage had become a national movement. Initiated in 2012 by New York City fast-food workers, it had quickly spread to workers in retail and home healthcare. Over the following years, several states and major cities had enacted the $15 minimum, and some large employers—including Amazon, Facebook, Costco, Target, and Wells Fargo—had agreed to it as well. Pressure was mounting for others to get on board.

There was little history of strong solidarity among the six Disney World unions (representing transportation workers, stagehands, custodial workers, food manufacturers, housekeeping, and food service employees) affiliated with the Services Trades Council Union. But from the outset of the $15 campaign, things felt different, with an unprecedented level of accord. "The idea of us all talking together freaked Disney out," Clinton explained, since the company was accustomed to picking them off with separate side agreements. According to UNITE HERE Local 737 president Jeremy Haicken, "We never broke ranks once."[21] Disney's initial offer—a dollar-an-hour raise over two years, coupled with a $200 signing bonus—was rejected by 93 percent of rank-and-file members. In the meantime, the company landed a $1.6 billion windfall from Donald Trump's corporate tax cuts and offered a $1,000 bonus to all of its 125,000 full-time and part-time employees in the US. But management also threatened to withhold these one-time bonuses from the 43,000 union workers unless they accepted the initial deal.

This effort to extort members backfired. The unions filed an unfair labor practices complaint for discriminating against cast members engaged in bargaining and decided to take the campaign public. Several small rallies culminated in a mass protest in 2017 at the Crossroads entrance to Disney World. (It looked for all the world like a picket at the dream factory gate, but, since the union contract forbids picketing, it was billed as a "parade.") In the spring of 2018, hundreds more marched toward the entrance to Disney Springs, holding picket signs and balloons. Faced with a potential PR debacle, management caved, agreeing to a series of 75-cent incremental hikes that would see the minimum wage reach $15 by October 2021.[22] It was a remarkable triumph. "Not one cast member I knew thought we could get $15," Gabby told me. She believes that the contract will "change the socioeconomic map around here" and that one of the immediate payoffs will be to see the people on her team "move off food stamps and into their own apartments."

Two months after the Disney World agreement was announced, the

UNITE locals called for Universal to match the raises, and issued a press release for a public march on the rival theme park. Just hours before the march was scheduled to begin, Universal announced a pay hike from $10 to $12 and an increase to $15 in 2023. "We won for everyone," the unions boasted, and it wouldn't take long for that proud slogan to come true. In the November 2020 election, Florida voters approved an amendment to raise the minimum wage to $15 by 2026 for the entire state, despite vigorous and well-funded opposition from the Chamber of Commerce, the Florida Restaurant and Lodging Association, and other tourist industry trade groups.

Corporations with large revenue streams can easily afford a $15 minimum wage. Smaller firms with thinner profit margins might have a tougher time. Yet if they cannot pay a living wage, they should not be in business. And if the pandemic had not dealt a grievous blow to Central Florida's workforce, the Disney wage hikes alone would have pushed an additional one billion dollars into the region's economy during the four-year contract. When the economy recovers, small businesses through-out the area will see more revenue from the additional spending. And for some Disney workers, the new union contract did allow them a pathway out of the motels. As the hikes began to kick in, I encountered several cast members who were able to make the transition. Ramona, the short-order cook, seized her chance to escape from HomeSuite-Home (now under new management as the Banyan Hotel). "My new apartment costs fourteen hundred dollars, which is still a stretch for me," she says. "But it's two bedrooms, and for the first time since I started work down here, I feel human—living in a home that gives me some self-respect." Another grateful cast member who made the move tells me: "We just had our first Thanksgiving dinner when we didn't have to sit on my son's bed."

Marie, an EPCOT greeter from Northwest Ohio, had a more mixed experience. When I first met her, she was paying $205 weekly in the Capri Inn for a room she shared with her estranged husband and was working evenings in the motel office to make ends meet. She had no trouble getting the Disney job. "I applied online when I knew I was moving to this area, had an interview the day I got down here, and was hired on the spot." She was a natural. "I'm a people person. I've always been that way, so I just took me to Disney, and I have had a ball for the last six years on the job—guests thank me for having the same smile on my face when they're leaving; they can't believe that I have it that late in the afternoon." The room-sharing arrangement was a strain, however, and her husband's income did not add enough to get them out of the motel. With the new union contract, Marie was now convinced she could make the move, and she sent for her thirty-five-year-old daughter to join her in Florida. They rented a trailer home together just off the strip. But her daughter could only find an eight-dollar-an-hour job with an hour-long commute, so she returned to Ohio after six months. Marie could not afford the mobile home alone, but the second step of the wage hike did allow her to get her own room at the Capri, without her ex and his contribution. "I have my own art on the walls," she points out, "my own quilt, my own hot plate, and enough money to splurge now and again."

Cast members who want to escape from rundown motels but cannot yet afford an apartment look at places like Backlot Apartments, a long-abandoned Travelodge undergoing conversion into three-hundred-square-foot studio apartments for rent. Its proximity to the theme parks, at the western end of 192, is a prime advantage. Backlot is the second motel property in the region to be repurposed by One Stop Housing, which mostly has units in Sarasota and Manatee Counties on Florida's Gulf Coast. The company presents itself as offering a "second chance" to working-class renters at risk of falling into homelessness. Applicants are screened for their rental and criminal history and rejected if they have an eviction within the past seven years. They must earn enough to cover a rent of $775 per month, inclusive of utility costs—a rate considered affordable to someone on the $26,000 median income of a service industry worker in Florida.

In Sarasota, One Stop Housing encourages residents to graduate from its studios to its one- and two-bedroom units. In Osceola County, the model would fit nicely with Disney's stepped wage hikes: cast members could move up to one- and two-bedroom apartments when their yearly pay increases kick in. But Backlot only has efficiency studios, so tenants have to transition to market-rate apartments elsewhere if they want to move up. In the meantime, though, they have a safe, stable residence that costs less than a motel (even if it still looks and feels like one), and they can build up their credit score along with their rental record.

Cole Washington and Kareem Burrow both moved into Backlot studios shortly after the building opened up, and they had just gotten their first Disney pay increase when I talked to them during a visit. Cole, a security officer, lived previously in a number of Kissimmee area motels, while Kareem had braved HomeSuiteHome for almost three years. They had been approved for Backlot on the strength of their pay hikes and were grateful that the manager only asked for the first (and not the last) month's rent along with the deposit. Cole is already looking to move up into a one-bedroom apartment, but he has run into a problem: when potential landlords "hear that I am Disney," he tells me, "I'm sure they jack up the rent." Kareem, too, has heard of landlords raising rents because Disney is raising wages. "There is a crazy perception that Disney workers are well off," he says. "And maybe we are getting paid more than the guy working at the Days Inn, but it's unfair to charge us more." It was the first time I heard about this practice, but other Disney employees reported similar stories about landlords trying to squeeze more rent from them. When I ask Gabby, she nods knowingly. "When wages rise like a helium balloon, rents shoot up like a Roman candle," she says.

Is it possible that the hard-won pay raise at Disney World will simply get absorbed by higher rents and retail prices? Opponents of minimum-wage hikes often make arguments of this kind, suggesting that businesses just raise their prices in response. In addition, they reason, increasing income without increasing housing supply puts more pressure on the low-end rental market, resulting in higher rents. There is no definitive data to either support or refute these arguments; since most pay increases kick in over a multiyear period, it is particularly difficult to track the impacts. Housing supply in the private market is also likely to shift during that period, in response to the prospect of tenants having more options. But in general, although minimum-wage increases promise working people a pathway out of poverty, on their own they are rarely enough to secure permanently affordable housing. Given the persistent failure of private housing markets to deliver, pay raises need to be coupled with effective rent controls and with sustained public investments in nonprofit, community-owned social housing in order to create permanently affordable units.

Besides, a $15 minimum wage may be a big hike in many localities, but it will not bridge the housing gap. According to the National Low Income Housing Coalition, in 2020 the fair market rent in Osceola was $989 a month for a studio, $1,064 for a one-bedroom, and $1,248 for a two-bedroom. To afford those apartments while spending no more than 30 percent of their income on rent, full-time workers would need wages of $19.02, $20.46, and $24.00 per hour, respectively.[23] Even when Disney cast members finally see that $15 minimum wage in their wage packet in the fall of 2021, a fair market studio apartment still won't be affordable for them. The magic they conjure up from their hearts is the monetary lifeblood of the company, underwriting its vast profits year after year. By any measure, they are owed a whole lot more than $15.

OUT OF WORK

The COVID-19 pandemic delivered a sharp blow to most employers, especially small businesses with scarce capital reserves. It also broke the momentum of rising wages across the country. After mass layoffs, the ready availability of workers desperate for jobs meant that demands for higher pay would be on mute for a while. During the first months of the pandemic lockdown, national unemployment levels went from record lows to record highs. LHT industry employees in top travel destinations like New York, Hawaii, New Orleans, Los Angeles, Las Vegas, Miami, Atlantic City, Myrtle Beach, Flagstaff, and Orlando were the hardest hit of all. When the theme parks closed in March 2020, Disney World unions pushed for employees to continue receiving pay during the shutdown. But that arrangement lasted only for five weeks, and then Disney furloughed almost all of its general workforce.[24] Almost every other big regional employer also furloughed or laid off workers en masse. In May, when the nationwide jobless rate stood at 13.3 percent, it reached 14.5 percent in Florida statewide, 22.6 percent in Central Florida, and a staggering 31.1 percent in Osceola County.[25]

Florida's unemployment benefits max out at $275 a week—one of the lowest payouts in the US—and its application system proved to be a nightmare. (Eventually, Governor Ron DeSantis was forced to acknowledge that the system had been explicitly designed by his predecessor, Rick Scott, to be dysfunctional, so that claimants would give up trying to navigate it.) A full month after the first wave of unemployment registrations, only 34,000 of the 850,000 pending claims had been paid, making Florida one of the worst states at meeting its obligations to the jobless.[26] Two months later, the glitches had still not been resolved, and many of those who did start receiving checks were being randomly kicked off the system. For those waiting on payments, it was simply impossible to make the rent. Orange County's rent relief and foreclosure prevention program was so overloaded with applications that it shut down, though its mayor pledged to use federal stimulus funds to "divert" evictions and keep a roof over some heads. In Osceola, which had even less funding available, the rent relief lottery for five hundred applicants filled up within minutes of opening on the first day of each month. Orlando's homeless shelters began to fill up with first-time homeless people, some of them from the Osceola motels.

Like many Republican-led states, Florida lifted restrictions prematurely in the first few months of the pandemic. By the time Disney World partially reopened in July, COVID-19 infection rates had risen sharply. Despite their economic suffering, almost twenty thousand cast members signed a petition calling, unsuccessfully, for the opening to be postponed until worker safety could be better guaranteed.[27] In a move that enraged the Actors' Equity union (representing onstage performers), Disney World decided not to provide COVID testing for employees, relying instead on temperature checks. Its rigorous cleaning and distancing protocols were designed primarily to reassure guests, and infections that spread among cast members went unreported for fear of keeping these guests away. Gabby contracted the virus in June—"I felt my body was encased in concrete," she says—and was still suffering from serious consequences, including loss of taste and smell, when I saw her in October. "Lots of my cast got sick; they just disappear for a while, and some die," she told me. "Everyone knows what's up, but there's no incentive for anyone to really talk about it." In many ways, Disney's cast members were the region's "essential workers," a core labor force around which Central Florida's economy revolved. Like the pandemic's frontline employees—nurses, grocery store clerks, deliverymen, farmworkers—they had little choice but to balance their livelihoods against the risk of dying on the job.

By the end of the summer it was clear that attendance numbers at theme parks were much lower than expected, so the company decided to lay off thousands of workers whom it had previously put on furlough. At Disney World, a fifth of the entire workforce—more than 8,800 of the furloughed part-time union employees, plus 6,700 non-union employees—was cut loose, adding to the already long lines at UNITE HERE's weekly food bank.[28] Many of these cast members had been with the company for ten years or more. The layoffs were a crushing blow to the region, especially small businesses reliant on the workers' consumer power.

Mike Beaver still had his job, but his living arrangements were becoming increasingly dire. Creditors and county authorities had finally caught up with the owner of the Star Motel, who now faced foreclosure on account of numerous code violations, loan defaults, and unpaid utility bills and property taxes.[29] Over the summer, a water main rupture flooded the property. The utilities were shut off, garbage mounds piled up, and sewage began to back up in some rooms. Mike hung on, though he was preparing for the worst. "I am doing spring cleaning and throwing things out in case I have to move suddenly," he reported. In September, the Star became national news when the *Washington Post* carried a story detailing the abandonment of its residents by state and county departments.[30] Shamed by the coverage, officials leaned on the Hope Center and other homeless advocates to help find temporary housing for some of the residents in other motels.[31] A new owner proposed to refurbish the Star and its sister property, the Lake Cecile Inn (abandoned months earlier), as a "transitional living" center, with solar panels and a community garden. Unpersuaded by this vision, the county commissioners cited the motels as a public health hazard in early 2021, and voted to condemn them.

Mike was the last of the remaining occupants to continue paying rent and performing basic maintenance on the building. "This is nothing compared to growing up in my Iowa town," he insists. "I get my sixty batteries from Dollar Tree to operate my fan, and I am helping to stock a food pantry" in one of the vacated rooms. "God has told me to stay here and to stand up for what's right," he proclaims, as we picnic on the grass verge outside the trashed-out motel. "I am rattling the cages of the politicians because I am in a position to put them on notice about the problems in the motels and the low pay of cast members." Two months later, when the preparations for demolition began, he was finally forced out and checked into the Sun Inn motel farther along the corridor.

GIVING, LENDING, OR TAXING?

Disney's response to its employees' acute housing needs has been dismal. What about other corporations in its league? When Amazon announced in November 2018 that it would build a second headquarters in Long Island City, realtors and landlords jumped to attention, and housing prices and rents in the area began to surge. A few months later, the company canceled the plan in the face of grassroots resistance driven by concerns about rent inflation and displacement of longtime residents. After its pullout, rental prices in the Queens neighborhood fell back.[32] However, the same frenzy seized hold of Northern Virginia's

Arlington County, where Amazon opted to locate the new campus instead. Reports of prices rising in anticipation of its arrival fueled the public perception that corporate giants, especially those with highly paid white-collar employees, are implicated in the housing crisis. If so, how should they be held accountable for helping to resolve it?

Back home in Seattle, Amazon was fighting tooth and nail to avoid any accountability. In May 2018, the city council unanimously approved a tax of $275 per employee on companies making more than $20 million a year, with the proceeds used to help fund housing for the city's burgeoning homeless population. In response, Amazon threatened to halt its downtown expansion and hinted it might leave Seattle altogether. Along with Starbucks and other affected corporations, it began a signature-gathering initiative to place a repeal of the tax on the November ballot. Cowed by the threats, the city council reversed its decision less than a month after putting the tax in place.[33]

Similar fights have been playing out elsewhere, with varying results. In San Francisco, a tax on big businesses to help fund homeless initiatives was opposed by several tech companies (including Lyft, Square, Stripe, and Twitter), but the proposition passed anyway in 2018. In Cupertino, on the other hand, Apple pushed back against a similar ordinance and won. While they fervently resist new taxes, the tech companies also avoid paying their fair share of existing ones, depriving local, state, and federal authorities of money they might use to address the housing crisis. Large corporations in general are notorious for tax dodging, of course, but even among that crowd the tech companies stand out. According to an estimate from the UK organization Fair Tax Mark, six Silicon Valley favorites—Facebook, Apple, Amazon, Netflix, Google, and Microsoft—managed to avoid paying more than $100 billion in taxes between 2010 and 2019.[34]

In 2019, in a major PR blitz, big tech launched a series of its own housing initiatives. That January, Microsoft announced it would invest $500 million on projects for low- and middle-income housing in the Seattle metro region. In June, Google made a billion-dollar commitment to help address the chronic Bay Area housing crisis; this was followed, in October, by a billion-dollar pledge from Facebook. In November, Apple upped the ante with its announcement of a $2.5 billion plan to tackle the housing crunch in Silicon Valley. Amazon belatedly joined the others in January 2021 with the announcement of a $2 billion commitment to three locations—Nashville, Seattle, and Northern Virginia—where it has large offices. But these sizable sums of money did not come in the form of philanthropic contributions. They are mostly for-profit investments or loans, and only a small share are being offered as outright donations or grants.

For example, almost all of Microsoft's commitment is for "below-market-rate investments," with only $25 million offered as direct aid to homeless initiatives. Three-quarters of the billion-dollar Google pledge is the assessed value of company-owned land that Google will lease to housing developers, while only $50 million is being gifted to nonprofits working on homelessness. Facebook is similarly repurposing $225 million worth of its land for developers of residential housing, while donating only $25 million to build housing for "essential workers." As for Apple's $2.5 billion pledge, $300 million of that is its own land being made available for development, $1 billion is for an open line of credit to developers of affordable housing, and another billion will go to financing for first-time homebuyers. Only $50 million is being granted to efforts to mitigate homelessness in Silicon Valley. Likewise, most of Amazon's pledge is in the form of below-market loans and lines of credit to private developers.

Even if the returns on these investments are below-market, it is difficult not to see them as an example of corporations making a profit by "fixing" the problems they helped to create in the first place. Despite Amazon's obstructive efforts, a version of Seattle's employee head tax was approved again in 2020, and it is a more forthright way of holding corporations accountable for their impact on local housing prices.[35] (It could have been more equitably implemented, however, as a payroll tax, pegged to income rather than simply the number of employees.) Cities like Pittsburgh and Denver already levy head taxes to help fund community services like firefighting or police, the need for which increases as populations grow. In Seattle's case, the revenue was aimed at assisting populations most vulnerable to eviction from rising rents. The countercharge that a head tax is a "job killer" is standard Chamber of Commerce fare, cynically masking the self-interest of its corporate members.[36]

Not all the blame for the housing crisis can be laid directly at the door of the big tech companies. However, they are an easy public target because it is widely believed that their high-wage employees contribute to gentrification, displacement, and rising rents in areas within commuting range of their workplaces. But what about large service industry employers like Disney? Their employees are much closer to the poverty line and experience homelessness on a routine basis. Surely addressing *their* housing insecurity lies within Disney's orbit of responsibility even more than obligation for housing in Seattle and the Bay Area lies with the tech giants? Yet there is no public expectation that Disney should help house the humans who don Mickey Mouse's costume every day, or that Walmart should provide accommodation, or even a housing allowance, for the millions of its warehouse and store workers.

Disney could easily make some of its large parcels of surplus land available for housing, either for its own workers or for others who need it. In Osceola, the company's land bank includes an undeveloped section of Celebration west of I-4, in a location that would be a short commute for its employees. In 2018, Disney purchased the 965-acre BK Ranch, just southeast of Celebration, which is already zoned for a mixed-use development of three thousand homes.[37] Offering some of that land would go a long way toward improving the company's shabby record of contributions to local housing needs. But instead, Disney has remained true to its Grinch-like reputation, which dates back decades. In 1989, the Reedy Creek Improvement District snagged all the tax-free bonds (valued at $57 million) allocated on a first-come, first-served basis to local Florida governments for affordable housing programs. Rather than constructing dwellings, the company used the funds to upgrade a sewage plant serving Disney World hotels.[38] In the mid-1990s, the city of Anaheim tried to extract five hundred units of workforce housing from Disney as part of a negotiation to upgrade its Disneyland resorts. The company refused, insisting that it was not a "residential builder," and instead offered $5 million for "neighborhood improvements."[39]

In response to some of the public criticism of its record, Disney has stepped up its charitable donations. In 2017, it contributed $3.7 million to Central Florida organizations fighting homelessness; two years later, it gave $5 million to the Orange County Housing Trust, an affordable housing initiative in Southern California.[40] During the pandemic, the company donated the coins thrown by guests into Disney World's various wishing wells and fountains to the Coalition for the Homeless of Central Florida; they added up to $20,000. In Osceola County, it donated a similarly meager sum of $50,000 to the Hope Center to help move some of their clients out of the 192 motels and into apartments. However, the company maintains the position that its primary contribution to the public good lies in creating jobs, and that the cost of servicing the housing and other needs of its employees is accounted for in the taxes it pays.

Criticism of these tightfisted policies sometimes comes from within the family—in the form of high-profile harangues from Abigail Disney, granddaughter of Walt's brother Roy and a notable filmmaker in her own right. She takes particular issue with the salary and bonuses of CEO Bob Iger, whose 2018 earnings of $65.7 million were 1,424 times the amount earned by a median employee. Disney, who describes herself as a "traitor to my class," said of Iger: "He deserves to be rewarded but if at the same company people are on food stamps and the company's never been more profitable . . . how can you let people go home hungry?"[41] After the coronavirus closed the theme parks in March 2020, Iger waived his monthly salary through the end of September, but he still earned $21 million for the year. Pay cuts to other executives were imposed but restored within a few months.

Abigail Disney is well placed to do this kind of public shaming, and as a member of the Patriotic Millionaires group, which advocates for steeper taxes on the wealthy, she belongs to an elite cohort of Americans pushing back against a system that generates so much inequality. Tarnishing the brand by flagging the disparity between CEO and median employee pay is a familiar move; in the 1990s, anti-sweatshop advocates contrasted Disney CEO Michael Eisner's salary with the low pay of Haitian workers sewing Mickey Mouse pajamas.[42] The tactic never fails to snag headlines, and it helped to win some improvements in workers' conditions. But it has had no appreciable impact on the salary ratios, which have only become more skewed over the years.

By contrast, the successful campaign for a $15 minimum wage showed the real leverage that labor power has over workplace pay. Winning the case for a secure roof over employees' heads is a more complicated business, however. In the early-twentieth-century heyday of benevolent capitalism, industrialists tried to stave off the threat of socialism by offering their workers a range of benefits, including housing them in compact and often well-designed company towns.[43] Today's corporate giants feel no such obligation to their workforce and instead have relied on the haphazard growth of linear quasi-dormitories like the 192 corridor. The knowledge capitalists among them are weaned on the dogma of problem-solving, so they are inclined to believe that their market innovations can produce solutions even to social challenges like the housing crisis. Yet the fledgling stabs at housing by California's tech mavens are neither innovative nor effective, let alone "disruptive" in the sense lionized by Silicon Valley culture.

The same goes for personal philanthropy, such as the Day One Fund created by Amazon CEO Jeff Bezos in the wake of bad publicity generated by Amazon's hostility to the Seattle head tax. Among other causes, the $2 billion fund donates to charities combating homelessness; one of its grants was a $5.25 million donation to the Homeless Services Network of Central Florida in November 2019. However, the funding came with strings attached.[44] The money can only be used to help the "literally homeless," those in shelters or on the streets. It does nothing to help people—many of them working in the company's own warehouses or distribution centers—trying to hang on in apartments, houses, and motels they could barely afford, even before the pandemic.

Philanthropic giving of this kind is not really intended to get at the root causes of the housing crisis. Rather, it serves as well-honed propaganda for figures like Bezos, who are prime beneficiaries of a system of undertaxed and unlimited wealth accumulation. The corporations that generate these spoils actively create poverty and then distribute scraps of money in well-publicized acts of charity to address the symptoms. Elected officials have been well tutored in this mentality. As a result, they eagerly compete to hand over jumbo tax subsidies to attract corporate facilities (as highlighted by the sordid inter-city contest to land Amazon's HQ2) and then express gratitude when the annual festival of corporate giving includes some contributions to local charities.

Despite Walt's 1960s musings about EPCOT's fix for "the problems of our cities," few today expect a company like Disney, which specializes in "imagineering," to come up with real-world solutions. And rightly so. At the end of the day, corporations cannot be trusted, nor should they be expected, to take up these kinds of challenges. Of all the remedies under consideration for employers, progressive taxation of company salaries and profits is the most equitable way of extracting the funds required to take housing off the market and make it available to those in most need. While the private real estate market has shown that it cannot produce housing that is truly affordable in the long term, corporate philanthropy and self-interested lending to developers are even less likely to make a dent.

As the tech giants take tentative steps into the housing business, Disney's record, as one of the few Fortune 100 corporations that actually has been a residential developer in its own right, is instructive. The prices speak for themselves. In the summer of 2020, the median home in Celebration cost $394,500, far more than most locals can afford. As for the three hundred homes in Lake Buena Vista's Golden Oak community, Disney's other residential venture, prices there start around $2.5 million.

ANDREW ROSS

6

Wall Street Comes to Town

CELEBRATION IS AN unlikely place to host stories about economic hardship and housing distress. Carefully designed and strenuously marketed
by Disney in the mid-1990s as an innovative, New Urbanist town for
twenty thousand residents, it quickly established itself as one of the
most commercially successful real estate developments in Central
Florida. With its neotraditional houses, compact urbanism, and tastefully landscaped acres, it was voted America's Dream Town in 2006.
Today, even its most modest dwellings and rental apartments command a price premium well above the county's median range. Locals
think of Celebration as a place of privilege, and rightly so.

It didn't have to be that way. Departing from the dominant suburban model of tract housing—with cookie-cutter houses and price
points—Disney's town was planned as a mixed-income community,
where households on a budget would mingle with the well heeled.
During its fledgling years the community managed to live up to that
ideal, thanks largely to the presence of renters in its downtown apartments. Take the family that lived next door to me while I was working
on *The Celebration Chronicles*: the mother was a middle school teacher
in Kissimmee, and the father worked part-time in a Macaroni Grill on
192. But it's been quite a while since a household like that could afford

to live in one of Celebration's central villages. Early on, Disney nixed the opportunity to build in permanently affordable housing, and over the years the company made only half-hearted efforts to retain lower-priced units as part of the housing mix.

Disney World's powers of self-government insulated the company from regulatory oversight by Orange County's elected officials, but the decision to split off Celebration's five thousand acres from the Reedy Creek Improvement District in 1994 meant that Disney had to nego-tiate all land-use provisions for the new town directly with Osceola County. At that time, large "developments of regional impact" were required to include some provision for affordable housing. For Cele-bration's planners, this proved to be a challenge. Their projected price points for a commercially successful development would, over time, put even the cheapest homes beyond the reach of most of the people likely to be employed in the town (as teachers and service providers, as well as retail and maintenance workers). Rather than build market-protected affordable housing on-site, the company opted to contribute to a fund providing down-payment assistance for low-income home buyers elsewhere in the county.[1]

When it came time to make that contribution, company officials bargained hard, and county representatives, unused to dealing with Disney, ended up accepting a lowball payment of just $300,000. Susan Caswell, the county's housing specialist, surmised that "the whole concept of housing mitigation"—a mechanism for developers to fund workforce housing—"was new to everybody, and there wasn't a real formula for how much you would pay for your impact, so they didn't know what would constitute a lot of money." In any case, the county was much more interested in reaping property taxes from Celebra-tion's promise of higher-priced homes. But the trifling sum Disney handed over would set the tone for its consistently miserly response to Osceola's affordable housing crisis as it mushroomed over the next two decades.

For the most part, Celebrationites have little contact with the pri-vation of those who live on or adjacent to route 192, though I did encounter several former residents of the town whose economic mis- fortune landed them in the motels and the woods. Nor, with the exception of the financial support and members' volunteer work pro- vided by Celebration's Presbyterian church for the Community Hope Center, has the town contributed much of its residents' ample talent, resources, and worldly connections to meeting Osceola's many needs.[2] Celebrationites tend to reserve their civic zeal for their own extensive system of community governance.[3] No residents have successfully run for office or served for long on the county's many standing and advisory committees.[4]

Though Celebration is socially distant from how the other half lives, it still belongs to Route 192, which runs along the town's northern bor- der. But the disparity between the town's high-concept urban design and the untidy landscape of the strip could hardly be greater. Indeed, though few motorists would notice it, the green signage on the portion of 192 that abuts Celebration land is deliberately inconsistent with the purple color scheme of the rest of the corridor. Linda Goodwin, for- mer mayor of Kissimmee and a longtime local power broker, recalls the heated negotiation between county and Mouse. "Celebration did not want purple poles, and I said, 'Why should it be any different?' Tom Lewis [president of The Celebration Company at the time] responded that 'we need this to say that this is really Celebration.' And so we went through some pretty interesting discussions. But boy, were they not going to let up. So we ended up having to cave."

Despite this standoffish attitude, it turns out that Celebration was not immune to the scourge of financialization—the treatment of buildings primarily as investment commodities rather than as places of human dwelling and social use—that has taken its toll on commu- nities in other parts of the county and the nation. The post-2008 wave of predatory investing by private equity firms was a kind of "hostile takeover" of many low- and middle-income neighborhoods, resulting in jacked-up rents and shrinking inventory of affordable housing. Most of the media attention to these raids has focused on the conversion of single-family homes into rentals. But in their pursuit of assets that will yield sizable short-term returns, Wall Street investors have also been busy capturing other classes of real estate—multifamily apartment buildings, condominiums, mobile home parks, build-for-rent subdivisions, student housing, assisted-living facilities, extended-stay hotels, master-planned retirement and age-restricted communities, along with the full suite of commercial properties.[5]

In Celebration's case, the target was its eighteen-acre town center, where apartments and offices sit above stores and restaurants in the mixed-use style of prewar towns. The revival of this traditional design was a leading feature of New Urbanist communities in the 1990s. The mixed-use center has become an increasingly common anchor feature of new suburban developments and is especially popular among younger people looking for walkability and higher levels of urban interaction. A traditional town center has hundreds of different owners, but the financing of real estate development today often allows for a single entity to own one of these large and quite complex properties. As odd as it might sound, an entire downtown area can now be bought and traded as a single commodity.[6]

To craft the streetscape of Celebration's town center, Disney executives took pains to recruit some of the most seasoned figures in architecture and community development. Its signature buildings—designed by starchitects like Michael Graves (who did the post office), Philip Johnson (town hall), Charles Moore (sales center), Robert Venturi and Denise Scott Brown (bank), and Robert Stern and Cooper Robertson (the master plan)—quickly became the object of highbrow architectural walking tours. This feature alone would have made Celebration's downtown a highly appealing chunk of real estate, likely to appreciate in value over time if properly maintained.

But most private equity firms are not really interested in investments that can accrue value over time. They are on the hunt for equity that can provide an outsize return within a few years, often by saddling the acquired target with debt, stripping off its most valuable assets, and discarding the rest.[7] Well-known retail brands have often been casualties of this approach, accounting for the downfall of companies like

Toys "R" Us, Payless, Nine West, Fairway, and Kmart. And few business sectors have proven immune to the plundering strategies of the
giant buyout funds. Hospitals and other healthcare practices acquired
by private equity have seen a marked inflation in common charges
and notorious increases in "surprise billing," when patients unexpect-
edly receive out-of-network services. Meanwhile, the pursuit of cost
efficiencies diminishes the quality of care. Philadelphia's 171-year-old
Hahnemann University Hospital, known for serving poor patients on
public assistance, suffered a widely publicized fate after private equity
tycoon Joel Freedman acquired it in 2018. Just a year after the acquisition, he placed the hospital in bankruptcy and closed it down, with the
intention of selling off the valuable underlying land to developers of
luxury hotels and condos.[8]

In real estate, private equity firms are especially attracted to housing
in a condition of "distress," whether from foreclosure or some other
reason for depreciation. But any kind of property is fair game if the
new owners can hike rents and fees while skimping on maintenance, or
if an "underperforming" tenant class can be flushed out and replaced
with a more lucrative one. Investors' interest in acquiring mobile home
parks, for example, is driven by the opportunity to push up rents that
owners pay on the land beneath their homes, boosting profits in a sector that already provides double the average real estate rate of return.[9]
The story of Wall Street's capture of Celebration's showpiece town
center is a cautionary reminder that such private equity profiteering
is not just an affliction at the lower end of the market. If they have
an eligible or vulnerable component, more upscale communities are
also exposed to rapacious investors with little interest in the general
well-being of residents. Celebration's town center proved to be that
soft spot, and it would be exploited according to a business model that
has played out in communities all across the country.

In this case, however, a small group of the residents fought back.
The struggle to hold on to their apartments was not a brawl on skid
row. Unlike the have-nots in 192's motels or the budget renters with
corporate landlords itching to evict them for a late payment, these

combatants were not on the brink of destitution, even though their adversary handed them substantial property and income losses and no small degree of suffering. Nor was their battle typical of the kind of condo association wars that have clogged the courts in Florida and other Sunbelt states since the 1990s. It was a face-off with the new breed of predatory investors who have grabbed vast bundles of residential and commercial property over the last decade and are poised to swoop down again in the wake of the looming coronavirus property meltdown. The fact that it occurred under Disney's nose and within one of Route 192's wealthiest zip codes goes to show that no one's dwelling is safe from the wolves of Wall Street.

THE GOLDEN TICKET

The best seats in the house for events in downtown Celebration are on Cookie Kelly's apartment terrace overlooking the lakefront. As an honorary member of Cookie's circle, I always have an invitation extended to me. Each time I climb the stairs to her place, I pass the balcony of the apartment in the adjacent building where I lived more than twenty years before and wince at the ever-larger hole in the base of the corner column and the advancing decay of the ceiling. On one occasion, in the pitiless heat and humidity of a storm-battered peninsular summer, the balcony looks more like a public safety hazard than a weathered fixture in a gracefully aging Florida lakeside town. Cookie takes a quick look and passes judgment: "It's melting. Literally melting."

The central location of Cookie's condo apartment lends some authority to her reputation, in some quarters, as the ungovernable "mouth of Celebration." Some town wags see her loose lips as a threat to their property values. But for many others, Cookie is the town's conscience, cherished for her vigilant defense of its founding New Urbanist principles and her spirited put-down of those who have forgotten them. I have seen her labeled as a betrayer ("why do you hate this town so much?") but also hailed as "our Erin Brockovich." Cookie herself has a sardonic literary bent, so she is more likely to compare her local standing to that of Silas Marner, George Eliot's tragic hero, unfairly accused and shunned by his neighbors.

It takes a while for her to respond to visitors at the door. This isn't because of her age—for all her seventy-six years, she is mentally sharp as a tack and as effervescent as a Magic Kingdom greeter. Rather, for several months she has been evading a process server, who regularly shows up to ring her doorbell. The efforts to serve a subpoena are part of a legal spat that has singled Cookie out for harassment but is also steadily consuming the lives of many of those who reside downtown or who use its facilities. The dispute is eating away at Celebration from within, but its crux is not a disagreement with a homeowners association or a local squabble so typical of small-town politics. The source is located a thousand miles away, in the Madison Avenue office of an entrepreneurial investment firm.

Everyone in Celebration agrees that the mess originated in Disney's 2004 decision to sell the entire town center to Lexin Capital, which specializes in "providing opportunistic real estate investments to a select group of private and institutional investors." The sale itself came as an unwelcome surprise to most townsfolk. There have always been grumbles that the retail businesses in the town center cater more to tourists than residents, but the downtown complex—which hosts stores, restaurants, offices, and more than a hundred apartments—is still the natural core of the community. Selling it off seemed crass to some, a violation of some tacit covenant between Celebrationites and the Mouse. Even those who chafed at the infamously strict regulatory hand wielded by Disney saw the company's withdrawal from its most high-profile managerial role in town as a dereliction of responsibility.

However, the property transfer was by no means a departure from Disney's business plan. It had always intended to sell off all of the town's developable acres, in choice parcels and preferably at the top of the market. The housing lots were sold to builders; the highly rated golf course was auctioned off in 2003; and in the years since, Disney has continued to divest itself of land in the commercial corridor along the town's northern boundary. But the buyers of the links had a forty-year record of golf course management under their belt. By contrast, Metin Negrin, the founding owner of Lexin Capital, was a novice in the business of community management, and Lexin itself was less than two years old. Why would Disney entrust the town's most Instagrammed location to a third-tier Wall Street investment manager who had built his reputation by buying and restructuring distressed properties for client-investors on the lookout for a fast buck?

Since no one I asked had a surefire answer to this question, cynicism ruled by default. Pat Schroeder, the former Colorado politician and Celebration's best-known resident, saw it as simply a transactional matter: "If you have a car that you just want to sell and a sixteen-year-old comes to you with cash, are you gonna go out for a spin with him and decide whether he's a good driver?" Given the secrecy surrounding the sale—the property was not put out to bid—there were also many rumors about how Negrin wielded influence at the top, especially with former Disney CEO Michael Eisner, whose architectural passions had underpinned the creation of Celebration.One of the more favored theories has to do with the property tycoon Al Taubman, a close friend of Eisner's whom Negrin identifies as his mentor.[10] In 1993, Taubman helped Negrin found his first company, Athena Group, to acquire real estate at fire-sale prices after the savings and loans collapse of the late 1980s. According to this theory, Taubman, who made a fortune as a shopping mall developer and also speculated in distressed properties, was all set to buy the town center himself but got sent to prison for a price-fixing swindle he ran as Sotheby's board chair. With the deal up in the air, Negrin stepped forward, presumably with Taubman's backing.

Other firms, much more qualified than Lexin, would surely have jumped at the prospect of acquiring such a prime piece of architecturally significant real estate if they had been given the chance. By 2004, members of the Disney Development Company team that created the town had spun off their own separate and independent enterprises, any one of which might have been better qualified to take over the property. There were even some well-connected Celebration residents who could have pulled together an offer. Lexin's portfolio at the time of the sale, meanwhile, was very slim. It included a handful of very recent Florida acquisitions, among them an eight-hundred-acre planned community in Palm Beach County, but the firm had no experience in managing complex, multiuse properties. In addition, although he was dealing with a notoriously hard-nosed seller, Negrin got away with a surprisingly low price. The record of sale shows that he paid only $21 million for the eighteen-acre combination of sixteen shops, six restaurants, 105 rental apartments, ninety-four thousand square feet of office space, and two adjacent parking lots. Even as a stand-alone financial transaction, it was a sweet deal. And the cachet of owning Celebration's trademark core would also greatly increase Lexin's ability to raise funds for other investments. In Cookie Kelly's words, "It was like winning the Golden Ticket."

THE BUSINESS OF EXTRACTION

It was a timely moment for Disney to step up its own planned exit from Celebration. The town had reached the stage that developers refer to as "control turnover," which is to say that residents now outnumbered Disney reps on the homeowners association board. Now that the acclaim for creating Celebration had subsided, Disney officials were happy to pass on the headaches of managing a community that is a favored source of "trouble in paradise" stories for the international media.[11] Plus, they could hand over the awkward legacy of oversights and flaws from the hasty construction of the town center almost a decade before. Twelve years after the sale, Negrin would blame Disney in a *Wall Street Journal* article about the physical deterioration of the buildings under his control. "No amount of maintenance could have avoided these kinds of issues," he declared, "because it wasn't built properly."[12]

In 2004, however, Negrin was not paying much attention to the original construction flaws. There was fast money to be made. According to Cookie, Disney offered, as part of the sale deal, to pay up to $750,000 for any infrastructure repairs related to construction, but

Negrin passed. "Lexin wanted to refinance as soon as possible," Cookie explains, "and they didn't want underwriters having to deal with the fact that there might be outstanding work tickets on it, so they just let that offer go." Negrin lost no time in making good on his investment. Within twenty-four hours of inking the purchase, he collected $20 million by selling the two parking lots for condo development, recouping almost all of his purchase cost. A few months later, he reaped further profits by converting the 105 rental apartments to condos for sale.

From the outset, it was clear that Negrin's goal was not to carefully and tastefully manage the legacy of Celebration's crown jewel. He was following the private equity playbook: exploit the acquisition for immediate gain, sell off its parts, and load it with debt. Within a year, he refinanced his new property with a $23 million loan, drawing off the equity for himself and his investors. Lexin proceeded to buy up other apartment complexes, both in Celebration and Orlando, and convert them to condos. With the Celebration town center as collateral, his firm was able to raise large sums of capital for real estate acquisitions across the country.[13]

This kind of debt-financed investing was not uncommon even before the 2008 financial crash, but in the years since then, it has increased in scale and intensity, with devastating results for the cause of affordable housing. Condos play a significant part in this story. The business of converting rental apartments into condominiums began in the 1970s as a lucrative exit strategy for landlords who lost their patience with collecting steady rents and grabbed at the chance to generate a large one-time return on their properties. But the condo boom really came into its own in the 2000s when the promotion of homeownership and the ready provision of cheap loans fueled the housing bubble. Given the short-term rewards on offer, investors and developers saw a bonanza. Sales were especially frenzied in Sunbelt states, and Central Florida was one of the busiest of all the nation's condo-conversion markets. Inevitably, condo owners caught in the bubble would be among the hardest hit by the financial crash. In a complete U-turn, condo *deconversion* became one of the most active trends of the real estate market in the decade following, as rentership began to rise, along with rents.

Affordable housing was one of the biggest casualties of the initial phase of conversions, which swallowed up traditional rental apartments. But the loss was compounded when Wall Street firms bought up condo units after the housing crash to convert them back into apartments for rental at inflated rates, with revenue now flowing directly to investors. This hostile takeover of condos was pioneered by Florida's statute 718, which allowed "bulk buyers" to terminate the condominium arrangement once they had acquired 80 percent ownership of the buildings, but it spread rapidly to other states after the crash spawned a multitude of distressed units. Investors would snap up the units at low prices, take control of the condo association, then raise the fees beyond what the remaining occupants could afford. Deconversion and gentrified rents followed, displacing what had been a relatively low-cost homeownership class. In many parts of the country, condo owners took to the courts to resist these aggressive raids. As litigation piled up, some municipalities, like Chicago, have tried to make the process more difficult by upping the percentage of owners required to approve.[14] But the coronavirus recession, which has seen commercial banks step back from lending, has put private equity even more firmly in the driver's seat.

What impact did the Lexin purchase of Celebration's town center have on housing availability in the town? The initial 2004 conversion of downtown apartments into condos resulted in the instant loss of Celebration's largest section of affordable housing. In return, tenants were given the opportunity, in a lottery, to purchase their units and enter the rapidly inflating condo market. But since they were among the town's least affluent residents, they were the most vulnerable to foreclosure when the housing bubble popped in 2007. Several years later, when Negrin found himself at war with the condo owners, he would try to buy them out in hopes of taking over and terminating the condominium. In the interim, their units were so devalued by the crash that they had once again become the cheapest housing available in Celebration. If he succeeds in turning them back into market-rate rental apartments, the units will lose their affordable status for the second time.

To be fair, Negrin is hardly alone when it comes to real estate speculation in Celebration. In the years before the crash, home flipping and asset leveraging to finance other purchases were almost as popular as day trading. Celebration residents with disposable capital did not hold back. Many bought up multiple units in town as investment rentals or to flip, and the town's original anti-speculation rules (no sales allowed before eighteen months of occupancy) were relaxed to grease the wheel. Celebration's prestige attracted its share of land gamblers, along with swindlers and con artists, some of them quite colorful characters with criminal records for fraud. Judged by the fly-by-night standards of this gold rush, Lexin's initial handling of the town center acquisition was not all that exceptional.

During those boom years, some residents filled out a real estate license application and set up shop. Originally drawn to the community for its New Urbanist philosophy, Cookie was one of them. "The running joke," she recalls, "was that you needed a realtor's license to live in this town." Reared in the Arts and Crafts utopia of Arden, Delaware, she and her family had gravitated toward Celebration's promise of good design and neo-traditional living. A sideline working as a Disney World costume character for nine years helped to sweeten the romance. "I played Mickey, Donald, Daisy, Dopey, Pinocchio, and Stitch, but Minnie mostly," she says. "When you're looking through her eyes, you see the most amazing things . . . but you have to look out for the thirteen-year-old boys; they are quite naughty." Once she got the Celebration bug, she quickly rose to become one of the town's ace realtors, selling almost $100 million worth of homes. "It was like shooting fish in a barrel. People already wanted to buy, but they needed a narrative to rationalize the extra price"—Celebration homes commanded a 30 to 40 percent premium over area comps. "I really started doing it to 'explain' the town, and what a great job of building the infrastructure Disney had done. I was passionate about it. At that time, I was a true believer."

It was largely because Cookie and other residents had such faith in Disney's promises that the Lexin deal did not set off alarm bells. As part of the sale, the company issued a new set of rules and regulations to protect the "orderly operation, maintenance, and future development" of downtown. Disney's standards are famously rigorous: the regulations for Celebration homeowners cover almost every plank and nail of their homes, even extending to their yards, where only approved shrubbery can grow. Owners of stores and restaurants are also bound by rules about the appearance of their storefronts and restaurants. So downtown residents were unconcerned about the transfer of the property to Lexin. Known around town as "the benevolent dictator," Disney would surely have vetted the new owner as a suitable heir, or so they thought.

But while Disney had an interest in keeping the town center shipshape, in order to help the company sell Celebration's homes, Negrin merely intended to drain as much short-term revenue as he could from the property, secure new loans on it, and then sell it off. Since the private equity business model is extractive in nature, there is little incentive for firms such as Lexin to maintain an asset in satisfactory condition, let alone spend resources on improving it. If anything, neglecting upkeep might make Celebration's town center look more attractive to a refi lender: on a spreadsheet, at least, the property would then look as if it had low operating costs, while turning a tidy profit from all the commercial rental and restaurant revenue. Since the town had the cachet of being Disney-built, anyone with doubts about the rundown condition of the buildings was more likely to give it a pass. And for more tough-minded lenders, Negrin could point out that if any repairs were needed, the owner (or a prospective buyer) had the power to assess condo owners for the lion's share of the costs.[15] Across the country, tenants of rental properties owned by the likes of Invitation Homes, American Homes 4 Rent, and Starwood Waypoint are all too familiar with the long inventory of repairs and basic maintenance tasks for which they are personally held responsible by their Wall Street landlords.[16]

If Negrin was planning to flip the town center, the optimum time would have been three to four years after the first refi loan was secured.

But his opportunity flamed out in the housing crash, which ripped through Central Florida's I-4 corridor like a hurricane, leaving a trail of foreclosures as wide and deep as anywhere in the badly clobbered Sunbelt. Celebration was not spared. The fallout affected the full range of homeowners, peppering the leafy porch-lined streets with For Sale signs. One in every twenty Celebration residents was foreclosed on in 2009 and 2010, compared with one per forty-eight in Florida as a whole.[17] When the dust cleared, Celebration property prices had fallen 60 percent from their 2006 peak. The downtown condo owners took the most brutal hit, emptying out a third of the downtown units.

Some of Lexin's other Central Florida investments went south, but its Celebration asset continued to be a money-spinner.[18] In 2015, the firm completed a second refinancing, taking out a still larger loan with the town center as collateral and distributing the funds to its investors. Cookie estimates that the town center's debt soared to $34,700,000. A stroll around the downtown buildings, many of them quite obviously in conditions of neglect and disrepair, would reveal how little of the money drawn from the loan had been spent on upkeep.

ORGANIZING THE NEIGHBORS

Among those who took advantage of recession prices to buy a condo in Celebration was Laurel Rousseau, a former travel agent with "Florida pioneer" roots in the area: her father used to drive dairy cattle up to Kissimmee when its Cowtown moniker still meant something. She and her husband had raised and homeschooled their children in Maine and New York, but Celebration caught their eye while they were on a Disney vacation. They scraped together funds to buy one of the foreclosed town center condos facing the Bohemian, the town's lakeside hotel, paying half of what it had fetched in Lexin's 2004 conversion sale. "The previous owner pulled out all of the fixtures," Laurel recalls, "so there were no appliances when we moved in. With all the empty units downtown, it was eerie, almost like a ghost town, and it got quite gritty and lawless in those days—you never saw a police officer. People were struggling to pay dues. And as for renters, you didn't say no to anybody."

Worldly wise from overseas sojourns, with eclectic cultural interests, Laurel had no particular yen for Celebration nor any long-term plan to settle there. When housing prices recovered, she figured, she and her family would move on. But their condo, located in a building with a defective roof, turned out to be an ill-fated purchase. Her efforts to remedy the problems would make her, along with Cookie, the leading figure in the residents' dispute with Lexin. "The first rain we got after we moved in, the roof leaked," Laurel recalls, "and that was really what started me on this journey."

Initially, like the other condo owners, Laurel filed independent complaints with Lexin. Most of these went unanswered. In 2014, water penetration got so bad that the company agreed to put on a new roof, but it leaked worse than the original. Eventually, growing frustration with Lexin's neglect and slipshod repair efforts prompted Laurel to join the condo association board. She requested files showing numerous complaints from others about water intrusion and rot, and she began to inspect some of the units. "It wasn't until I had started climbing through the attic spaces of these buildings that I saw the full amount of damage and decay," she relates. "In many of them it almost looked as if fires had happened, the wood and the trusses were so rotted. And, of course, termites and roaches had taken over because it's the perfect living environment for them."

After knocking on neighbors' doors and comparing notes, Laurel realized the problems were widespread and that taking on Lexin would require coordinated action. She ran successfully for president of the condo board, replaced the other board members, and fired the condo association's lawyer, accountant, and management company. "Then I started looking for litigating attorneys," she explains, "because at that point I had enough information that I felt there was a greater level of wrongdoing and neglect." Laurel turned out to be a natural leader in the conflict with Lexin, bringing discipline and clarity of purpose to the condo association members. With her scrupulous sense of fairness

and dogged pursuit of a reasonable solution, she would come to command the loyalty of fellow residents who risked their financial stability
to follow her.

Once Laurel had taken over the board, she teamed up with Cookie,
who became the part-time manager of the condo association, and
whose deep, practical knowledge of real estate finance and development was a perfect complement for her own people skills. "I'm more
heart and she's more brains," Laurel explains. Always good for a
punch line, Cookie quips: "It was stunning that we found each other—
otherwise we'd both be at the bottom of the lake right now, wearing
cement shoes." Together, they set out to expose Negrin's negligence.
Reviewing the records, they found that Lexin had spent only $300,000
in maintenance on its twenty-one buildings over the course of five
years, and much of that was for trash collection, insurance, and utility bills. This paltry sum alone helped explain the cascading problems
experienced by residents.

Laurel and Cookie encouraged condo residents to document the
damage, and they compiled a visual archive in preparation for a lawsuit.
One of the earliest and most avid documentarians was Jesse Opalka, a
mild-mannered graphic designer who bought a Market Street condo in
2004 because it reminded him of Savannah. He noticed the water intrusion early in his occupancy. Some of it, he discovered, was due to the
lack of flashing on the roof—an original Disney oversight that afflicted
more than one downtown building. "I am handy," Jesse notes, "and I
could have fixed some of the holes and cracks I found up there, but
Lexin told me I could get sued for trespassing." Water penetration got
so bad that, during thunderstorms, "a waterfall effect" appeared in his
apartment.[19] By 2015 he had to move out to a nearby unit. His original
apartment, when he showed me around in 2018, was a picture of dev-
astation; walls had been ripped apart in an effort to expose the rot and
stem the water flow. The only visible efforts at remediation undertaken
by Lexin were blue tarps applied to the roof, which could be seen, from
below, fluttering ineffectively on the downtown skyline.

Stories like his were legion among condo residents who had to move because of accumulated mold or were advised to stay off their balconies and stairwells because of unsafe conditions. One contractor, hired to open up the walls of a downtown apartment for inspection, found that termites had chewed away all the studs and joists. "It's all mulch," he reported. Debie and Don McDonald, prominent among the "founder" families in town, opened an antique map store in the town center in 1998. Under Disney management, they recall, "If you had a lightbulb out, they'd come in that second and bring flowers." Under Lexin, it was a quite different story. "They didn't keep it clean or care about the leaks we had. They just ignored us completely." By the time the McDonalds ended their lease in 2008, Debie could no longer work in the store. "The water would pour down between the balcony and the wall," she reports. "The mold was so bad that every time I went in I would have trouble breathing, feel sick, then go home and feel better."

Cookie and Laurel began to spend long evenings poring over records and documents. Their detective work turned up details that led them to believe Lexin may have cooked the books in preparation for the second refinancing review. Alerted to their sleuthing, Negrin put them on the defensive by imposing on the condo owners a $4 million assessment for repairs to be made on several buildings. It was a rare acknowledgment that the repairs had to be taken care of, but the request that condo owners foot the entire bill, to the tune of $50,000 each, was seen as an affront. In fact, it was a routine private equity move, shifting the costs onto occupants themselves, and Lexin had the legal right to do so.

Riding the tide of owner resentment, the condo board decided to sue. In 2016, it filed a lawsuit in Osceola County Ninth Circuit Court over Lexin's "negligent maintenance" and "breach of fiduciary duty," alleging that the condo units were in a "colossal state of disrepair" and had suffered from "pervasive sustained moisture intrusion with resulting rot of structural components and of interior components with related termite infestation." The primary threat from the lawsuit was to Negrin's plans to prepare for a third refinancing. But as the dispute intensified over the next few years, spawning several related lawsuits and strategic attempts to outmaneuver each other, the face-off took on a personal, vendetta-like character. As Laurel later observed, "I sensed there was a real irritation, on his part, that it was two females taking him on and besting him on some level . . . I just don't think he expected us to match his tenacity or his wiliness—he didn't expect that from a woman."

Over those same years, large Wall Street landlords like Invitation Homes (owned by the Blackstone Group) and American Homes 4 Rent were also being sued for a litany of complaints very similar to those in Celebration: negligent maintenance for mold, water penetration, infestations, and defective fixtures. There were also complaints of fee stacking—such as charging a late fee for nonpayment of a previous late fee—and of price gouging on rents. Stories about chronic neglect by corporate owners emerged across the entire housing landscape, from rural towns to urban sprawl. In its marketing materials, Invitation Homes boasted of providing a "worry free" living environment with "peace of mind" through "exceptional resident services," including "24/7 emergency maintenance."[20] Yet tenants experienced service more akin to that of a slumlord, with long waits for major repairs, and most other maintenance jobs left in their own hands. With investors to please, the companies had trimmed management costs and cut corners to boost revenue, generating a slew of class action suits in response.

For companies like Blackstone, fast becoming the largest real estate company in the world, with holdings on every continent, the litigation was simply part of the cost of doing business. Tenants, for their part, were misguided in thinking that their well-being was ever a priority for Wall Street. For private equity firms, their client is not the tenant but the investor.

THE CAMPAIGN TAKES ITS TOLL

Over the next four years, Laurel and Cookie put pressure on Lexin by taking their fight to a variety of public as well as legal forums. Airing the town center's dirty laundry within Celebration earned them friends and foes in equal measure.[21] Then they went outside what residents call "the bubble," bringing in local news crews and a *Wall Street Journal* reporter to cover the story of the damage.[22] Aside from the primary litigation, several other supporting lawsuits were filed and contested in Osceola courts. Along the way, they tried to pull the town's most prominent voices into the dispute by showing up with their allies at meetings of Celebration's many governance committees to secure backing from the movers and shakers on their boards.[23]

There were some wins but many more setbacks. Celebration's homeowners association declined to take up their cause, legal costs piled up, and it was more and more difficult to see a way out that did not land the condo owners with a hefty bill. With the fight eating up their days and hours, the experience of being hung out to dry by some of the town's most well-known figures reinforced their sense of isolation. Of the two, Cookie took on the mindset of the justice warrior, driven by a righteous resolve not to cave in to someone she viewed as a vulture capitalist. Laurel, meanwhile, agonized day and night about her fiscal responsibilities to members of the condominium association. "Being right in the end isn't going to save our buildings," she muses, "and any gains have to be weighed against how many will fall along the road." For her, every meeting with the members where she had to urge them to stay in the fight and foot the legal bills was "a do-or-die moment." With the exception of only a handful who had opted out, they stuck by her.

Sabina Mohammadi, the owner of my former apartment, now worth a third of what she paid for it in 2006, was one of the arch loyalists. Toward the end of a lunch meeting in Tampa, where she runs her own real estate business, she pinpoints what, for her, is the most galling part of Negrin's management setup. "Our money was used by him to buy new properties, so in a way we are all owners or stakeholders in his investments," she says. Though owners like her draw no benefits from being leveraged in this way, she reckons that "we have all become his business partners, effectively." It is a telling insight into how business-minded residents like her view the venality of private equity's real estate business model.

After the homeowners association decided to take a pass, the two women began petitioning Disney to step in directly. Disney officials often take advantage of the perception, shared by not a few residents, that the company no longer has much of a stake in Celebration. But in reality, the voluminous town charter gives it the right to step in if its regulations are violated and to take action if a property owner such as Lexin fails to maintain the "community-wide standards" laid down in the founding documents. Unusually for a developer, Disney retains the right to exercise veto power over Celebration's affairs for the long term.[24]

Privately, Laurel and Cookie tried to persuade Disney to play the white knight. "They talked about writing the narrative that they wanted written," Laurel recalls, "and then they could spin the story that everybody would want to hear about Disney saving the town." But the attorneys in Burbank nixed the idea. Eventually, the pair did persuade the town's nonresidential owners association (still dominated by Disney reps) to file a lawsuit against Lexin, but it turned out to be a lightweight affair, covering only a fraction of Lexin's violations of the codes governing property maintenance.

Why did Disney decide not to intervene more forcefully? Stepping up to save the day would have been a prime PR opportunity to create fairy-tale headlines. But there were more downsides, including risk to the Disney brand if its name were mentioned in stories about calamities traceable to the original construction of the town. So, too, any Disney intervention to remedy the town center woes might have encouraged litigation over its responsibility for construction flaws in other parts of the town. Many law firms would relish taking on a company with the ability to pay out in case of a massive judgment against it. By comparison, Lexin has relatively few unprotected assets to go after. Nor does its business depend on branding: its portfolio of debt-leveraged properties in Florida, Arizona, New York City, and overseas is a scattershot collection of investment "opportunities" and does not amount to a coherent brand profile.

The Great Recession placed many of Celebration's condo owners under *financial* stress, but Negrin's neglect of building maintenance was turning their condos into *physically* distressed properties, giving him new opportunities to take advantage of their vulnerability. As Laurel shrewdly notes, Negrin's business is to "know the various ways to make a distressed property valuable to him." After threatening to foreclose on several units, he pressured several owners to sell to him, hoping to win enough votes to take over the condo association and convert the units back into rentals. The legal doctrine of economic waste—which holds that it's unreasonable to require repairs when their cost is much greater than the lost value of a structure—might even let him rebuild the town center in a more profitable format. "The key legal question," according to Laurel, "is whether he can be liable for making it a distressed property and then profiting from it."

Ultimately, if her members get landed with $100,000 bills and nowhere to go, Laurel could imagine going for what she describes as the "nuclear option" of direct action. Celebration rules prohibit protests in the streets, and most of the condo owners are loath to get into what she calls "a public slugfest." (Indeed, many of them would only speak to me off the record.) However, if all else fails, a banner drop coordinated with national news reporters would deliver some damaging publicity for Disney. Cookie, for her part, vows to "strap myself to D'Antonio's restaurant sign with a lightning rod in my mouth and just hang there."

DARK SCREENS AND A PYRRHIC VICTORY

A stroll around the corner from D'Antonio's takes visitors past the town's two-screen movie theater, designed by Cesar Pelli as a classy retro tribute to the prewar Art Moderne style. With its twin spires and streamlined marquees, it is arguably the most joyous building in Celebration. But since 2010, when the theater chain AMC shuttered the building, it has also been Celebration's shame.[25] As part of its original Disney lease, AMC was barred from showing films with violent or sexually explicit content, so attendance was always thin. Eventually, AMC closed the theater to cut costs. At the same time, though, the chain renewed the lease with Lexin, continuing to rent the building for more than $20,000 a month to preempt any competition for its other screens in the region. Over the years, residents have floated proposals for turning it into a community arts center, among other uses, but Lexin's refusal to compromise on the rent stands in the way.

Empty theaters are a common sight in hollowed-out downtowns all across America, and the pandemic recession is consigning many more to oblivion. But here, at the center of Celebration, the spectacle of dark screens and blank marquees is jarring. Storefronts on Celebration's main street frequently sit empty as well. In contrast, the several retail units that Lexin has converted into restaurants, adding hundreds of seats while netting 5 percent of their gross receipts, are usually bulging with patrons. The disparity only reinforces the perception that Negrin's sole interest in Celebration's iconic core lies in hauling off the maximum amount of revenue, while keeping ground rents high in order to look good to big lenders. The inability of townsfolk to reclaim the theater for community use also underlines how much the character of the town is still largely determined by remote corporate decision makers for whom Celebration is simply a bundle of income streams on their balance sheets.[26]

Cookie Kelly is still a Magic Kingdom fan, regularly visiting with grandkids on her annual pass. She has Disney posters on her apartment walls, including a charming Cubist depiction of Donald Duck. So it pains her to watch the company walk away from the care it put into Celebration's design. "François Truffaut said that every time he started out to make a masterpiece, by the end, he was just glad to have film in a can," she tells me. "And so that's what I say to Disney. 'Now you're just putting film in a can. You just don't care anymore.'"

Over the years, Cookie and Laurel pursued many different legal channels—construction law, property law, condo law—to go after Negrin, only to discover time after time that Florida law was usually on his side. Their big lawsuit, amended several times, took a painfully slow path through the courts, and then the pandemic backlog pushed the trial date from November 2020 into the following year. In the meantime, Negrin slapped another large assessment for repairs on the condo members and hiked the condo fees by 80 percent in one year. Would the owners be able to survive until they had their day in court, or would they be forced to sell their units to him at markdown prices?

After the pandemic struck, some Celebration businesses shuttered their doors for good. Lexin's revenue from commercial rents and sales plummeted, and it was hit even harder when AMC declared bankruptcy and stopped paying its hefty rent on the cinema. Cookie and Laurel speculated that Lexin might have to go into bankruptcy itself. The hardship of the condo owners was now being shared by their Wall Street adversary. For its part, the condo association had spent a whopping $1.2 million in legal fees. It seemed like the time to push for a settlement.

By June 2021, after several prolonged rounds of mediation that Laurel described as "negotiating divorce with a partner you don't trust," it looked as if an agreement might be in sight. The adversaries were so far apart that significant concessions would have to be made on both sides in order to reach a final settlement. But the condo owners, who had consistently found that Florida's developer-friendly laws cast them as the weaker party, would likely take the bigger hit. After five years in the trenches, which she blamed for several deaths and actual divorces among her association members, Laurel was determined that a settlement would at least save them from financial ruination at Negrin's hands. Cookie, less willing to entertain the prospect of compromise with her archenemy, was anticipating a "Pyrrhic victory."

As the dispute with Lexin unfolded over the years, owners of dream homes in other parts of Celebration had looked on with varying degrees of empathy, most of them thanking their lucky stars that they didn't live in the town center. Though they were not directly involved in the conflict, their property values were not entirely immune to the fallout. Celebration was sold to them with the promise that it would be a real community in charge of its own destiny, not a jumbo subdivision run by an impersonal management company. Yet the looting of the town center, and Disney's disinclination to rein it in, showed that the

Celebrationites are still subject to the agenda of far-flung corporate entities who answer primarily to anonymous shareholders and investors. One company built and promoted Celebration as a sustainable, community-minded town but then made a woeful error by selling the town's centerpiece and refused to correct it. The other had no interest in the place at all other than to suck it dry.

The battle over Celebration's town center was not the first condo war in town and is unlikely to be the last. Indeed, the Water Street condos, where Cookie herself moved just before the pandemic, fought for seven years to get a settlement from the developer who converted the units in 2003 and bequeathed a laundry list of construction flaws. But the town center ruckus was a different kind of conflict. In this case, the adversary was not a builder in a hurry to get the job done and leave before the defects were discovered. Rather, Lexin had come to town as a real estate raider, seeking only to ruthlessly exploit an asset. Unlike the developers, the company added nothing to the built environment.

Given his heavy reliance on debt financing—even the initial $21 million sale was financed with a $19.1 million GMAC loan—Negrin and his partners probably did not even have much skin in the game. What makes the private equity business so attractive for investors is that the potential downside for those involved is quite limited. The firm puts very little of its own money into an acquisition, operating it as a vessel for transferring funds from lenders to investors while extracting hefty management and performance fees for itself. The investors, meanwhile, are only risking whatever money they have put in; liability for the massive loans taken out on the property they acquire is assumed by a subsidiary company (in this case, Lexin Celebration Commercial, LLC) set up for the purpose. If the property goes bankrupt, only this subsidiary is affected, while the investors and the private equity firm itself are shielded from exposure.

This principle of limited liability has long been central to the world of finance; advocates argue that without it, no one would take on the risks of investing in a business. However, it has only recently become a significant feature of residential real estate, with Wall Street's voracious entry into the housing sector. By 2018, over 16 percent of rental properties in the US were owned by a limited liability corporation, or LLC. When counting rental *units*, almost half were owned by institutional investors with some element of limited liability.[27] Under such arrangements, landlords are less likely to be accountable. When the risk from tenant litigation or code enforcement fines diminishes, there is less incentive to maintain properties in a safe and healthy condition. One study of Milwaukee housing records showed that when properties change hands to LLC ownership, the rates of disrepair and deterioration shoot up.[28]

But there is an even higher price to be paid for treating housing like any other kind of investment, and it has become all too apparent in the destructive role that corporate investor ownership has played in deepening the housing crisis. To put it simply, housing is different from other commodities because everyone needs it. Housing can and should be a human right, not an opportunistic wager on the finance markets.

In a 2019 letter to the Blackstone Group, Leilani Farha and Surya Deva, two human rights specialists at the United Nations, reinforced this point by calling out the "egregious" practices of the new corporate landlords. "Real estate equity firms have an independent responsibility to respect human rights," they wrote, "which means that they need to conduct human rights due diligence in order to identify, prevent, mitigate and account for how they address adverse impacts on the right to housing."[29] But nothing could be further from the mind of the private equity investor, for whom housing has become just another cash cow.

ANDREW ROSS

Your Home Can Be a Hotel

To ENSURE IT would remain a community of permanent residents and not a vacation or snowbird colony, Celebration used to have strict regulations against home rentals. These days, long-term leasing is allowed, but short-term rentals are still prohibited, as is common in many communities run by homeowners associations. Celebration, however, sits within one of the country's largest concentration of homes catering specifically to rentals of a week or a few days. There are as many as fifty thousand of these properties in Osceola County, mostly owned by out-of-towners and rented to vacationers looking for an alternative to cookie-cutter hotel rooms.[1] The rapid growth of this kind of real estate is one of the reasons why affordable housing is not being built for the local working-class population.

During the Great Recession, when credit for building and buying residential housing was tight, big money was still flowing into the construction of these vacation homes. The cow pastures at the west end of the 192 corridor rapidly morphed into shiny new subdivisions of barrel-tile-roofed houses. Upscale "purpose-built communities," with cheerful names like Reunion, Encore, and The Retreat at Champions Gate, attracted a new class of investors riding a boom in the vacation home rental (VHR) sector.[2] By 2017, the VHR market in the United

States was valued at $17 billion, with rosy growth estimates for the next decade.[3] Like the overseas buyers who snapped up high-rise real estate in Manhattan and Miami, many investors saw Central Florida's vacation homes as a safe haven to park their capital, and so they lined up to make all-cash purchases.[4] Thanks to the boom, an ever greater share of the county's housing stock is now reserved for the needs of visitors, owned and operated for the financial benefit of far-flung investors. In Osceola, VHR properties have a 45 to 55 percent average occupancy rate (60 percent is considered good business), so on any given night, while the woods people sleep in their tents, thousands of VHR rooms sit vacant.

Entire floors of Manhattan's soaring ultra-luxury condo towers also lie empty while the city's homeless shelters are overflowing.[5] Unlike Osceola's vacation homes, these palaces in the sky were not built to be occupied: they are safe deposit boxes for the capital gains of tycoons, princelings, and oligarchs from Russia, Asia, and the Middle East. But in both locations, the gulf between existential need and market speculation is an extreme symptom of the housing crisis. And while neither Manhattan's luxury condos nor Osceola's vacation mansions appear at first to have much in common with the more ordinary single-family houses snapped up by corporate landlords across the country, all of these dwellings are versions of the same phenomenon: the financialization of housing. Whether the focus of investors is on rental revenue and debt leveraging, or tax shelters and money laundering, or the appreciating asset of the underlying land, these interested parties look upon housing as merely a commodity investment, not as actual homes for people in need of shelter.

Struggling to recover from the recession, Osceola's officials bet on a new branding initiative in a bid to compete with the tourist attractions and big hotels of neighboring Orange County. Osceola's tourism bureau began to promote the county as the "Vacation Home Capital of the World" and trademarked that slogan for good measure.[6] Guests in vacation homes were spending more than twice as much as typical tourists, so it made economic sense to funnel incentives toward that sector. At the same time, the county's record on making affordable housing available for the employees who manage, clean, and service these properties has been woeful.

The result is a tourist and hospitality industry that disregards the needs of locals while channeling the lion's share of its proceeds elsewhere. According to the tourism bureau, visitors to Osceola spent $3.8 billion in 2018, supporting forty-five thousand tourism-related jobs. Yet most of the revenue from VHR rents and fees is sucked out of the county by distant owners. As for jobs, the property management companies that have sprung up to maintain the vacation homes do employ a multitude of cleaning, catering, landscaping, and other service workers. But the depressed wages on offer don't go far, so the gap between these workers' own places of residence and the homes they service could hardly be greater. These disparities are by no means unique to Osceola's VHR sector. They are a stark consequence of national economic policies that have punished working people while rewarding those with the disposable capital to invest in housing as a financial play.

BESPOKE

None of the cleaning staff on duty for Jeeves Florida Rentals have heard of the fictional figure whose name the company bears. But when I describe P. G. Wodehouse's literary character—the gentleman's refined, all-knowing valet—they want more detail about the services he provides for his bachelor employer Bertie Wooster. Is he a live-in butler? Is he well paid? What is their relationship like? I explain that Jeeves is a servant who is infinitely smarter and more capable than the unworldly Wooster, and that the wealthy have always depended on such people. Francisco, the crew's supervisor, nods and smiles knowingly. Beatrice, busy wiping the kitchen surfaces, comes forward and asks me to write down the names of films in which Jeeves features.

The staff are working on a "back-to-back," speed cleaning a palatial house in the hours between the departure of one set of guests and the arrival of the next. Francisco's crew of three has a mere five hours to scrupulously clean a nine-bedroom mansion, as big as one of the minor country houses that populate Bertie Wooster's world of the idle rich. This one, in the ultra-luxury community of Reunion, is fully loaded with amenities for fortunate twenty-first-century children and for adults with the money and the inclination to spoil them rotten. A twenty-seat home theater is tricked out with a Steamboat Willie theme and a Hogwarts Express entrance. Down a long hallway, an extravagant immersive environment called the Enchanted Forest beckons the questing child, while several game arcades boast state-of-the-art machines. The bedrooms are elaborately themed with Disney characters, including a full-sized Dumbo head in one of them, and decor that depicts specific (commercially licensed) scenes from movies. The sprawling entertainment areas of the house flow into broad patios and multilevel swimming pools.

In her office, Jeeves's CEO Sharon Harley describes, in a matter-of-fact voice, some of the features of an even larger house just added to her inventory. "It has two automated bowling alleys, thirty-two pairs of shoes in varying sizes, an indoor spa, and an indoor basketball court where you press a button to make the hoop go away and it becomes a racquetball court." Another house in the Jeeves inventory has a synthetic ice skating rink. "The boundaries are moving all the time," Harley notes. "We've actually got one under construction at the moment that will have laser tag." Our conversation about these custom-built properties inevitably veers toward the most expensive and over-the-top one in Reunion: a 23,000-square-foot home, with fifteen bedrooms and seventeen bathrooms, that rents for $50,000 per week and just went on the market for almost $10 million.[7]

The services offered by Harley's property management company go far beyond the valet role of the fictional Jeeves, though she points out that "we do provide butlers to guests who want them, and the butlers sometimes stay in the home with them." Naturally, her company can also meet other concierge requests—for bespoke chefs, nannies, party planners, scuba divers, chauffeurs, dog sitters, Maserati rentals, VIP tour guides, and the like. "Our guests are members of the public that normally would only consider going to a Ritz-Carlton, a Four Seasons, or a Waldorf," she explains. Jeeves offers them the "discretion" of a private home with all the amenities of a luxury resort. "And no matter how wealthy or famous you are," she says with a smile, "everyone has to do that trip to Disney."

The servants in the classic aristocratic country house lived downstairs, but in today's version they are far removed, geographically, from their wealthy clients. The small army of cleaners, gardeners, inspectors, technicians, drivers, caterers, and fixers who service homes in this league live well off-site and endure punishing commutes along 192 from Kissimmee and towns even further east, like Buenaventura Lakes and St. Cloud. Most are subcontracted, like Beatrice's cleaning crew, so they work on demand whenever a back-to-back opens up. Standards for keeping properties like this shipshape are exacting, and the repercussions for failing to meet them are severe. If a Jeeves inspector finds so much as a stray hair left behind on a bedspread or, worse yet, on a pillow, the cleaners may be called back to do an extra unpaid shift. During one of my visits, a crew member fishes out a candy wrapper from under a sofa cushion. Everyone is relieved. "It may look clean," Francisco says, "but we can always find something, believe me." With a noiseless intensity, they push on, from room to room, dwarfed by the colossal dimensions of the house.

Francisco is part of the "elite team," so he is one of the company's client-facing employees. He welcomes guests, attends to their whims, and troubleshoots their problems. Tall, alert, and debonair, with the body language and charm of a seasoned handler, he is a graduate, not surprisingly, of Disney's customer service training. When I talk to him he is preparing for Passover, a massive date on the Jeeves calendar, as extended Jewish families from New York and New Jersey come to occupy the mansions. "I take care of all the difficulties," he assures me. "I am on call directly, 24/7." Francisco is also responsible for interpreting the guests' "experience" and communicating with the owner of the home about suggested improvements. "The most common complaint is about sound systems," he reports. "I often recommend upgrades to the owner." Guests want them completely up-to-date, he says, not from a year or two before.

Like many of his coworkers, Francisco has more than one job. He is also a boxer, a motivational speaker, and a mentor for youth. We talk about the challenges faced by Osceola's young Puerto Rican men. Francisco has a younger brother in jail, so he is all too familiar with how a low-wage economy can feed the cycle of incarceration. His parents lost the family house to Hurricane Maria, and he has many friends who joined the migration of climate refugees to Kissimmee in 2017. They are only the latest arrivals since Disney began to recruit aggressively from the island in the 1990s. Multilingual Disney-trained Puerto Ricans like him (sometimes referred to as "Mickey Ricans") are prized in Central Florida's tourist industry, where Spanish is the language of service workers and also of many overseas guests.

Francisco and his employer have seen their share of whining from entitled guests, not to mention bizarre demands. "We've had guests who come to Reunion in July," Harley tells me, "and they complain that the outside fireplace is not working, and that's the reason they booked the house. Seriously? In the middle of summer at ninety degrees?" Harley herself is not to the manor born. A native of Wales, she and her husband poured their savings into a failing business called Jeeves, "mostly because we liked the name, since it's synonymous with good service." To begin with, she did the housekeeping herself, and her husband maintained the homes. "Our idea when we moved here was to get fifty properties to manage and live the American dream," she says. Now she has more than four hundred and runs a real estate subsidiary to sell clients' homes for them.

Focusing on the many needs of the super-rich leaves little time to learn how the other half lives. For Harley, Hurricane Maria was "when it first occurred to us that a lot of our staff really struggle because that's when we realized that people living in mobile homes were being warned to move out of them." Subsequently, she and her husband visited a homeless center. "That was also a real eye-opener for us," she recalls. "We told our staff how it affected us, so now we donate all the stained towels and linens, unused toiletries, and leftover items." Harley has ridden the VHR boom to great heights, but she is also aware of its impact on the housing needs of her own employees. The boom "has not made it easy to get staff that are local because there's no affordable housing for those people to live in," she says. "It has all become prime real estate for vacation rental."

Harley's acknowledgment of this problem is not common among her peers. The owners, investors, and managers in the red-hot VHR sector have a vested interest in seeing their properties as a niche real estate class, walled off from the market for long-term rentals and owner-occupied homes. For the most part they are in denial about their industry's role in deepening the county's housing crisis, or else they keep mum about it. Yet there is no doubt that VHR development gets preferential treatment from county officials. Some of these perks come in the form of economic concessions. To finance new schools, for example, the county requires developers to pay impact fees of almost $12,000 per single-family home. When Osceola commissioners last increased these fees, builders and other VHR industry stakeholders lobbied officials to waive the increases for vacation homes, since those do not house any schoolchildren. In 2018, the commissioners rewarded them in a controversial decision that not only spared short-term rental properties from the hikes but actually cut their impact fees by 38 percent. A newly designated category of "vacation villas," meanwhile, was declared exempt from such fees altogether.[8]

Arguably the biggest subsidy comes in the form of hands-off regulation. Neighboring Orange County, like many jurisdictions around the country, sets strict limits on nightly rentals. (Until 2018 they were prohibited entirely.) Osceola, however, only lightly regulates their terms of business. As a result, vacationers searching online for a rental home in Orlando will most likely end up at an Osceola location, thirty miles south of the city. The county saw a 500 percent increase in such units over the five years from 2014 to 2019, and the vast majority were for entire home rentals. In some of the VHR communities, no mailboxes are visible for blocks on end.

By 2016, the VHR properties were delivering more tourism taxes than the county's hotels and motels.[9] This gave the sector's advocates some bragging rights and helped counter criticism that the VHR boom was not offering many benefits to the local service workforce. Unfortunately, under state law none of the tourism tax revenue can be used for general-purpose spending. Instead of helping to fund infrastructure, housing, education, or social services, it has to be reinvested in supporting tourism; technically, the 6 percent surcharge is called the Tourist Development Tax. In Osceola, the revenue is spent mostly on advertising and marketing by its tourist bureau, though it can also go to capital construction of tourist-related facilities. In Orange County, it's similarly used by Visit Orlando, a nonprofit group overseen by a board of tourism executives.

How do VHRs impact the rest of the housing market? Nationwide, there is growing evidence that when short-term rentals reach a critical mass in any given neighborhood, they contribute to rising rents, loss of general housing inventory, and the displacement of long-term residents.[10] In tourist destination cities, for example, it is not uncommon to find apartment buildings that used to house waiters, bartenders, and hotel workers now being utilized entirely for short-term rentals. Buildings that start out with one or two Airbnb listings tend to turn into "cottage hotels" when it becomes more lucrative to list every unit for nightly rentals. Local employees are displaced and forced to commute long distances to work.

Localities differ, however. In Osceola County, with lots of open land available to developers, there is less evidence of *active* displacement. Most of the upscale vacation home rentals are clustered in the western end of the county, in a specially zoned Short-Term Rental Overlay District; unlike urban Airbnb units, they are, to some extent, spatially segregated from long-term rentals or owner-occupied housing. What's more, many vacation homes are new units, with no prior occupancy. But displacement of residents is not simply a matter of moving long-term tenants out and nightly renters in. Studies show that the mere presence of short-term rentals in a locality can push up rents.[11] And

there is also the impact on builders and developers, who are irresist-
ibly attracted to the lucrative VHR product. When Central Florida's
single-family home market was still recovering from the financial crash,
major home construction companies like Lennar and PulteGroup were
all too happy to churn out upscale homes for the VHR market. With
ample profits flowing from these contracts, there was little reason to
build anything in the "missing middle"—the multiunit housing types
such as duplexes, fourplexes, and bungalow courts that traditionally
provide more affordable housing.

Concessions extracted from the county by these builders are often
offset by burdens placed on other kinds of housing. At the same time
that Osceola County commissioners waived impact fees for developers
of "vacation villas," they increased them by 87 percent on builders of
multifamily apartments. As a result of the decision, Osceola's impact fees
for such apartments ($11,362 per new dwelling unit) are now the highest
of any Florida county, and the burden of paying them falls unfairly on the
builders of units most likely to yield affordable rents. Not surprisingly,
this has helped to stifle investor interest in such projects.

THE DISTRIBUTED HOTEL

Long before Walt Disney decided to locate a theme park in peninsular
Florida near the crossing of two highways (Interstate 4 and the Florida
Turnpike), the lakeside town of Kissimmee was a well-known tourist
destination. Its nineteenth-century resort hotels played host to digni-
taries and moneyed travelers, offering alligator hunts and steamboat
trips on the Kissimmee River, which meandered more than a hundred
miles down to Lake Okeechobee. In the wake of the Seminole Wars,
these visitors were drawn by the thrill of sampling the southern frontier of American settler colonialism, on the edge of a tropical expanse
that the Spanish bluntly called Los Mosquitos. Feral hogs left behind by
Hernando de Soto blazed trails through the palmetto and scrub pines
that would eventually morph into six-lane highways. But in the 1880s,
Kissimmee was as far as the railroads, and the visitors, came.

The town was also the headquarters for Hamilton Disston's massive effort to drain the river valley's floodplains and open up a canal route to Tampa Bay. Disston's 1881 purchase from the federal government of four million acres, at twenty-five cents an acre, made him not only the largest landowner in the US, but also the most prolific real estate salesman. He set up sales offices for investors all over Europe, and settlers arrived in droves to stake out their parcels of reclaimed land. They joined the homesteaders and Civil War veterans who were being offered scrubland by the US government for virtually nothing while the Seminoles were being forcibly evicted. Disston set in motion Central Florida's first land and construction boom. Many more would follow, using the same ingredients—out-of-town investors and buyers, oversold lots (some of them literally underwater), strategic dredging, and slick promotional fantasies of a tropical paradise where the living is easy. In a portent of the fate that lay in store for so many other land speculators, Disston lost his shirt and took his life when the financial Panic of 1893 was followed by the destruction of the citrus industry in the Great Freeze of 1894–95.

The second tourist wave followed the 1920s construction of the two-lane Dixie Highway, which brought the masses. "Tin Can" travelers arrived in Ford Model Ts to pitch their tents in camps around Kissimmee. By then, part of the attraction was seeing real cowboys, since Osceola had now become the cattle empire of the South. Kissimmee continued to build on this reputation even after Disney World's 1971 opening ushered in yet another wave of visitors. But as the main action shifted to Orange County and the sprawling theme park zone to the south of Orlando, the town steadily lost its cachet. By the early 2000s, Kissimmee was hollowing out as a commercial center. It had become a commuter town for LHT workers, and Osceola County—deprived of the lion's share of the tourism industry's swelling tax base—was starved of revenue for schools, services, and housing needed for its fast-growing population.

In 2012, the county's marketing agency renamed itself Experience Kissimmee to distinguish the location from Orlando in the tourist mind and began plugging Osceola's VHR offerings at every opportunity. This reboot coincided with a widespread surge in renting out private homes (or rooms in them) to travelers. Airbnb, the poster child of the sharing economy, led the pack in urban areas. Other online platforms, such as HomeAway, VRBO, FlipKey, TripAdvisor, Vacasa, and Expedia, made it easy for second-home owners in traditional tourist destinations to book nightly renters. Demand for local property managers and service firms increased. Almost overnight, VHR became an industry, albeit with little in the way of professional norms and standards.

The "ownership society" promoted by George Bush in the early 2000s has steadily lost ground among its middle-class aspirants since then; the meaning of "home" has slipped from the warm, wholesome sense of a haven, lurching more and more in the grubby direction of retail. In the heady lead-up to the housing crash, owners began to treat their homes as assets for leveraging equity. They still lived there, though, and cherished their private space. In the decade since then, as the "renter nation" and the sharing economy took hold, every corner of the home became fair game for being booked as long as the price was right. Suddenly, everyone could be an amateur landlord. By 2020, the sanctity of the owner-occupied home, preached by generations of national moralists openly shilling for the real estate industry, had faded significantly.

Historically, renting out a room or a bed was not uncommon among working-class families, who often took in boarders or lodgers to make ends meet. As the housing crisis intensified, the extra bodies were friends or relatives evicted from foreclosed homes or unafford-able rental units. But the explosive post-2008 growth in nightly rentals involved more upmarket accommodations, artfully curated by own-ers to catch the eye of discerning travelers. And what started out as a way for individuals or families to earn supplemental income by sharing their dwellings has increasingly become a professional hosting enter-prise. Just as private equity firms like Blackstone snapped up bundles of foreclosed homes for the purpose of long-term rental, institutional bulk buyers and bookers quickly moved in on the short-term rental market. In many locations, listings are now dominated by multiple "unhosted" units owned by the same person or enterprise, often with an out-of-town address. It is estimated that less than a third of Airbnb's US listings are from hosts with a single property, while a full third are from hosts with more than twenty-five properties.[12]

Concentrations of these properties are an obvious threat to the business of hotels and B and Bs, especially because their owners are not required to abide by the regulations applied to commercially zoned lodgings. Many cities with strong hotelier lobbies have therefore started prohibiting short-term rentals entirely, or at least are trying to distinguish between owner-occupier hosts, who are merely aiming to augment their household income, and professional landlords, who are entirely absent from the properties in their portfolios. In New York City, for example, it is now illegal to rent out an entire apartment or home for less than thirty days, and renting out a room for a shorter period is only allowed if the host is present during the guest's stay. In Santa Monica, Airbnb hosts must live on the property during the renter's stay, register for a business license, and collect a 14 percent occupancy tax on the city's behalf. Orlando limits bookings to half of the rooms in a house and requires hosts to obtain notarized permission from their landlord or homeowners association to operate as a home share rental.

In European cities suffering from overtourism, authorities are also taking steps to reclaim the private housing market from domination by investors buying to rent. Amsterdam has restricted sales of newly built housing to owner-occupiers and banned Airbnb from the city center altogether. Barcelona has cracked down on Airbnb for hosting illegal, unlicensed apartments, imposed fines on several investment funds for leaving downtown apartment buildings vacant, and threatened to take over units unless they are leased out for long-term rent. In 2019, those two cities plus eight others—Berlin, Bordeaux, Brussels, Kraków, Munich, Paris, Valencia, and Vienna—demanded that the EU take a stronger regulatory stand against Airbnb. "European cities believe that homes should be used first and foremost for living in," they declared in a joint statement. Introducing a ban on professional Airbnb hosting, the mayor of Prague declared that the trend had effectively turned his city into a "distributed hotel." During the pandemic lockdown, Dublin and Lisbon, among others, ordered landlords to find long-term tenants or forfeit their units to the city.

Such regulations are cheered on by housing advocates, who blame Airbnb and other nightly rental platforms for driving up neighborhood rents and removing affordable units from the market.[13] A 2019 study by the Economic Policy Institute showed that the entry of Airbnb into a community reduces the stock of long-term rentals, creating economic costs that outweigh the benefits of increasing tourism.[14] A detailed McGill University study of New York City showed that two-thirds of Airbnb revenue came from likely illegal listings and that Airbnb rentals had removed as many as 13,500 units from the long-term rental market. The result was a $380 rent increase per year for the median tenant in New York City overall and an increase of more than $700 per year in some Manhattan neighborhoods. The study also found a racially disparate component to Airbnb's impact: the neighborhoods where Airbnb properties were far more profitable than long-term rentals, placing them at particularly high risk for losing rental housing, were 72 percent nonwhite.[15] Overall, the retailing of space inside private homes has morphed into a commercial opportunity for professional hosting firms or speculators who commandeer ever-greater portions of housing stock.

The VHR sector is following a similar path. After 2008, owners of second homes, long accustomed to using them only sporadically for personal recreation, began to rent out their properties for portions of the year. At the turn of the century, eight out of ten owners never rented their properties. By 2018, two-thirds were doing so, and new markets aimed at pure rental profit were emerging. Vacation homes were being built and sold solely for returns on investment, and large commercial players moved in to control the all-important booking marketplace. Several of the leading online travel agencies underwent consolidation: Expedia swallowed up VRBO, HomeAway, ApartmentJet, and Pillow (along with full-service agencies like Orbitz, Hotwire, and Travelocity) in order to compete with Booking.com and Airbnb in a three-way race to dominate the distribution of short-term rentals. Each of these companies is now moving into the real estate market itself, by building or investing in residential housing and shared living space. Google, Amazon, and other corporate giants are in close pursuit.

From 2016, start-ups began to attract significant quantities of venture capital to compete in this scramble.[16] Even at the height of the coronavirus lockdown, plans were announced for Central Florida's first "build-for-rent" subdivision, a professionally managed community type that has now emerged as the next fast-rising asset class in this league.[17] While the pandemic hit the sector hard, Osceola strenuously lobbied Tallahassee for a fast reopening of its top-priority VHRs. In May 2020, it became the first Florida county to be approved to do so. Shying away from hotels for the duration of the COVID health crisis, vacationers decided that VHRs, with their self-contained kitchens and private spaces, were a safer option and flocked to them when the theme parks reopened. Year-on-year bookings showed a rise, while many owner-occupiers, suffering pandemic hardship themselves, transitioned their homes to short-term rentals to capture income from the increased traffic.[18]

As it happens, Osceola County has its own claim to be the historic birthplace of the sharing economy. In 1982, the sixteen-unit Westgate Vacation Villas opened a mile south of Disney World, introducing a new kind of lodging model: time-shares. (Today, the company boasts more than 400,000 members, 14,000 luxury villas, and 25 condo resorts across the country.) Strictly speaking, time-shares and vacation rental homes are different markets: Westgate's customers are hosted in cookie-cutter condos or villas on-site and don't overlap much with the families seeking out customized accommodation in vacation homes or Airbnbs. But the housing crash (and then the pandemic) hit Westgate hard, and so it began to advertise vacant units for short-term rent, in direct competition with the VHR sector. At the same time, the big hotel chains, like Wyndham, Marriott, and Choice, are rapidly moving into the VHR market in pursuit of customers who left them to go there. All of these owners, large and small, act on the assumption that an area's land and property are a prime investment opportunity for out-of-towners to exploit. Wherever the market and lawmakers' minimal regulations allow, these assets are being requisitioned or withdrawn from the needs of local populations and auctioned off or leased to outsiders.

To its credit, Westgate did mount a philanthropic initiative to combat homelessness: Hospitality Helps, founded by Mark Waltrip, the company's chief operating officer, helped several hundred families transition into apartment housing. But when I visited Waltrip in his office, he was unwilling to acknowledge that Westgate's own vacation housing model might be a contributor to the problem. Instead, he blames Osceola's motels for becoming "low-income housing projects," proclaiming that Central Florida has become a "dumping ground" for the homeless of the entire East Coast. "If you don't stop these hotels from operating illegally, they're going to continue to be festering grounds," he tells me.

Waltrip's views, absent the colorful language, were shared by other leading figures in the region's VHR business whom I interviewed. One exception was Rembert Vonk, the owner of Excellent Vacation Homes, who was more ready to acknowledge VHR's impact on the mainstream housing market. "The vacation market boom is great for the economy," he notes, "but because it's so much more attractive for the county and builders to do vacation homes, we have created quite an affordable housing challenge." As a native of Amsterdam, he is accustomed to generous state outlays on social housing. Perhaps thanks to that background, he is able to take off his industry hat and question the policy of capturing bed taxes for the exclusive purpose of promoting the tourism industry. "Speaking as a concerned resident," he says, he would like "for these tax dollars to be spent on things like better transportation, affordable housing, you name it."

HOSPITALITY IS A VIRTUE

In the property management business, back-to-back cleaning sessions are always rush jobs, but they are usually straightforward. That said, some guests have their own quirks, and others cause havoc. On this occasion, in a house not far from Kissimmee, a departing Brazilian family has left behind not only food spattered all over the kitchen, but a mess of broken glass: several windowpanes, sliding doors, and glass inserts in the coffee tables were all shattered. Tammy, the house cleaner having to deal with it all, offers the obvious explanation: "Maybe they had a fight." But there is also a chance that this was an outside job, an act of random vandalism. Regardless, there are some peculiarities to add to the forensic evidence. One door handle is missing; so is a doorstop on another door. And while the family had several children, "it looks as if they all stayed in the master bedroom," Tammy notes.

Whatever the story, it is an onerous cleanup for her. A former property manager herself, Tammy is, by her own admission, getting too old for jobs like this one. Facing an arduous commute from Lake County, she is scaling down the number of properties she cleans, but cannot afford to give up the work entirely. Her employer, Lance Boyer, who is listening to us, points out that she has become "part of the struggling underclass." He assures me later that Tammy is a valued employee. For the most part, he says, "it's impossible for us to find good help because all the good people go to Disney—you cannot match the Disney benefits. So we generally get the Disney rejects applying for our jobs."

Lance and his wife, Karin, formed the Florida Dream Homes property management company in the late 1990s, at the dawn of the region's VHR business. They had just succeeded—against Disney's wishes—in launching a Montessori school in Celebration (a story I documented in *The Celebration Chronicles*), and they took a neighbor's advice to generate income by booking area rentals for European visitors. Up until then, Lance recalls, vacation rentals for Americans "meant cabins in the woods where people would go hunting or to the lake, and you brought your own sheets." Within a couple of years, the Boyers were booking a million dollars annually in reservations and gradually went into the business of managing the properties themselves. At its peak, the company had more than fifty properties, but as Lance and Karin approach retirement, they have reduced the list by half. It's still mostly a family business: Lance oversees the bookings, Karin does the inspections, their son Brandon troubleshoots the technology, and their other off-spring, Amber and Colin, lend a hand when needed.

As the business grew, the Boyers and other property managers formed their own trade group, which would become the Central Florida branch of the Florida Vacation Rental Managers Association, to promote their interests. In neighboring Polk County, the association helped to elect friendly officials who promptly relaxed some restrictive VHR regulations. Osceola commissioners welcomed VHR from the outset, but to Lance's great annoyance they used bed taxes from the industry to build pork barrel projects—a seldom-visited Museum of Military History, along with a new rodeo arena in Kissimmee, in deference to the county's powerful cattle ranching families. On the bright side, Lance claims that the Experience Kissimmee slogan, "Vacation Home Capital of the World," was originally his idea. He pitched it to the county, he claims, through the trade association.

Unlike many of their peers, the Boyers have long resisted being sucked into the more lucrative, but ethically compromised, business of selling the homes they manage. Instead, they insist they are in business to help people, not to maximize their profits. As Lance puts it, "We are constantly focusing on things that we feel have an impact on making society better." Of course, serving the customer is a staple rhetoric of property management, but Lance and Karin really do seem to have brought their own family's hospitality ethos into their work. According to Karin, "Our guests are practically part of our family. They come back to us over and over again because they know we care about them—and I want to treat them the same way I would want to be treated." The Boyers' office, in an annex of their own home, is crammed with the luggage and personal effects of guests who make twice-yearly visits, and they regale me with tales of their close personal relationships with many of these clients. Karin attributes this fellow feeling to their former work in a psychiatric hospital, which is where she and Lance met: "We learned how to deal with all stripes of people in a loving way."

Despite their distaste for profiteering, Lance also frames their aptitude for hospitality as a business advantage. "Can you get a cheaper property than ours?" he asks. "Sure. Can you get a better one? Sure. But you will not get someone who cares as much or provides the same kind of personalized service as we do." He adds, "Renters know when you are faking it." Looking after guests and cleaning up after them does not generate much cash flow, but it is the best way to "control the guest experience." Like other property managers I spoke to, Lance reaffirms that "you cannot charge enough money for a home to cover the cost of presenting that home to the guest . . . which is why you need a slice of the bookings." As corporate players like Expedia take ever more control of these bookings, the margins for small family firms like Florida Dream Homes keep getting tighter.

Among my interviews with property managers, the Boyers stood out for their candor about the industry and their passion for the comfort of guests. Their approach reminded me of the pride that amateur Airbnb hosts often take in opening their home to strangers. Welcoming guests with respect and curiosity about their person is a golden rule in most cultures and a deep virtue in many faiths. Introducing any kind of monetary exchange into the host-guest relationship is detrimental, of course, and especially so when the owner or occupant is not present to welcome and attend to visitors. But the final blow to any semblance of authentic hosting comes when multiunit owners or institutional investors get involved. When more and more of the revenue from visitors is sucked away and distributed around the globe, tourist sectors like this become a parasite on the surrounding area. Having local property managers means that at least someone is acting like a host, even if only deputizing for owners thousands of miles away. The Boyers and their contract cleaning crews are still part of a real local economy, drawing down incomes and providing jobs.

STOPPING THE CONTAGION

For now, the individual ownership model is still the standard in Osceola's VHR subdivisions and master planned communities. Some owners have multiple units, but so far there has been no major corporate takeover. Even so, the west end of the 192 corridor, with the more upscale vacation homes, is starting to attract mega-projects, marking the entry of big investor money into the VHR market. The largest of these is Jimmy Buffett's Margaritaville resort, with a thousand "vacation cottages" and three hundred time-share units for sale. When I posed as an interested buyer, the salesperson told me that if I wanted to be able to rent out my unit, I would have to choose approved furnishings, in order "to maintain a guest experience consistent with the brand." Any artwork I wanted for personal decor would have to fit inside the "owner's closet" while the unit is being rented.

As for foreign capital, Brazilian investors are funding several hundred "condotel" units in the rental townhome community of Magic Village resorts and are bankrolling the eighty-seven-acre Magic Place, dubbed "the Dubai of 192" on account of its initial plan for ten tower blocks stretching up to twenty-five stories.[19] Such developments are corporate variations on the alternative-lodgings model of VHR. They are also sizable capital investments in need of protection from the "contagion" of the motel people further along the corridor. The county's efforts to do exactly that began in the depths of the Great Recession in 2012, when an economic advisory board was appointed to recommend upgrades that would draw investors to the stretch of Route 192 that runs from Kissimmee city limits to the Lake County line.

The board's study divided this fifteen-mile stretch of road into three sections: the westernmost one near Disney World, the easternmost one near Kissimmee, and a segment in the middle. According to the board's report, the easternmost portion was in a downward spiral, with its motels hosting "non-permitted extended stays" as a "last resort" for people under "economic stress." The study lamented the state of these "vacant structures, under-performing businesses, and discount-based marketing strategies," and concluded that 192's "inconsistent signage and poor maintenance" had resulted in "an irregular and visually unappealing commercial business corridor." Urgent measures, it continued, were needed to prevent this "blight" from spreading west to the other two sections, including the more affluent precincts closer to Disney World. The board envisaged a cohousing pilot program to look into retrofitting the motels for standard use as apartments and otherwise assisting residents "to find more permanent, safe, and appropriate housing." A community land trust was also mentioned as a feasible way to "to acquire and hold land for affordable housing."[20]

While these findings were presented in an evenhanded way, business journalists were more candid about the board's recommendations. As one article put it, "the county is considering potentially drastic surgery on 192—amputating one section to save the other two from a spreading infection."[21] Investors and business owners with interests on the west side lobbied for a new agency to administer the surgery, and the following year saw the formation of the W192 Development Authority. Given powers to levy special taxes and to deploy eminent domain to seize rundown properties, the authority would preside over Florida's largest community redevelopment area, encompassing nineteen square miles. The seven board members, all owners or managers of local enterprises, were given a rare opportunity to make over 192 in their common business interests. Ordinary residents who lived on the corridor, or adjacent to it, were not represented at all.

The lion's share of the agency's attention was focused on the prosperous western segments of 192 and on improvements aimed at further gentrification of that end of the corridor. Celebration had been the first of the west side's glittering prizes, and since the 1990s it has helped to anchor the district as a domain of relative affluence—though Disney's plans for the community were not always seen that way. "When Celebration was first pitched to the county, the tourist industry fought it tooth and nail," recalls Hector Lizasuain, who oversaw W192's controversial beautification campaign. "They wanted 192 to be a tourism-only environment, and Disney was selling a lifestyle there for permanent residents." Over the years, the growth of Celebration's retail component assuaged any such worries, and when the district began to gentrify commercially, the upmarket tone that Celebration lent to the neighborhood proved to be an asset.

Lizasuain, a former engineering technician with a golden tongue

and what he calls "a passion for 192," served for more than a decade as
the mediator between government and the corridor's business stakeholders. He is now deploying these skills as director of planning and
government affairs for the Brazilian investors behind Magic Place.
With homes designed by the high-end Italian firm Pininfarina, this
development—"the first branded home product in Central Florida,"
according to Lizasuain—is being promoted as a milestone in luxury
vacation rental housing. It is slated to include upper-end retail, including a gourmet food hall—a step beyond anything else on 192, currently
known for its chain restaurants and dollar stores. High-rolling Brazilian
tourists, Lizasuain notes, average more than $5,000 in consumer spend-
ing for a typical visit: "They're the ones with seven or eight suitcases,
in plastic wrap." And aside from them, the upmarket retail plans for
Magic Place are neatly tailored to Celebrationites, who live in the near
vicinity.

In contrast to the go-go growth in the west end of 192, effectively
steered by the development authority and by Experience Kissimmee,
the economic advisory board's recommendations for the depressed
eastern end of the corridor, with its rundown motels and unsuitable housing, have not gone very far. According to David Buchheit, the authority's former director, the blame lies in large part with the moteliers.
"I'm being blunt," he tells me. "There are owners that are slumlords
masquerading as a hotel or motel. If they don't elevate their brand,
they shouldn't even be in business."

The motel owners are an easy target, but it would be a mistake
to think that the growth of vacation homes is disconnected from the
housing distress further along the corridor, or that they are in two different real estate markets. Susan Caswell, a housing specialist in Osceola
County government, has spent long-suffering years trying to encourage developers to deliver the kind of housing the county desperately
needs—"zeroes and ones," as she puts it (referring to bedrooms), not
the "twos and threes" of single-family homes that the large national
firms are hardwired to build. In 2018, her team of planners introduced
new zoning regulations that encourage mixed-use development and

more diverse, high-density housing products, hoping that builders will take the bait. "We now have fifty thousand acres of land that are zoned for mixed-use," she notes. "But we don't have any mixed-use developers in Osceola, so we are working on educating them."

Caswell concedes that "the market is never going to provide for people earning less than $25,000." But in Osceola and other regions like it, the most pressing housing need is actually for households earning between $25,000 and $35,000. These are the tourist and service industry workers, the elderly, and single-parent families—"not the middle-class, nuclear families who are a match for the 80 percent of housing product in this county." Caswell beats her head daily against the "fundamental mismatch" between builders' supply of these multi-bedroom single-family homes and the demand from lower-income households for smaller units. "Production is keeping up," she points out, but "a huge percentage of it is for vacation rental units. That's where the money is, and that's the market failure."

This mismatch between supply and demand is only magnified by the surge in absentee ownership and short-term rentals—not only in Osceola, but across the country. From 2000 to 2009, when the Census Bureau's American Community Survey last gathered reliable data, absentee ownership in Manhattan swelled by 70 percent; by 2010, one in every twenty-five units had an owner or renter who lived there less than two months of the year.[22] In the decade since then, the numbers more than doubled, though purchasing through anonymous LLCs has made ownership difficult to track.[23] Builders of new apartments and houses are meeting a demand from out-of-town buyers willing to pay through the nose, but they are not catering at all to the local need for workforce housing. And while this imbalance is most visible in heavily visited destinations like New York or Central Florida, those locations are hardly anomalous. After all, the shortage of affordable housing is everywhere, in almost every county in the US.

So where does the "market failure" lie? Not in the markets themselves, which in this case are reliably responding to the most profitable source of demand. The fault lies in the assumption that markets

are actually capable of meeting the needs of large sectors of the population. That is plainly not the case, because in most instances, markets are the cause of, and not the solution to, the housing crisis. But
the neoliberal belief that every problem has a market-based solution
has so permeated the public mind that the ever-wider divide between
dogma and reality has not yet forced a reckoning. Housing's recent
takeover by finance gave a fresh boost to the romance with markets,
even though the outcome—the severing of land and realty prices from
local incomes—has been calamitous. The only silver lining to the pandemic recession is that its shock impact, heralding a spate of evictions
and foreclosures, serves as a vigorous reminder that alternatives to the
market delivery model for housing are desperately needed.

ANDREW ROSS

The Battle of Split Oak

AT THE EASTERN end of Route 192 lies a vast expanse of undeveloped land that stretches from St. Cloud all the way to Osceola's border with coastal Brevard County. Locals refer to it as "Mormon country" because it is occupied by a colossal ranch owned by the Church of Jesus Christ of Latter-day Saints (LDS). Environmentalists prize this domain for the rich diversity of its flora and fauna and are fighting to conserve as much of it as they can. Developers see a future empire of low-density housing to peddle to Central Florida's steady flow of new arrivals. The outcome of this tug-of-war will lock in the destiny of these lands for the rest of the century, potentially hobbling the region's fledgling affordable housing efforts.

In the suburban sprawl of the Sunbelt's boomburgs, there are always more green fields just beyond the metro fringe for developers to plow under and jerry-build subdivisions of tract housing. Because the land is cheaper than in urban areas, construction should, in principle, yield more affordable units. But the overall costs of sprawl, to residents and nonresidents like, are prohibitive, amounting in the US to more than a trillion dollars a year.[1] And the financialization of the housing market means that the payoff for individual home buyers is by no means guaranteed. In the years before 2008, for example, lower-income prospective buyers of single-family homes were advised to "drive until you qualify"—only to find themselves saddled with subprime loans and stranded out in the foreclosure belts after the housing crash, dozens of traffic-choked miles from places of employment. Developments under construction became "ghost subdivisions," riddled with weed-strewn lots and unfinished roads.

Opponents of auto-dependent sprawl routinely denounce that pattern of low-density growth beyond the metro edge as environmentally catastrophic. In common with many housing advocates, they favor instead the smart growth approach: building more diverse kinds of housing units in infill areas, upzoning already developed land to increase densities, and retrofitting abandoned malls. To give this formula some teeth, sympathetic local governments have adopted the planning tool of the urban growth boundary (UGB), which prohibits development outside a given line. UGBs are supposed to be a check on sprawl, preserving rural land and encouraging more compact building closer to jobs, stores, and schools.

Such growth boundaries do not by themselves automatically yield affordable housing. But when they are combined with land-use regulations that guide development toward higher urban densities, housing is more likely to be cheaper per unit, and the cost of public services and transportation is also reduced. However, in many jurisdictions across the US, and in almost every Florida county, officials tend to regard the lines drawn by UGBs as provisional, subject to revision whenever an overriding development need or request arises. County commissioners are especially responsive to landowners who donate to their election campaigns and then ask for their developable acres to be included, undercutting the intent of the UGB.[2]

Osceola is no exception, and the story of its expanding UGB is a clear warning about the damaging habit of allowing powerful developers to bend the rules and influence decisions about land use. A campaign by local environmentalists to preserve a forest in the northeast of the county has exposed the collusion between landowners, officials, and developers. A loss for the environmentalists is likely to further

undermine efforts to encourage more efficient and inexpensive building within the footprint of Osceola's developed, semi-urbanized areas.
It is a story involving Florida's largest single landowner, and it takes
place against the backdrop of rising seas and populations fleeing the
ruinous impact of climate change.

SCRUB JAY

"We just moved from recovering sandhill through some scrub," notes
my guide as we follow a trail through Split Oak Forest. "Now we're
heading into what I would say is wet flatwood, and over there is cypress
dome, which has been here forever." Split Oak is a nature reserve a few
miles beyond the eastern urban fringe of Central Florida, shared by
Orange and Osceola Counties. Technically, this refuge land is a mitigation bank to offset ecological damage caused by highway construction,
established as part of a statewide wave of environmental conservation
in the late 1990s. Quite modest in size, at 1,700 acres, the forest is playing an outsize role in the bitter fight over development in the region,
and the state as a whole. The same could be said for my guide, Valerie
Anderson.

Ambling further into the forest, through what she identifies in turn
as pine flatwoods, oak scrub, and sandhill longleaf, we make our way
north to Lake Hart, an upper headwater of the Everglades. Valerie,
who has closely studied the history of this terrain, notes that "the water
here used to be four feet higher" before Hamilton Disston's colossal
dredging projects in the 1880s changed much of the topography of
peninsular Florida. "He drained Lake Hart here into East Lake Toho,"
she explains, "and then into Lake Toho, and then into the Kissimmee
River, and then all the way down into the Everglades." Commercial
turpentine and cattle operations on these lands preceded the establishment of the reserve, so it is far from pristine. But if you know where
to look, she assures me, there are ancient flora and fauna everywhere.

Along the way, our path is temporarily blocked by a gopher tortoise
shuffling toward a food source. Valerie is excited about the encounter

("he is our mascot"), though she is disappointed that we don't spot any scrub jays, the only bird species endemic to Florida. "These jays," she explains, "just do really poorly when they are adjacent to people; they're not very adaptable." Both the scrub jay and the tortoise are federally listed as endangered. The jay's survival is tied to the sandy, scrubby habitat of Split Oak, and gopher tortoises are a keystone species: hundreds of other species in the ecosystem make use of their burrows.

Valerie and I are here because Split Oak and its at-risk species (others include Sherman's fox squirrel and the swallow-tailed kite) are being threatened by developers' intrusive plans, and she is leading the charge to stop them. It's a standoff you can find almost anywhere in the US: a local growth machine, aided and abetted by developer-friendly officials, encroaching on environmentally fragile lands. The rural eastern portions of Central Florida have long been considered off-limits, but a proposal to ram a parkway through this forest would open them up to low-density development far from established urban centers.

Valerie did her master's thesis at USC on the ecology of Split Oak, and in the few years since graduating, she has almost single-handedly jump-started the effort to save the forest. She has garnered the support of seasoned environmentalists, some of whom refer to her affectionately as Scrub Jay, while the dealmakers who preside over breakneck growth in the region now recognize her as a dogged adversary. "Everybody in Central Florida who wants to develop things knows who I am now," she chuckles. "When I walk into a public hearing, complete strangers come up to say 'hello.'" For this Daytona native, raised as a Jehovah's Witness, who self-describes as a "tech-y, athletic-y millennial," the adjustment has been sharp. "I wasn't the captain of the volleyball team. I wasn't the first chair flute. Nobody was ever, like, you're a natural leader," she says. Now she is in a position where powerful people ask: "What do you want, Valerie?"

After our forest walk, Valerie and I attend a meeting hosted by the League of Women Voters of Orange County, the organization's largest county chapter in the US, and one of her key allies. Some of the chapter's most active members have come to talk shop about the defense of Split Oak, discussing legal research and political strategy.[3] One figure roundly denounced by a variety of speakers is Charles Lee, Audubon Florida's director of advocacy. He has made a career out of brokering deals between environmentalists and developers—mostly in the interest of the latter, according to those at the meeting. Lee has played his hand on Split Oak as well. In return for his prized endorsement of the parkway route, he helped negotiate a 1,550-acre mitigation area of additional protected lands to be donated by the highway's immediate beneficiary: Tavistock, the developer of a 27,000-acre community called Sunbridge, on the other side of Split Oak. Lee touts the result as the "best deal" the public can get. The environmentalists at the meeting see it as a blatant sellout.[4]

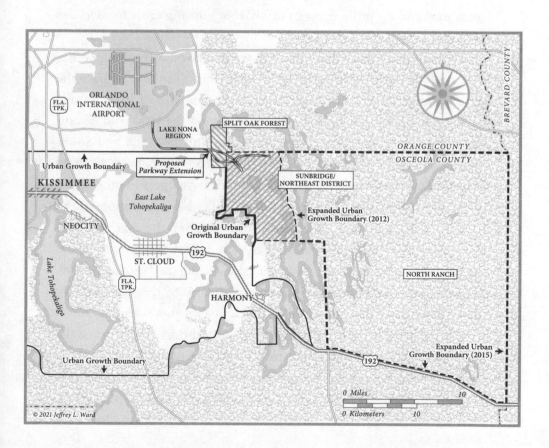

Valerie seems pleased about the tenor of the discussion, but no one doubts that officials in both Osceola County and Orange County will approve the proposed parkway; indeed, they both do so within a week. But approval for the highway's cross-forest route is only one move in a much larger game being played by Osceola. For some time, the county has been an active partner in the LDS church's plan to develop its vast land inventory in the east. The centerpiece is a blueprint for what would be Florida's single largest development: a new city for half a million residents, currently designated as North Ranch. It is to be located on a 133,000-acre site that is part of the church's capacious 290,000-acre Deseret Ranch. The location is in the middle of what Karina Veaudry, president of the Florida Native Plant Society's local chapter, calls Florida's "last remaining wilderness."[5] So, too, the decision to allow development so far from the region's urban service areas may end up prolonging its affordable housing crisis for decades to come.

The construction of the new city would have far-reaching consequences, filling in the last gap in the thick belt of growth that spans the state's central section. Development would then stretch from Tampa Bay all the way to the Space Coast, threatening the vital wildlife corridors that allow species to move between North Florida and South Florida. In addition, approval to ride roughshod through a conserved area like Split Oak would be a green light for developers in other parts of Florida to make inroads on conservation lands that are supposed to be fully protected by the state's constitution. Given the milestone status of Florida's land conservation program, it may reverberate across the country. Public lands that were set aside during the 1980s and 1990s, including national parks and monuments, many of them Indigenous sacred sites, have been under direct attack in almost every state.

The 27,000 acres due to be developed as Sunbridge were part of the Mormon ranch until being sold to Tavistock, Central Florida's most powerful land developer. The proposed parkway through Split Oak is the gateway to Sunbridge, and the building of Sunbridge will trigger construction of North Ranch, so all three projects are intimately connected and interdependent. Both Sunbridge and North Ranch lie far outside Osceola's original UGB, drawn up to encourage more compact development inside the county's urban areas. Attempts to regulate developers into building cheaper housing units in more dense clusters or in infill areas are undercut when construction is allowed well beyond the urban fringe. The result is leapfrog development, the scourge of anti-sprawl advocates, and a headache for planners hoping to contain service costs and reduce the carbon footprint of settlement. "Why," Valerie asks, "would you develop infill in downtown St. Cloud when you can build a new downtown on a floodplain out there near Split Oak?" There is no guarantee that private development on infill will be affordable in the long run; that outcome can only ultimately be ensured by forms of nonmarket housing. But building on ecologically fragile land far outside the existing service infrastructure is the worst option of all.

The outcome of the battle of Split Oak will shape any initiatives to address Osceola's housing problems through tighter regulation of land use because it will send a message about the continuing ability of developers to get whatever they want from elected officials. It will also affect the balance of power between environmentalists and pro-growth coalitions throughout the state. Republican lawmakers have already made it easier for remote development to be greenlighted solely on the basis of projections of future population growth and land capacity. But the future is far from stable, as COVID-19 reminds us, and the impacts of climate change will hit Florida harder than almost anywhere else in the US. How will the chronic housing challenges described in this book play out amid rising sea levels, ever-stronger hurricanes, water shortages, and more lethal pandemics?

CHURCH AND STATE

Walt Disney's Florida land grab of 30,000 acres made all the headlines in 1965. Fifteen years earlier, when the LDS church bought a much larger chunk of the region—54,000 acres of range, pasture, and cutover timberland—the acquisition attracted hardly any attention, but it may prove just as consequential in the long run. Over the years, the original parcel has been augmented by other purchases through AgReserves, the Mormons' agricultural investment wing, growing into today's vast Deseret Ranch. Contrary to its tourist iconography, Florida is one of the country's most important beef cattle states; by the 1990s, Deseret was the biggest ranch east of the Mississippi, boasting the largest cow-calf herd in the US.

Despite aerial evidence of extensive denuding of land, Deseret officials have long vaunted their responsible stewardship of the property. Yet, as with many rural landowners, when the urban fringe creeps closer, the siren call of developer dollars becomes difficult to resist.[6] According to some projections, the population of Osceola will more than triple over the next four decades, and the Deseret lands are an attractive greenfield site for developers to profitably meet the housing, commercial, and transportation needs of these incoming residents. With planners trying to escape Central Florida's traditional pattern of piecemeal, sprawl-driven growth, a single large landowner amenable to a *unified* development plan would have a clear advantage in any approval process.

In 2007, Osceola County revised its Comprehensive Plan for land use, encouraging developers to submit large-scale "conceptual master plans" based on smart growth principles. This gave the LDS church the perfect opportunity to step forward with a proposal for development of a swath of Deseret Ranch directly to the east of Split Oak Forest. In the 1990s, this portion of the ranch had been among the biodiversity hot spots targeted for public acquisition through an ambitious Florida initiative to conserve environmentally significant lands. The land was key to the statewide connectivity of ecological corridors, and so conserving it in perpetuity would have been in keeping with LDS church principles of environmental stewardship. The state tried to acquire this ecological jewel for over a decade, but the church repeatedly refused to sell, electing instead to wait for the right time to develop the land.

Charles Lee, Florida Audubon's master deal broker, told me that

Osceola officials were more than ready for Deseret to step forward with its development plans when that moment arrived. "Osceola County decided that its growth path lay to the east [in Mormon country] and not to the south," he says, despite pressure from "venture capital and large ranch owners" to go in that direction. As Lee sees it, this was a providential decision because the southern part of Osceola, "a tremendous reservoir of wildlife and species diversity," was hosting the effort to restore the Kissimmee River and save the Everglades. But environmental surveys show that both of these regions—in the east and in the south—are very high on the biodiversity index. By framing the decision exclusively as a choice between development in one region or the other, Lee's logic essentially demanded that one of them be sacrificed at the altar of growth.

Deseret's proposal to develop the Northeast District—which Tavistock would brand as Sunbridge—was especially attractive to Osceola's economic development managers because the developer vowed to create 44,000 jobs in industrial and commercial facilities, whetting the county's appetite for high-wage employment. There was a biomedical research cluster being built in the community of Lake Nona, just across the Orange County line, and it held out the promise of becoming a new economic engine for Central Florida. Jeff Jones, a regional planner recruited by Osceola to be its "change agent" and coordinate its "Go East" policy, recalls the excitement generated by the prospect of joining in that bounty. "It looked almost like it was 1968 and Disney is coming—and now Osceola had a chance to be part of that."

Inconveniently, the Northeast District fell outside Osceola County's UGB, so in 2010 the county commissioners proposed to amend the boundary, extending the urbanized area by more than 12,000 acres. This move generated stronger than usual opposition from environmentalists. The Sierra Club and the Florida Native Plant Society, along with a coalition of concerned citizens, filed an official objection with Florida's Department of Community Affairs (DCA), an agency set up in the late 1960s to oversee land-use planning and act as a check on runaway development.[7] The DCA required a "demonstration of need" in order to approve a large development plan, and the Northeast District plan was put forward just as the post-crash storm of foreclosures blew through the region; seldom has the need to build tens of thousands of new homes seemed more redundant. The environmental groups noted that the county already had a large surplus of approved but unbuilt residential units—62,356 of them—*inside* the UGB, in addition to 25.8 million square feet of similarly unused commercial space, so there was no demonstrated need to extend the boundary for further development.[8] The agency agreed, ruling that Osceola's proposed amendment was unnecessary, environmentally damaging, and likely to promote urban sprawl since it would remove any incentive to develop the "vacant underutilized land" that lay within the UGB.[9] In other words, if the Northeast District plan were approved, Osceola would be pulling the rug out from under the smart growth commitments it had made only three years previously.[10]

Luckily for the developers, the agency's days were numbered. In early 2011, as one of his first acts in office, incoming governor Rick Scott abolished the DCA and replaced it with a new division that looked and behaved like its exact opposite: a Department of Economic Opportunity, mandated to enable and accelerate growth and development. According to Ralf Brookes, the environmental lawyer who filed the objection with the DCA, one of the first casualties of the shake-up was the requirement for justifying growth. "It was turned upside down, just like Alice in Wonderland," he recalls. "Instead of demonstrating the need for more land, the new requirement was that counties had to demonstrate they had put aside enough land to accommodate the projected population growth over twenty-five or thirty years, even when they didn't need it now." Within the year, a settlement agreement for the Northeast District was signed between the LDS church, Tavistock, and Osceola, and the county continued to amend its Comprehensive Plan at the request of the developer. "We really don't have a comprehensive plan," Valerie points out. "Whenever a developer wants a change, we make one."[11]

Osceola is not the only place where UGBs have come under assault from the real estate industry. In Portland, one of the first US jurisdictions to adopt the anti-sprawl measure, there is a heated debate over whether its UGB is responsible for jacking up the price of developable land inside the boundary. Whether Portland's UGB has in fact made its housing less affordable is a fiercely contested topic; for example, the bull market in housing and the appeal of the city's dense, transit-friendly infrastructure to younger buyers are contributing factors in the rise of its home prices. But it is hard to imagine that Osceola's UGB is responsible for its lack of affordable housing: within the original boundary line, Osceola still has 64,400 acres of developable land available outside its two cities, Kissimmee and St. Cloud.[12] With that ample supply, land prices are not rising rapidly. The county's efforts to encourage compact, mixed-use development would have had a better chance of succeeding if it had held the line. Whether the private market is capable of delivering housing at reasonable prices and maintaining those rates over the long run is another matter.

After eliminating the DCA, Scott gutted many of the initiatives that had made Florida a national leader in growth management. Among them was a regulatory measure that required large-scale plans like Sunbridge (with 28,000 homes and 9,000 multifamily units) and North Ranch (with 180,000 housing units) to include some provision for affordable housing.[13] Now, the best that housing officials like Susan Caswell can hope for is that "if the diversity of product is there, it will be more affordable." Charles Lee was more blunt by far when I asked him to hazard a guess about the likely price points of housing in the Deseret projects. "People who work at Disney," he pronounced, "are not going to be able to afford to live in the Northeast District."

NORTH RANCH

After the Northeast District plan was in the bag, Deseret sought approval for the much larger North Ranch project. Once again the scheme was aided and abetted by the governor. In late 2013, Scott established a task force on opening up East Central Florida for development and formally requested Osceola County to work as partners with Deseret on the project. Only a few days later, the LDS church's AgReserves division announced a mega-purchase of 382,000 acres in the Florida Panhandle. Sitting on a total of 670,000 acres, the church was now the largest private landowner in the state, putting it in prime position to wield even more political influence in Tallahassee.[14] In the tradition of Hamilton Disston, who acquired millions of acres without generating any revenue for Florida, the church was now the latest out-of-state investor to extract and repatriate a fortune from a land empire without giving much back.

In a matter of months, Osceola and Deseret fast-tracked a plan to be sent for approval by Tallahassee. It included a provision for the county's UGB to be expanded yet again, now as far east as the Brevard County line. Once more environmentalists stepped forward to oppose the amendment, though this time Audubon took the lead. In a letter of objection, Charles Lee pointed out that, far from being urban and compact, the plan for North Ranch development was more characteristic of low-density, linear sprawl. In fact, overall residential density in the plan was for just five housing units per acre, more typical of an American suburban subdivision than an urban center. Lee also argued that the plan's intention to conserve only 28 percent of the North Ranch area (mostly wetlands) was too low, with unacceptable harm done to wildlife corridors, aquifer recharge areas, and fragile watersheds.

Utah's Mormon authorities, on the other hand, regarded the 28 percent of conservation set-asides—recommended by Deseret's own environmental consultants—to be far too high. According to Jeff Jones, the Osceola "Go East" planner, the church's response to the conservation proposal was "something along the lines of 'You're giving up how much land? Are you insane?'" Osceola commissioners tried to resolve the impasse by soliciting an independent review from a trio of highly respected Florida ecologists, but their report came down decisively on the side of the environmentalists who were pressing for more set-asides.[15] Their most significant recommendation called for adding a minimum of 19,100 acres of conserved lands, many of them upland

areas abundant with at-risk species, including the crested caracara, bur-
rowing owl, Florida sandhill crane, and Eastern indigo snake.[16]

Unused to outsiders having a say in the use of their land, the LDS
top brass began talking about dropping out of the deal entirely. But
according to Jones, just when it looked like the Mormons "might pull
the plug," Charles Lee "got more involved," playing his accustomed
role as a go-between. The other environmental groups were steadfastly
opposed to any horse-trading, but Lee brokered a deal with Deseret
that added a mere 3,000 acres of land to the main wildlife corridor at
the southern end of the property. Lee himself told me that he was
"far from happy" with the arrangement but saw it as the lesser evil.[17]
("Deseret was in the driver's seat," he told a reporter. "They could have
walked away any day and said, 'OK, we'll do what other developers do
and develop 500 acres at a time.' And for the environmental outlook,
that's the worst outcome.")[18] His intervention proved decisive. As Jones
put it, Lee "is the voice of the environmental community, and if he's
OK with it, that's what everybody is looking for." The Osceola County
commissioners promptly approved the plan.

After my conversations with Lee and Jones, I drove across the
Deseret Ranch, which spreads out serenely and abundantly from the
eastern limits of St. Cloud. Clocking mile after mile of tidy roadside
fencing, I passed solitary herds of cattle and feedlots and cut through
the woods, pasture, and marsh that make up the signature mosaic of
uplands and wetlands. For now, high-grade utility lines are the only
other intruders on this vast expanse. It is eerie to think that more than
180,000 housing units of housing will be built here, more than the
county's entire inventory right now.

At the ranch I meet with Don Whyte, a seasoned community planner recruited by Deseret to negotiate and deliver the North Ranch plan.
Although he is not an LDS church member, he has prior experience
working in Mormon country, on Utah's 4,000-acre New Urbanist community of Daybreak. A jovial greeter, with scads of information to
impart to me about Deseret's cattle breeding methods and productivity
feats, he is careful to specify that he speaks only for himself and not for

the church. Recalling the controversy over the conservation set-asides, Whyte concedes that asking for "the ecologists' review was probably ill-advised, frankly. If you ask an environmentalist, 'Did these guys offer enough land?' what do you think their answer is going to be? They will always say no because all they want is more." As for the protection of endangered species, Whyte asserts, despite proof offered by Valerie and others, that "no scrub jay has actually been seen"—though he later acknowledged that the ranch has some land "suitable for their habitat."

Whyte also plays down the significance of widening the wildlife corridors. "Species coexist post-development in lots of communities," he ventures, pointing out that, on the ranch, animals cross roads all the time. "Occasionally, a Florida panther wanders up here from the south, looking for a girl panther, and then it wanders back when it can't find one," he breezily notes. It is a flip comment on a matter that is given the highest priority by environmentalists who oppose the North Ranch plan. Panthers are not only charismatic; they are an umbrella species, which means that their fate affects many others in an ecosystem.[19]

Jones, for his part, says that after decades of trying with limited success to regulate the scattershot advance of low-density sprawl, he sees North Ranch as a unique opportunity to do regional planning on a grand scale. For that reason alone, he believes it was worth making some concessions, such as extending the UGB to the very edge of the county. That was done "for public purposes," he insists, not simply "for the benefit of a single landowner." Another concession concerns the development timeline: while the initial plan stated that North Ranch would not break ground until 2040, the final version ties the construction date to the progress of the Sunbridge build-out and does not rule out an earlier start.[20]

Ultimately, the building of North Ranch is dependent on the approval of three major highways slated to crisscross the area. These roads would eliminate what was described in Scott's 2013 executive order that established the East Central Florida Corridor Task Force as a "connectivity gap" between metro Orlando, its international airport, and the Space Coast.[21] Environmentalists insist that construction of the highways would actually *create* a more damaging connectivity gap—between wildlife habitats.[22] Unlike Deseret's existing two-lane rural roads, six-lane highways are a death sentence for highly mobile species. There are only 120 Florida panthers left in the wild, and 23 died in 2019 alone from vehicle strikes on the state's major roads. Underpasses or bridges decked out in native flora—the best of the solutions for highway crossings—are a weak substitute for preserving wildlife corridors intact, and there are few more vital than the ones running through the North Ranch property.

The threat to wildlife habitats got a public airing in the wake of Tallahassee's controversial, fast-track approval in 2019 of three new major toll highways elsewhere in the state. They will run, for a total of 330 miles, through remaining rural lands and waterways of Old Florida and endanger wildlife corridors in the southwest. The plan for these new roads in previously undeveloped areas was promoted by an army of industry lobbyists, and it was savaged by environmental and civic groups. In the thirty years before Rick Scott's administration, Florida had done more than almost any other state to conserve its unique biodiversity, but the reversal of those policies over the last decade has been relentless, and the damage is not restorable. As Florida Native Plant Society's Karina Veaudry puts it: "You cannot re-create nature. You can't re-create upland and wetland mosaics. These systems were created over millions of years, and the plants and animals that inhabit these lands have specialized relationships. There are certain insects and birds that only eat certain native plants, and so they have relationships. Once you break these apart, you can't re-create them."

CLIMATE GENTRIFICATION

When these fragile wildlife habitats get bulldozed for the 180,000 homes of North Ranch, who will occupy those houses? This question was never asked during the rancorous public hearings about the development of East Central Florida.[23] Don Whyte told me that Deseret had done no market research on customer demand for the new city. Local environmentalists, though, had an answer in mind. As Valerie

Anderson puts it, "Miami is going to have to go somewhere." She and her allies think that the residents of South Florida will move to North Ranch when their own cities are inundated by rising seas.

This belief is sometimes hedged by comments about the survivalist LDS mentality, which harks back to the formative experience of Mormon settlers struggling to subsist as religious refugees after they crossed the Great Plains to populate the valleys of the Rocky Mountains. The church has a tradition of establishing industrial welfare farms, intended to feed its members "should there come a time of need."[24] This has led the LDS church to acquire rural lands in many countries, making it, for instance, the biggest foreign landowner in the UK. Building a sanctuary for the climate refugees of the future is not inconsistent with this tradition, nor is it at odds with the theology of preparing for a Second Coming, which in LDS doctrine would be heralded by hurricanes and other natural calamities. Florida has almost 160,000 LDS church members, so it is possible that many could flock to North Ranch. Whyte assured me, however, that Deseret did not have this target customer in mind. Nor is North Ranch being designed, as some LDS communities still are, according to the church's signature "plat of Zion."[25]

He confirmed, however, that Deseret's consultants did look at projections of sea level rise and concluded that the North Ranch site is protected on its eastern boundary by the St. Johns River. But the river itself is under threat from climate change, as rising seas push salt water further upstream and inland.[26] Saltwater intrusion is more difficult to predict than sea rise, and a prolonged drought (such as those that plagued the region in the 1990s and 2000s), or simply an overdraft of water for urban supply, could hasten its advance. It is by no means certain that the water supply of North Ranch will be secure by the end of the century, when its build-out is projected to be complete.

Even if it is not a perfect sanctuary, North Ranch might still serve as a destination for Floridians displaced by climate change. Refugees, wherever they are, seldom move very far from their homes, even when the odds on their return are low. Affluent residents of South Florida's threatened coastlines are already migrating to higher ground, where, historically, African Americans were consigned, through redlining and other kinds of racial zoning.[27] The displacement of minority and lower-income residents from Miami neighborhoods like Little Haiti, Overtown, Liberty City, and Little Havana is well underway, as part of a pattern that has been termed "climate gentrification."[28] But relocating within the city will not be enough: sea levels for Miami-Dade County are projected to rise as much as seventeen inches by 2040 and fifty-four inches by 2070.[29] Most estimates see the entire coastal urbanized area underwater by the end of the century. According to one study, 2.5 million people will have to flee from the region that includes Miami, Fort Lauderdale, and West Palm Beach, and many more from coastal areas to the west and north.[30] A new city in East Central Florida would be a prime spot to relocate to, at least for those who can afford the move.

No one can predict the housing market of 2040, let alone 2070. But in the event of population pressure from climate change, the price of entry to North Ranch is certain to rise, filtering out poorer migrants and pulling in well-heeled families looking for an eco-haven from Florida's submerged coastal cities. It is much less clear how other classes of climate refugees will fare or where they will be housed. Many of those who fled from Puerto Rico to Central Florida in the wake of Hurricane Maria in 2017 ended up in motel rooms on Route 192, paid for initially with FEMA vouchers, or else doubled up in the cramped homes of relatives. The effort to provide shelter for these refugees and accommodate their children in the schools proved a massive burden on the resources of Osceola County.

To be sure, having to instantly absorb a population in urgent need is quite different from a carefully "managed retreat" from inundated coastal counties. But in any event, not everyone displaced by climate change is likely to be welcome. While Puerto Ricans can freely move to the US mainland, there are many obstacles in the path of refugees from other Caribbean islands threatened by increasingly severe hurricanes. Florida is already an immigration battleground, hosting detention centers that have been described as "prisons by any other name," and the state has a well-established record of preferential access for those

with money and/or light skin.[31] Cuban businesspeople and professionals were warmly received in the 1960s, but their lower-income brothers and sisters from the 1980 Mariel boatlift were disparaged. More
recently, moneyed exiles from Venezuela have been welcomed, but
Haitian victims of the 2010 earthquake faced deportation and stigma to
add to their trauma, and Bahamians fleeing Hurricane Dorian in 2019
were barred from entering the US without visas.

The storms of the future will be more intense and ruinous, and
populations in their path are almost certain to be dispersed and segregated according to skin color and wealth. This pattern of separation
can rightly be called eco-apartheid, and it is already well established in
many American cities, where affluent, resource-rich "green enclaves"
coexist with the sacrifice zones of the less fortunate struggling to find
fresh air and clean water on the other side of the tracks.[32] If North
Ranch does indeed turn into a realtors' plan B for inundated South
Florida, the odds are that it will not be for everyone. The LDS church
may end up creating a new ark for the self-chosen.

BLUEPRINTS AND REALITIES

During public hearings, the North Ranch project was promoted as a
forward-looking solution for absorbing the explosive growth of Osceola County's population. Advocates also cited two other benefits: they
argued that employment centers in North Ranch and Sunbridge would
provide the high-wage jobs that have long eluded Osceola County, and
that the pedestrian and transit-oriented character of both communities would be more sustainable than the current sprawl patterns on the
developed portions of the county. In blueprints, both of these claims
held up, though the estimates of benefits did not take into account
the full cost of building new infrastructure in open space. So, too, in a
state notorious for its history of real estate scams, developers are well
versed in the art of embellishing the plans they are trying to peddle,
and officials are adept at allowing them to renege on the more alluring
promises.

For sure, Osceola is badly in need of higher-wage employment and sustainable growth since its record on trying to deliver either is well below par. Its past efforts at economic development include attempts to build a spring training facility for the Washington Nationals and to lure Colt to relocate its gun manufacturing operations from Connecticut; neither came to fruition. Hopes for NeoCity, a five-hundred-acre high-tech campus east of Kissimmee anchored by a semiconductor fabrication facility, have similarly fallen short. When the NeoCity blueprint was presented to Osceola commissioners in 2017, the principal architect described it, naturally, as "visionary and game-changing."[33] The cluster was projected to create more than 34,000 direct and indirect jobs, many of them to be filled by Osceola residents who currently commute to Orange County. But within months, the high-tech booster talk gave way to a more conventional retail offer, as the county threw its hat into the ring with a bid to host Amazon's second headquarters. Forget the semiconductors and futuristic tech: Osceola's pitch was now "NeoCity is made for Amazon HQ." The county was prepared to offer Amazon one hundred ready-to-build acres of NeoCity free of cost and throw in more than $200 million in tax abatements, plus other exemptions on overheads, utility costs, and corporate expenses.[34]

None of these enticements proved enough for Amazon, of course, and NeoCity is still struggling to find its footing. By some estimates, the commissioners have sunk as much as $200 million into building out the semiconductor facility in hopes of attracting investors. In February 2020, the facility's key partner, the University of Central Florida, walked away from the project after having spent more than $25 million on it, abandoning it four years into a forty-year lease. (The university subsequently transferred its lease to Minnesota-based Skywater Technology, at the cost of an additional $15 million.)[35] High-tech clusters are very difficult to pull off, and they usually require unaccountably large amounts of public funding to sweeten the pot for corporate investors.[36] Is Osceola County in a position to succeed where countless others had failed? For NeoCity critics, at least, it looked as if commissioners were neglecting urgent needs in housing and service infrastructure to make a risky long-term bet on the future.

Approval for the two Deseret developments was similarly tied to the promise of high-wage jobs. Officials had particular industry clusters in mind: life sciences and allied health services, information technology, chemical and plastics manufacturing, and more. According to Jeff Jones, this was the first time in Florida that a development plan was "tying jobs to land use." Yet while the county is hoping for what he calls "real jobs, like industrial and white-collar," he concedes it is already proving difficult to hold the developer accountable.[37] The conceptual plan for Sunbridge, for instance, states that after the initial construction stage, phase two of the development can only break ground once 4,000 of these jobs are created, and phase three after a further 10,000 jobs. Yet it is by no means clear how the count will actually be conducted and who is responsible for ensuring that the developers do not cut corners to evade their commitments.[38]

As for the county's record on sustainable growth, Celebration made waves in the 1990s as a New Urbanist model of "traditional neighborhood development," notable for mixed-use buildings, higher density per acre, street connectivity, and pedestrian-friendly principles. But twenty-five years after its founding, for all its virtues, no one would describe the town as an attainable model for anyone on a budget. Like Celebration, Sunbridge and North Ranch may turn out to have lower internal carbon footprints than the typical sprawl subdivision, but they will be primarily marketed to higher-income buyers. Is sustainability to be measured only by metrics like neighborhood walkability, reduced water consumption, and increased number of solar roofs? In a context of extreme housing inequality, such well-meaning physical goals cannot be disconnected from economic ones. The quest for low-carbon, sustainable living has to be affordable, or it will simply magnify the gap between those who have the means to achieve the green American dream and those (more than a third of US households) who were already struggling to pay the rent and utility bills even before COVID-19 entered the picture.

To their credit, Osceola's planners acknowledged this problem in an acclaimed 2017 study, *Strategies for a Sustainable Future*. The report reaches far beyond the typical green focus on physical issues, like energy use and resource conservation, by presenting a *fiscal* blueprint for shifting the county's growth patterns away from its dependence on low-density sprawl.[39] High on its list of recommendations is improving the county's jobs-to-housing balance, increasing employment diversity, and enhancing housing options for households with incomes of less than $35,000. The study could have been used as a local version of the Green New Deal touted by leading national politicians. But its authors were well aware of the limitations on what planners can actually achieve, especially when their regulatory efforts are routinely preempted by a state legislature beholden to the real estate industry, and by county commissioners prone to granting variances to developers. Ultimately, their plans are only aspirational. As Susan Caswell puts it, they often consist just of signaling to investors that "we are interested in this particular kind of development."

The arrival of COVID-19 was a further reminder of how unforeseen events can subvert planners' ideas—though it did bring some good news for Split Oak. Faced with a sharp fall in revenue from its toll roads, the Central Florida Expressway Authority decided in June 2020 to postpone its plan to expedite the highway extension through the forest.[40] The reprieve, which could allow more than a decade of breathing space, was a blow to developers and the Osceola commissioners backing them. So, too, was the decisive vote by Orange County's charter review commission to place an amendment on the November ballot to protect that county's portion of Split Oak from encroachment.

The Osceola commissioners hit back with a brazen attempt to kill the neighboring county's amendment, suing Orange County to prevent it from printing it on its ballots.[41] A judge blocked Osceola's last-ditch effort, though, and, in November, Orange County voters approved, by a large majority, the measure to protect the forest. Valerie Anderson and her allies celebrated their first major win in the battle of Split

Oak. But given that they have picked a fight with Central Florida's most powerful developer and its political allies, none of them doubt that the conflict will continue.

BEACH OF THE FUTURE?

Most visitors to Central Florida are unaware that it was the first part of the state (a landmass sometimes referred to as Orange Island) to emerge above the primeval seas as the earth's climate cooled during the Oligocene epoch, about thirty million years ago. But those paying close attention to the landscape can spot reminders that Florida has frequently been underwater. The biggest giveaway is the ubiquity of sandy soil, poking through the grass and foliage. In Osceola County, the most striking prehistoric remnants are the deep sand dunes that stretch out on either side of the Cypress Parkway as it rises to the west of Poinciana. The dunes are a prominent feature of the 150-mile-long Lake Wales Ridge, which runs down the spine of the Florida peninsula—in essence, an ancient Pleistocene shoreline right in the geographic middle of the state. They are the oldest beaches in a state that owes its modern economic growth to two thousand miles of welcoming sand on its shores.

As master practitioners of the art of dredge-and-fill, Florida's twentieth-century developers conjured scores of beaches, islands, and finger-canal subdivisions out of submerged land. The humorist Will Rogers once declared the dredge to be "the national symbol of Florida." Generous riparian rights allowed landowners to fill in freshwater and tidal land out to the navigable channel; even more land could be claimed if a developer's plans were in the service of "improvement" or the "public interest."[42] In the hands of the swamp merchants, the bay muck gave way to golden beaches with imported sand. Three-quarters of Florida's population is now concentrated in coastal counties that depend economically on the attraction of beach and waterfront life. But in many of these communities, these cash-cow strips of sand are increasingly at high risk. Today, almost $50 million of state funds, most of it matched by federal grants, are sacrificed annually to shore up and replenish beaches that will soon disappear beneath the rising seas.[43] The US Army Corps of Engineers, tasked with the Sisyphean job of "renourishing" the eroding beaches, is applying techniques of water control that are destined to fail.

Many American rivers are already being restored to their natural channels after decades of ecological damage from damming, channelization, and wetland drainage; the Corps of Engineers has now reversed its disastrous flood control projects in the Everglades and the Kissimmee River. In the case of the beaches, they won't have to undo their own work: climate change will do it for them. Meanwhile, Miami-Dade County has exhausted the reserves of offshore sand it dredges to replenish its storied beaches, and the Broward and Palm Beach inventories are also nearly gone. They are all desperately seeking to buy sand from less affluent counties elsewhere in Florida, or even from island nations in the Caribbean.[44] Federal law currently prohibits the Army Corps of Engineers from acquiring sand from foreign sources, but Florida senator Marco Rubio has twice introduced a bill to repeal the regulation.[45]

Occupying the highest ground in the state and located as much as seventy miles from either coast, Lake Wales Ridge is not only a memory of Florida's oceanic past, but also a powerful allegory for the resilience needed in the decades ahead. Eighty-five percent of Florida uplands have already been lost to citrus groves and housing development. The survival of the remainder depends on conservation efforts that are increasingly out of favor with lawmakers. If the dunes of the Lake Wales Ridge survive, will they once again be a shoreline? There's not much to stop that from happening. With Florida's relatively high groundwater table, rising seas will push saltwater further inland through the aquifers and up through the honeycombed limestone platform on which the state is perched and which renders the building of sea walls futile.

Long before the salty waters reach the central ridge, they will top the Atlantic Coastal Ridge, whose shell rock base made it possible to build the East Coast Railway and the high-rise resort towns of the Atlantic Coast. Then they will flow across the St. Johns River floodplain and lap over the smaller sand pine ridges (former shorelines themselves) that run down the length of the Deseret Ranch property. Their next stop will be Lake Tohopekaliga, the site of Hamilton Disston's massive dredging campaign to open up the Florida interior to colonial settlement. Coursing westward, their last phase of reconquest before they reach the Lake Wales Ridge dunes will be the man-made lands and artificially blue lakes of Disney World, engineered to allow so many visitors to believe they could be somewhere else. It will be an ironic fate for a land empire created through the legal mechanism of a drainage district, with miles of levees and canals constructed to stop or divert the natural flow of water. When the sea finally arrives, Epcot's massive aquarium, originally branded as The Living Seas, will no longer be a synthetic microcosm. It will be the real thing.

Homes for All

A FEW WEEKS before the 2020 election, I checked into a Route 192 motel that had hardly seen a tourist booking in two weeks. The local guests, who occupied about half of the rooms before the pandemic, were barely hanging on. A few doors along from me, an elderly resident named Latoya Blaine was parked in a wheelchair outside her room. She wanted me to know that, no matter how many others left, she was staying put. "I have nowhere else to go, and anyway this is my home," she declared. Unlike some of her neighbors who had been served with eviction notices, she was not behind on rent but worried that the owner was going to give up and sell off the property. "Everything's gonna change around here, in every place like this," she predicted, waving her arms at the motels nearby. She added, more ominously: "People don't know what's coming, but it will come."

Blaine's sense of foreboding was widely shared on Osceola's main thoroughfare. Few wage earners or small business owners could say with any certainty what the next few months would bring. Even for those whose livelihoods were still intact, and who could see the COVID-19 vaccines coming, the future was still a short-term horizon. The same could not be said for real estate investors and developers, eyeing the same landscape and seeing gilt-edged opportunities. They were busy making deals, snapping up land parcels, filing for permit approvals, and signing building contracts. Unlike during the Great Recession, the flow of credit had not dried up, though less of it was now being issued by commercial banks and more by private equity investors.[1] The machinery of finance was still up and running, and cheap money was on tap. In the months ahead, the region's housing market would see record sales growth, with all-cash purchases driving the prices up. The Dow Jones would reach its all-time high. Seldom has there been such a gulf between the "real" economy, where the people who produce things or perform services were close to the edge, and the "paper" economy, where the people who collect unearned income through stock wagers and land ventures were sitting pretty.

The pandemic took a sharp toll on minority households in particular. During the Great Recession, when more than ten million homes were foreclosed, African Americans were the worst hit by far. Their decades-long efforts to build middle-class security through homeownership were crushed, resulting in a loss of more than 50 percent of their net worth. COVID-19 served up a fresh shock to households already buckling under financial pressure. Not only did African Americans suffer rates of infection and mortality three times higher than whites, but minority employees were often the first to be laid off and the last to be rehired. The federal moratorium on mortgage foreclosures helped keep the sheriffs at bay for a while, but it only applied to federally backed loans. Low-income home buyers who had been obliged to take out subprime loans had little protection, and again they were disproportionately African American and Hispanic.

Renters were even worse off. In August 2020, it was estimated that thirty to forty million tenants, or about a third of all renter households in the country, were at risk of eviction.[2] In Florida, as many as half of the state's renters were at risk.[3] At the end of the summer, Donald Trump temporarily banned the eviction of renters for nonpayment, using his broad authority through the Centers for Disease Control (CDC). The ostensible reason was to slow the spread of the coronavirus, a backhanded acknowledgment that housing is a form of healthcare. But only those who could demonstrate that they faced homelessness as a result of COVID-19 financial hardship were covered, and the adjudication of their cases was left in the hands of local courts. Unscrupulous landlords, who were not required to inform tenants about the CDC order, took advantage of any confusion. In the first six weeks following the CDC eviction moratorium, large corporate landlords issued ten thousand eviction notices just in the Sunbelt states of Florida, Texas, Georgia, Arizona, and Tennessee.[4] For those who did escape eviction under the moratorium, the rental assistance on offer from stimulus funds did not keep up with the steadily mounting level of missed payments (an estimated $57 billion by the beginning of 2021), and many landlords refused the offer, hoping to replace their current tenants with those who could pay more.[5] Once again, the pressure was racially skewed: the missed payment rate for nonwhite renters was nearly 50 percent higher than that for white renters.[6] Aiming to reduce that gap, the Joe Biden administration enacted additional rent relief after a federal judge struck down the CDC moratorium in May 2021.

Even if the worst-case scenarios of mass evictions and foreclosures can be staved off, it is almost certain that rentership will continue its steady rise. Before COVID-19, renter households were already predicted to outpace owner-occupied units by 66 percent over the next fifteen years. And for many "starter" households who had expected to enter the housing marketplace over the next decade, the pandemic recession may have deprived them of the income to do so.[7] Despite low mortgage rates, they are likely to join the Generation Rent millennials blocked from homeownership by crushing student debt burdens and the precarious character of the gig economy. Just as long-term job security has disappeared for most American workers, the opportunity to stabilize a family life through homeownership will become a thing of the past for large sectors of the population.

The pandemic exposed many long-standing deficiencies in the quality of American life. A dysfunctional for-profit healthcare system cost hundreds of thousands of lives, while the pitiless norms of at-will employment laid waste to the livelihoods of many others. The heightened insecurity of renters and homeowners brought home the ruinous consequences of four decades of favoring the market monopoly over public or social housing programs. (Social housing, far more widely implemented in Europe than the United States, comprises dwellings owned and managed by nonprofits, limited-equity cooperatives, or mutual associations.) It was always misguided to expect the real estate industry to deliver adequate housing for all household classes, and especially minority groups, whose historic exclusion from land and home ownership by realtors and government agencies was a flat denial of their civic personhood. Developers and the private housing market have never met that expectation, and never will.[8] Since Wall Street entered the picture, the odds have only dwindled. As more and more homes fall into the hands of private equity and institutional investors, land is increasingly traded as just another asset in the global marketplace, and rents and house prices have been decoupled from what local wage earners can afford.

Hard-hit locations like Osceola County make that decoupling all the more visible. We must learn from these places if we want to fulfill the aspiration of "a decent home and a suitable living environment for every American family"—the goal set by the landmark Housing Act of 1949, a core accomplishment of Harry Truman's Fair Deal.[9] The public housing and urban renewal projects ushered in by that legislation were flawed in their implementation and were anything but fair in their impact on minority populations. But the stated goal was a righteous one and comfortably attainable for the richest country in the world. Today, the ambition of the 1949 act is carried on by the housing justice movement, with its renewed focus on renter rights, tenant organization, and the rallying cry of "Homes for All."[10]

THE DIFFERENT FACES OF A CRISIS

Although it is national in scope, the US housing crisis looks quite different from place to place. Housing markets are intensely local, so pricing and rent gaps can vary greatly even within a single metro area, and even more so between them: consider the great disparity in housing affordability between, say, Boston and Detroit, or between space-starved cities in the Frostbelt and those in the Sunbelt regions with room still to spread out. In strong metro markets, like Austin or San Diego, homeownership is increasingly out of reach for middle-income earners. Unable to buy, those households are confined to the rental market, which in turn encourages landlords to jack up rates and effectively eliminate great swaths of affordable housing stock.[11]

By contrast, many parts of the country do not have a middle-class housing problem. In Osceola County, residents with household incomes of $50,000 a year can readily find housing. But as we have seen, there is a meager inventory of units for those earning less, especially households that earn above $20,000 (thus making them ineligible for subsidized housing) but less than $35,000 a year. They are badly underserved by a construction industry hardwired to churn out ever-larger single-family homes on a low-density pattern, which still accounts for up to 80 percent of units in production nationwide. Supply is especially tight for elders like Latoya Blaine, who make up almost a third of the county's cost-burdened population. "Before my husband passed, we had an okay apartment in Kissimmee," she tells me. "But then two checks became one, and this room here was all I could find to afford." She adds, "I worked hard all my life. I deserve better." Her circumstances have little in common with those of the more comfortable retiree class driving golf carts and taking tai chi classes an hour to the north in The Villages, an "active adult retirement community" that is now the fastest-growing metro area in the US.[12]

In addition to housing, access to employment and transportation also varies considerably across metro areas, and especially across county lines. Many of Florida's counties and municipalities enjoy home rule powers over zoning, taxation, housing ordinances, and other fiscal matters, so where you live matters a lot. These variations make it difficult to apply one-size-fits-all remedies to the problem of affordability. For example, the debate about rent control is red-hot among housing advocates in New York, California, and Oregon, each of which approved rent caps or rent stabilization laws in the past few years, but discussion of this topic is almost nonexistent in most parts of the country.[13] In one of my conversations with Osceola's housing specialist Susan Caswell, I asked her what rent control would look like in her neck of the woods. "That's so foreign to me," she said, eyes widening. "I can't begin to say. It's not even a thing that's talked about around here."

In fact, Florida is one of thirty-seven states where rent controls are prohibited or preempted. The Tallahassee legislature routinely kills any bill remotely sympathetic to the goals of the housing justice movement. In 2019, Organize Florida activists proposed a "Housing Bill of Rights" that included rent control, and they persuaded some state lawmakers to draft a bill, but it did not get a hearing. In a response that appeared to be punitive, the GOP-dominated legislature then passed a sweeping act that blocks counties and municipalities from mandating the inclusion of affordable housing units in future developments.[14]

At the national level, federal policy for the past four decades, under Democratic and Republican administrations alike, has looked to the for-profit market as the principal provider of housing. This reliance on private developers extends even to government-assisted low-income housing. Subsidies typically carry a sunset provision allowing units to revert to market-rate rents after ten, fifteen, or twenty years, so they are only temporarily affordable.[15] Nonetheless, talk about national rent caps and government housing was in the air even before the pandemic. New York representative Alexandria Ocasio-Cortez proposed such a cap in 2019, and national rent control was on the campaign platform of Bernie Sanders's 2020 presidential bid, along with promises to build ten million new units of public housing through his and Ocasio-Cortez's Green New Deal for Public Housing. Other presidential candidates, while less ambitious than Sanders, also proposed a variety of programs aimed at reducing some of the housing cost burdens, ranging from universal housing allowances and stronger tenant rights to reparations for residents of redlined neighborhoods. And Biden's $2 trillion infrastructure plan, unveiled in March 2021, included a whopping $213 billion to address the nation's housing needs.

Arguably the most contested approach to remedying the housing crisis is to simply increase the supply.[16] There are fewer homes per capita being built now than at any time since World War II, and many of those currently in production are a mismatch for the nation's real housing needs. Advocates argue that more deregulation would allow developers to increase and diversify production, especially in jurisdictions where zoning prohibits multifamily units or disincentivizes other types of affordable housing.[17] Faced with a giant bottleneck in supply, Portland and California (which faces a housing shortage of 3.5 million homes) have moved to eliminate restrictive zoning in order to encourage more varied housing types, including accessory dwelling units, garage apartments, backyard cottages, granny flats, and tiny houses. In 2019, Virginia lifted a ban on duplexes, while Maryland introduced legislation to facilitate upzoning—changing building codes to allow developers to build taller and denser—and to create a significant number of social housing units. The previous year, Minneapolis became the first city to end single-family zoning, which effectively prohibits the construction of anything other than a detached single-family home in a given neighborhood; in many cities, 75 percent of the residential land is currently zoned in this way.[18]

There is no doubt that large numbers of new housing units are desperately needed. But the record shows that measures like upzoning (intended to increase supply) do not automatically drive down housing prices. In desirable neighborhoods, the outcome is just as likely to be an increase in land and property prices, along with area rent inflation. In many locations where upzoning has been tried, even with a requirement for a certain percentage of affordable units, landlords and for-profit developers have been the primary beneficiaries.[19] As a result, grassroots activists in New York City have successfully opposed several high-rise projects intended for low-income neighborhoods, arguing that their "affordable" units would still be too expensive for most people in the area, while land speculation in the neighborhoods around the towers would drive out longtime residents.[20]

Lobbyists for the real estate industry, meanwhile, see arguments for increased housing supply as an opportunity to prise more money from the government. They insist that tax breaks, fee waivers, density bonuses, and similar measures are what's needed to wean developers off their addiction to the single-family home. But the industry already receives vast subsidies: everything from federal mortgage insurance to the mortgage interest tax deduction supports homeowners at public cost. The hundreds of billions spent on highway construction and the government policies designed to ensure cheap gas are also immense subsidies to land developers. The scope of the affordable housing shortage demands a government response far beyond the reflex action of just offering more sugar for developers to jump into the game.

Simply building more housing units will not provide long-term security for low- and middle-income households without additional guarantees of rent stability or protections against eviction and displacement. Nor will a new commitment to public or social housing succeed unless it is accompanied by policies designed to lift incomes up from decades of wage stagnation and ensure inexpensive access to other public goods like education and healthcare. In response to the soaring costs of those social goods, "Medicare for All" and "College for All" have steadily risen to the top of mainstream progressive policy goals; both were primetime talking points in the 2020 electoral race. "Homes for All" still lags behind, though its promotion by the housing justice movement has resulted in several legislative efforts to capture the appropriate scale of government response needed to address the housing crisis.[21]

Housing advocates have also launched a variety of initiatives, including a social housing development agency, designed to purchase distressed real estate and finance its transfer into the hands of cooperatives, nonprofits, community land trusts, or public authorities.[22] None of these proposed measures rise to the level of establishing housing as a *right*, as suggested in Truman's Housing Act of 1949, and explicitly named by Franklin D. Roosevelt in his Second Bill of Rights speech in 1944. But they are helping to challenge the consensus, long protected by powerful real estate lobbies, that housing is best regarded as a private-sector commodity, to be built, traded, and rented out on terms set by the market. This consensus about the wisdom of markets is a mentality that has permeated all levels of government in the neoliberal era. But it has not paid off for working-class people and for some time now has been failing large sectors of the middle class as well.

BABY STEPS

The modest shifts in policy that I have described, such as the end of single-family zoning in Minneapolis, all occurred in states and cities with a history of public or social housing programs and tenant activism. But how are other, less progressive localities responding to the housing crisis? What headway has been made in places like Osceola County—where there is no public housing at all, and elected officials have long been beholden to private developers—and what more could be done?

Even before Central Florida appeared at the top of the National Low Income Housing Coalition's 2019 unaffordability list (*Orlando Business Journal* ran the headline "It's Good to Be No. 1, Except When It Isn't"), the region's business leaders were pressuring local officials to step up efforts to address the troublesome problem on their doorstep. After several years of deliberation, an Orange County task force called Housing for All released a ten-year action plan aimed at helping developers produce more than 30,000 new affordable units. The task force had been mandated by officials to consider only "market-based" solutions through the existing "housing delivery system."[23] The local business press hailed the plan, but critics quickly pointed out that the proposed housing was hardly "for all." Nearly two-thirds of the proposed units are for those who earn between $83,000 and $97,000, a range well above the county's median income of $58,600.[24] At the same time, given that as many as 1,500 people are moving to the region every week, 30,000 homes would not be enough to even absorb a year's worth of growth, let alone a decade's.

Stephanie Porta, director of the activist group Organize Florida, points out that the task force was overwhelmingly made up of corporate execs, developers, and realtors, with renters wholly unrepresented. "They have their own self-interest," she says, "and that interest lies in lining their own pockets." For their part, task force members touted the proposal as the "most comprehensive housing plan developed by the county to date." If true, this claim speaks volumes about the stunted ambitions of a local government, scrambling to offset the callous neglect of a GOP-dominated state legislature disinclined to tackle the housing crisis.[25] Central Florida is no longer ranked as the area with the biggest shortage of affordable housing in the country, because the number of extremely low-income households in the region has dipped. But the people missing from that column are not necessarily earning more: it is most likely that they have moved farther away in search of apartments or motel rooms they can afford, or they are experiencing homelessness.[26]

Compared to Orange County, Osceola sees very little pressure from organized advocates and has fewer disposable resources to address its chronic housing needs, so its response has been even more low-key. Over the years, I have watched the county's planners play the cards available to them. They have simplified building and parking regulations, streamlined the building permitting process, lowered impact and mobility fees for smaller, cheaper, and more densely located units, and facilitated adaptive reuse, especially of motels and ghost malls.[27] They have also tried to lure out-of-town developers to build more diverse and compact housing products rather than the business-as-usual subdivisions of tract homes on freshly bulldozed greenfields. And they have encouraged the county to cobble together funds to subsidize the building of a few affordable complexes. But even with access to bigger pots of government assistance, the supply of privately built affordable residences is guaranteed to lag far behind demand.[28]

In the meantime, nonmarket alternatives have struggled to get off the ground. The concept of a community land trust, for example, is wildly popular among housing advocates across the country as a tool for ensuring that units remain affordable in perpetuity. But its underlying premise—to remove land from the market and cap the resale values of property built on it—is not well understood by Osceola's elected officials. (It doesn't help that many of them maintain a career in real estate development and sales, and so have a professional interest in protecting the private sector's monopoly on housing.) Custom builder Karl Theobald, a leading local proponent of affordable housing, worked with an area realtor to set up the legal structure for a community land trust in Osceola, but it has not yet been put to use. "We go to the county's inventory every year, but what it has in its land bank is useless," he explains. "Pieces get donated to them, or they take ones that are left over, but these are all little splinters, and there's not enough that's usable."

As for the motels on 192, the case for converting them into affordable apartment units is as strong as anywhere in the country. Theobald himself was contracted by a nonprofit to retrofit one motel property into an apartment building, converting its fifty-two rooms into twenty apartments in a range of sizes. The result, named Victory Village, is a fine example of permanent supportive housing, assisted by county and federal grants. The residents I interviewed were mostly low-income veterans and formerly incarcerated persons, and each had a history of moving from motel to motel, interspersed with spells on the street or in the woods. With Victory Village rents at $750 for a two-bedroom apartment, they could finally feel at ease. "This place is a mansion compared to what we are used to," one of them tells me.

But despite the efficiency of the conversion—it took only six months, by Theobald's estimate, and cost 30 percent less than a new build—retrofits like this have taken a while to catch on.[29] As long as the county allowed decrepit motels to bend the law and sustain their business through extended-stay rents, owners either held on to them or sold to other moteliers. Only when occupancy rates plunged during the pandemic did more of them decide to throw in the towel. If the county had wanted to move faster, it could have used the power of eminent domain to seize failing properties (including not just motels but also shopping malls emptying out under pressure from the "retail apocalypse") and convert them into social housing.[30] Likewise, officials could have tried to persuade VHR property owners to lease their underoccupied units to locals, as happened in some European cities.[31] Instead of allowing housing courts to evict occupants, the county could have helped tenants take over and self-manage their buildings.[32] But while the need could hardly be greater, the political will to take such measures is not yet there.

Like many suburban strips, Route 192 is itself an inefficient use of space, crying out for a wholesale redesign. The deep land parcels adjacent to its six-lane right-of-way are dominated by low-rise single-use buildings and surface parking lots, and there are many large pockets of unused space. Large parts of the corridor are ripe for redevelopment as sites for affordable multifamily complexes, with a rapid transit system running along its length. A study of a similar suburban arterial corridor—California's El Camino Real, stretching forty-three miles from Daly City to San Jose—showed that as many as a quarter-million housing units could be accommodated though a more efficient use of land along that commercial strip.[33]

Big steps like these would require a breadth of vision not readily available in a county struggling to manage its rapid growth and shifting demographics while transitioning from conservative rural ways. In a state that levies no personal income tax and taxes corporate investors very lightly, local governments like Osceola are forced to prioritize revenue from property and sales taxes. Dependence on those sources of public money tends to dictate the policy decisions of officials, limiting their ability to make bold moves. But Central Florida is hardly alone, as I have argued in this book. Versions of its housing emergency are evident in almost every part of the country, and so innovative alternatives to the status quo of private market delivery are urgently needed. If not now, when?

INCLUDE THE DWELLERS

Everyone remembers Dwight Eisenhower's warning about the expanding power of the "military-industrial complex" over government policy. Few recall his predecessor's persistent complaints about the meddlesome influence of the real estate industry. In 1947, as he sought to

preserve wartime national rent controls and save his emergency housing campaign for returning veterans, Harry Truman even sent a "special message to Congress" about the "stubborn obstacles" posed by
what he called the "real estate lobby":

> Its members have exerted pressure at every point against every pro-
> posal for making the housing program more effective. They have
> constantly sought to weaken rent control and to do away with nec-
> essary aids to housing. They are openly proud of their success in
> blocking a comprehensive housing program. This group has sought
> to achieve financial gains without regard to the damage done to
> others. It has displayed a ruthless disregard of the public welfare.

The lobby's "brazen operations," he concluded, were essentially anti-
democratic: "Nothing could be more clearly subversive of representative government."[34]

In the decades that followed, the industry's advocates found an
inside track within the corridors of power, and its members profited
handsomely from federal backing of mass suburbanization programs.
The legacy of that cozy relationship lives on, as does the lobbyists'
tradition of blocking rent controls, construction of public or social
housing, and tenant self-management. More recently, we have seen the
emergence of a new kind of obstacle to sound housing policy: the gal-
loping acquisition of housing stock by private equity, which is playing
an ever-greater role in shaping the real estate market and determining
rents and land prices. Revenue from these assets flows to investors all
over the world, and, as with many of Wall Street's activities, oversight
and regulation in the public interest is weak.

For much of the twentieth century, financing the construction and
purchase of a house in America was a relatively stable process—and
therefore, from Wall Street's perspective, a boring backwater. Commercial lenders, backed by government insurance, made steady but
unspectacular returns from mortgage loans. This long-standing formula
began to falter when middle-class and working-class household incomes

stopped rising in the 1970s and 1980s. Homeowners were forced to look for larger and more risky returns on resale, juggling debt to finance house flipping, while the large investment banks jumped in to package mortgage loans as an instrument for generating fast income streams.

After the crash of 2008 devastated homeowners, private equity firms rushed in, snapped up, and rented out distressed properties, opening a new door for Wall Street's profiteering. Most of the private equity purchases have been in the bottom third of the price range, blocking many first-time home buyers in markets where those acquisitions are concentrated.[35] Some of the big investment groups—Carlyle, TPG, Apollo, and Blackstone—have moved further down-market and are now purchasing large tracts of mobile home parks.[36] Contrary to initial forecasts, the era of the corporate landlord has not been a short-lived play by opportunistic investors, and thanks to COVID-19 these firms are now poised to take advantage of a fresh round of housing distress. This time around, foreclosed properties of owner-occupiers are not the only targets; many small landlords are at risk of going under as well, so their buildings will also be ripe for acquisition.

If we are to achieve the goal of homes for all, it is essential to de-financialize housing and pivot away from the failed market model. Housing stock needs to be democratically owned and properly protected from predatory investors, and elected officials should commit to a National Homes Guarantee. Truman's "decent home and a suitable living environment" should be promoted as a basic right, and instruments such as rent controls, community land trusts, and cooperative ownership ought to be widely encouraged and adopted. We need restitution programs to repair the damage from decades of racial exclusion, when the real estate industry and government regulators colluded with discriminatory practices like racial zoning and redlining.[37] Public housing programs should be relaunched on a mass footing, social housing initiatives must be favored and expanded, and adequate levels of household income should be guaranteed for people to keep themselves housed.

But these efforts will all stumble in new ways if they do not place dwellers at the center, as active participants rather than as passive recipients whose presumed needs are managed from above. The history of public housing offers some obvious lessons. Many of the myths about its "failure" are ideologically driven and inaccurate. But among its real weaknesses is that the authorities have routinely regarded residents as beneficiaries or dependents, not as partners or collaborators in the business of housing themselves.[38] That mentality must change.

Reflecting on the successful efforts of ordinary people to rebuild their communities after an earthquake devastated the Peruvian city of Arequipa in the late 1950s, British architect John F. C. Turner wrote an influential essay titled "Housing as a Verb." He asked readers to set aside their notion of houses as objects and to consider housing as a process, one best undertaken by occupants themselves in pursuit of their real needs and hopes. His controversial argument is that "when dwellers are in control, their homes are better and cheaper than those built through government programs or large corporations."[39] An admirer of the self-organized shantytowns of cities in the Global South, many of which turned into fully serviced suburbs over time, Turner pointed out that in rich countries only the well-off have any real say in the shape of their custom homes, while the rigidity of codes and permitting standards actively discourages most others from building for themselves.

But Turner was not suggesting that all people should be their own DIY homebuilders. His main point is about the benefit of having "users" be central to the whole process of housing. The ability to exercise an active role, he suggests, makes "user-controlled housing . . . far superior as a vehicle of personal, family, or social growth or development than housing which is merely supplied." By contrast, public housing authorities tend to decide exactly what dwellers ought to have, while private corporate builders offer only a narrow range of menu choices to potential buyers. Neither starts from what occupants really want or need from a home. Attention to the public and private sectors leaves little room for what Turner called the popular sector, which in subsequent decades became known as "third sector" housing.[40] With control of housing ever more concentrated in the hands of large firms and investors, and tenant rights under attack, it is even more difficult to realize his ideal.

As I end this book, which draws on the experience of so many dwellers trapped by circumstances beyond their control, I recognize that few of the people who appear in its pages are participants in Turner's sense. The only ones who are able to design their own homes according to personal needs are living in the woods, mostly under conditions not of their choosing, and they have fashioned their dwellings far outside of any approvable process. What does it say about the failure of American housing that only the unhoused and the very wealthy, in their architect-designed homes, can exercise that kind of freedom?

Interest in reviving and refashioning the cause of government-funded housing is growing, and it is influenced by the continued success and popularity of European social housing, which is often available to people of all incomes.[41] But before any new program gets underway, or defaults to a cheap production model of standardized habitats, we have to guarantee that would-be residents—who live in a variety of household types and have a diverse range of life and work needs—are more fully involved in the planning process. Conventional nuclear families, for example, are increasingly thin on the ground these days, while multigenerational units, including the "grandfamily" (in which children are raised by their grandparents), extended or reconstituted families, and other forms of shared living are on the rise. Meanwhile, the dispersal of employment options far outside of the public workplace means that more and more people require homes that can accommodate income-generating activities.

New paradigms of public and social housing should reflect these diverse arrangements by incorporating cohousing, granny flats, communes, single-room occupancies, intergenerational group dwellings, and a range of hybrid quarters that anticipate and facilitate how we are likely to occupy, as well as earn a living in, our homes. Risk-averse developers are loath to build for this kind of variety because it upsets their established formulas for profit. The next generation of American housing must take on that challenge. But it will only succeed if it is genuinely centered on people's needs and aspirations.

NOTES

INTRODUCTION

1. Andrew Ross, *The Celebration Chronicles: Life, Liberty, and the Pursuit of Property Value in Disney's New Town* (New York: Ballantine Books, 1999).
2. The arrival of the motel children in Celebration's schools came as a culture shock to the relatively affluent community. Today, Celebration High has 71 percent minority enrollment, and half its students are eligible for free or reduced price lunch, while the numbers for the K–8 school are 43 percent and 20 percent, respectively.
3. The term began to circulate in the immediate wake of the housing crash but was given legitimacy by a Morgan Stanley housing analyst who subsequently formed his own equity group, Sylvan Road, to buy up distressed homes for the single-family rental market. Oliver Chang et al., "A Rentership Society: Housing Market Insights" (New York: Morgan Stanley, 2011).
4. After placing the foreclosed FHA homes in its Distressed Asset Stabilization Program, the Obama administration sold them to private equity firms. Before they underwent consolidation, these companies included Blackstone, Colony Capital, Starwood, Waypoint, Silver Bay, Main Street Renewal, Tricon, Freo, Progress Residential Trust, Beazer, Wynkoop, and American Residential Properties. See Tony Roshan Samara, *Rise of the Renter Nation: Solutions to the Housing Affordability Crisis* (Right to the City Alliance, 2014).

5. Just as in the lead-up to the crash, these schemes included financial "innovations," such as leveraged purchasing, private-label lending, nonperforming loan acquisition, and, inevitably, rental bonds, through the market trading of rent-backed securities. Desiree Fields et al., *The Rise of the Corporate Landlord: The Institutionalization of the Single-Family Rental Market and Potential Impacts on Renters* (Homes for All and Right to the City Alliance, July 2014), https://homesforall.org/wp-content/uploads/2014/07/corp-landlord-report-web.pdf; Sarah Edelman with Julia Gordon and David Sanchez, "When Wall Street Buys Main Street: The Implications of Single-Family Rental Bonds for Tenants and Housing Markets," Center for American Progress, February 27, 2014, https://www.americanprogress.org/issues/economy/reports/2014/02/27/84750/when-wall-street-buys-main-street-2/; and Rob Call with Denechia Powell and Sarah Heck, "Blackstone: Atlanta's Newest Landlord; The New Face of the Rental Market" (Occupy Our Homes, April 2014), https://homesforall.org/wp-content/uploads/2014/04/BlackstoneReportFinal0407141.pdf.

6. Richard Florida, "How Housing Wealth Transferred from Families to Corporations," *Bloomberg CityLab,* October 4, 2019, https://www.citylab.com/life/2019/10/single-family-house-rental-recession-homeowner-management/599371/.

7. Andrea Eisfeldt and Andrew Demers, "Total Returns to Single Family Rentals," Working Paper 21804 (Cambridge, MA: National Bureau of Economic Research, December 2018), https://www.nber.org/papers/w21804.pdf. The 2015 American Housing Survey showed that, of the 48.5 million rental units in the US, more than half (25.8 million) were corporate owned.

8. Alana Semuels, "How Wall Street Bought Up America's Homes," *The Atlantic,* February 13, 2019, https://www.theatlantic.com/technology/archive/2019/02/single-family-landlords-wall-street/582394/.

9. Desiree Fields, "Automated Landlord: Digital Technologies and Post-Crisis," *Environment and Planning A: Economy and Space* (May 2019), pp. 1–22.

10. Francesca Mari, "A $60 Billion Housing Grab by Wall Street," *New York Times Magazine,* March 4, 2020, https://www.nytimes.com/2020/03/04/magazine/wall-street-landlords.html; and Aaron Glantz, *Homewreckers: How a Gang of Wall Street Kingpins, Hedge Fund Magnates, Crooked Banks, and Vulture Capitalists Suckered Millions out of Their Homes and Demolished the American Dream* (New York: Custom House, 2019).

11. Aaron Glantz, "Unmasking the Secret Landlords Buying Up America," *Reveal*, December 17, 2019, https://www.revealnews.org/article/unmasking-the-secret-landlords-buying-up-america/. In a series of investigative articles, Louise Story and Stephanie Saul exposed the operations that laundered ill-gotten tycoon cash through luxury real estate in New York and California: "Towers of Secrecy: Piercing the Shell Companies," *New York Times*, 2015–18, https://www.nytimes.com/news-event/shell-company-towers-of-secrecy-real-estate.

12. McKinsey Institute, "Tackling the World's Affordable Housing Challenges" (October 2014), https://www.mckinsey.com/featured-insights/urbanization/tackling-the-worlds-affordable-housing-challenge.

13. Miloon Kothari, "The Global Crisis of Displacement and Evictions: A Housing and Land Rights Response," Rosa Luxemburg Stiftung, December 2015, http://www.rosalux-nyc.org/the-global-crisis-of-displacement-and-evictions/.

14. Leilani Farha and Surya Deva, "Letter to Stephen Schwarzman" (March 22, 2019), https://www.ohchr.org/Documents/Issues/Housing/Financialization/OL_OTH_17_2019; and Patrick Butler and Dominic Rushe, "UN Accuses Blackstone Group of Contributing to Global Housing Crisis," *The Guardian*, March 26, 2019, https://www.theguardian.com/us-news/2019/mar/26/blackstone-group-accused-global-housing-crisis-un. The same year, Raquel Rolnick, who succeeded Kothari in the UN position, published a book that drew on her experience reporting on the violent entry of globalized finance into housing in Europe and the Americas: *Urban Warfare: Housing under the Empire of Finance* (New York: Verso Books, 2019). Also see Samuel Stein, *Capital City: Gentrification and the Real Estate State* (New York: Verso, 2019).

15. The decline was most evident in new housing. By 2014, only 59 percent of the houses built over the previous decade were owner occupied, as compared to a historical ratio of 77 percent. Mary Shanklin and Charles Minshew, "Homeownership Fades in Central Florida," *Orlando Sentinel*, December 18, 2014, https://www.orlandosentinel.com/business/os-homeownership-rentals-htmlstory.html.

16. National Association of Real Estate Brokers, "African American Homeownership Falls to 50-Year Low" (2016), https://www.nareb.com/african-american-homeownership-falls-50-year-low/.

17. Jung Hyun Choi, "Breaking Down the Black-White Homeownership Gap," *Urban Wire*, February 21, 2020, https://www.urban.org/urban-wire/breaking-down-black-white-homeownership-gap.

18. Irina Lupa, "The Decade in Housing Trends," *RENTCafé*, December 16, 2019, https://www.rentcafe.com/blog/rental-market/market-snapshots/renting-america-housing-changed-past-decade/#rentergrowth.

19. Executive Summary Report, Regional Affordable Housing Initiative (City of Orlando and Orange/Osceola/Seminole Counties, May 2018), p. 25, https://www.ocfl.net/Portals/0/Library/Board%20of%20County%20Commissioners/docs/Regional%20Affordable%20Housing%20Executive%20Summary%20Report%2005-2018-Final_web-Cert-CERT.pdf.

20. Lupa, "The Decade in Housing Trends."

21. Joint Center for Housing Studies, *America's Rental Housing 2020* (Harvard University, 2019), https://www.jchs.harvard.edu/sites/default/files/reports/files/Harvard_JCHS_Americas_Rental_Housing_2020.pdf.

22. Randy Shaw, *Generation Priced Out: Who Gets to Live in the New Urban America* (Berkeley: University of California Press, 2018); and Patrick Sisson, Jeff Andrews, and Alex Bazeley, "The Affordable Housing Crisis Explained," *Curbed*, May 15, 2019, https://www.curbed.com/2019/5/15/18617763/affordable-housing-policy-rent-real-estate-apartment.

23. National Low Income Housing Coalition, *Out of Reach* (2020), https://reports.nlihc.org/oor/about.

24. Tim Henderson, "Rural America Faces a Housing Cost Crunch," *Stateline*, an initiative of the Pew Charitable Trusts, March 25, 2019, https://www.pewtrusts.org/en/research-and-analysis/blogs/stateline/2019/03/25/rural-america-faces-a-housing-cost-crunch. Suburban poverty has grown at twice the rate as in cities over the last two decades. By 2013, the numbers of suburban poor surpassed those living in big cities or in rural areas, 16.4 million compared to 13.4 million and 7.3 million, respectively. See Elizabeth Kneebone and Alan Berube, *Confronting Suburban Poverty in America* (Washington, DC: Brookings Institution Press, 2013); and Scott W. Allard, *Places in Need: The Changing Geography of Poverty* (New York: Russell Sage, 2017).

25. As early as 1990, Paul Groth estimated that "hotel residents numbered between one million and two million people," and concluded that "more people lived in hotels than in all of America's public housing": *Living Downtown: The History of Residential Hotels in the United States* (Berkeley: University of California Press, 1994), chapter 1.

26. Pete Reinwald, "Amid Troubling 1st-Time Homelessness, Orlando Shelter Provides Lens into the Pandemic," *Spectrum News 13*, September 28, 2020, https://www.mynews13.com/fl/orlando/news/2020/09/28/amid-1st-time-homelessness--orlando-shelter-provides-lens-into-pandemic.

27. By the end of January 2021, landlords in the twenty-five cities tracked by Princeton's Eviction Lab had filed almost 250,000 eviction cases; see https://evictionlab.org/eviction-tracking/. According to the University of Florida's Shimberg Center, more than 57,000 evictions were filed in the state from March to mid-December 2020.

28. Jim Parrot and Mark Zandi, "Averting an Eviction Crisis," Moody's Analytics, January 2021, https://www.moodysanalytics.com/-/media/article/2021/averting-an-eviction-crisis.pdf.

29. Chris Cumming, "Private Equity's Trillion-Dollar Piggy Bank Holds Little for Struggling Companies," *Wall Street Journal*, June 28, 2020, https://www.wsj.com/articles/private-equitys-trillion-dollar-piggy-bank-holds-little-for-struggling-companies-11593212136.

30. Katherine Kallergis, "Sternlicht on Starwood's Hunt for Opportunities," *The Real Deal*, May 7, 2020, https://therealdeal.com/2020/05/07/when-its-really-ugly-its-a-good-time-to-invest-sternlicht-on-starwoods-hunt-for-opportunities/.

31. Quoted in Kriston Caaps, "What the New Federal Eviction Moratorium Means," *Bloomberg CityLab*, September 2, 2020, https://www.bloomberg.com/news/articles/2020-09-02/trump-eviction-moratorium-brings-new-questions.

32. National Low Income Housing Coalition, *The Gap: A Shortage of Affordable Rental Homes* (March 2019), https://reports.nlihc.org/gap.

33. Heart of Florida United Way, *ALICE in Florida: A Financial Hardship Study* (2020), https://www.hfuw.org/alicereport2020/. According to the Shimberg Center's 2019 *Rental Market Study*, Osceola also topped the Florida list of counties with the highest percentage of cost-burdened renters, at 32 percent. "Florida's Affordable Rental Housing Needs: 2020 Update" (Shimberg Center for Housing Studies, University of Florida, 2020), http://www.shimberg.ufl.edu/publications/fl-rms-brief-2020.pdf.

34. During my research for this book, I was often casually told that one in a hundred homeless children in America lives in Osceola County. But that statistical rumor is more accurate when based on the numbers of homeless children in the Central Florida region as a whole, estimated in 2017 to be almost fifteen thousand. Kate Santich, "Central Florida's Homeless Students Top 14,000," *Orlando Sentinel*, October 10, 2017, https://www.orlandosentinel.com/news/os-homeless-students-central-florida-20171006-story.html.

35. Jim Robison, *Kissimmee—125 Years of Its People and Progress* (Virginia Beach, VA: Donning, 2008), p. 26.

36. In March 2021, one of the larger agricultural properties, the 6,000-acre Green Island Ranch, which had been in the "pioneer" Partin family for more than a hundred years, went on the market. It will yield between 13,000 and 17,000 homes. Laura Kinsler, "Osceola's Nearly 6,000-Acre Green Island Ranch Hits the Market for $140M," *GrowthSpotter*, March 24, 2021, https://www.growthspotter.com/news/osceola-county-developments/gs-news-green-island-20210324-x6ybf4yewncfde4o2fja46luua-story.html.

37. Kyle Arnold, "Orlando-Area Rents Rising Faster Than Any Other Big City," *Orlando Sentinel*, December 20, 2018, https://www.orlandosentinel.com/business/os-bz-rising-rents-orlando-20181219-story.html; Kim O'Brien, "Orlando Remains Nation's Top Major Market for Rent Growth," *Real Page*, August 1, 2018, https://www.realpage.com/analytics/orlando-remains-nations-top-major-market-rent-growth/. For a comparative national picture, see Patrick Sisson, "Central Florida's Boom Shows True Picture of U.S. Real Estate Trends," *Curbed*, April 23, 2019, https://www.curbed.com/2019/4/23/18511006/orlando-tampa-real-estate-housing-development.

38. Caroline Glenn, "Orlando's Housing Supply Hits a Record Low This Year," *Orlando Sentinel*, March 3, 2020, https://www.orlandosentinel.com/business/real-estate/os-bz-housing-supply-keeps-dropping-20200303-qee2i75b4jfe7noeeipdasex5m-story.html.

39. Alex Soderstrom, "Buyers Increasingly Use Cash in Orlando's Competitive Housing Market," *Orlando Business Journal*, March 22, 2021, https://www.bizjournals.com/orlando/news/2021/03/22/buyers-increasingly-use-cash-for-orlando-housing.html.

40. Scott Maxwell, "Orlando Has Lowest Wages of Any Big City in America . . . Again," *Orlando Sentinel*, April 5, 2019, https://www.orlandosentinel.com/opinion/scott-maxwell-commentary/os-op-orlando-lowest-wages-america-scott-maxwell-20190405-story.html.

CHAPTER 1: A MOTEL IS NOT A HOME

1. Many motels from the midcentury heyday have not survived the shake-out. See Mark Okrant's loving portrait, *No Vacancy: The Rise, Demise, and Reprise of America's Motels* (Concord, NH: Plaidswede, 2013). For more documentation of the history of motels, see John Jakle, Keith Sculle, and Jefferson Rogers, *The Motel in America* (Baltimore: Johns Hopkins University Press, 2002).

2. Alex Smith, "Caught in the Extended Stay Motel Trap," *NPR*, July 11, 2018,

https://www.npr.org/2018/07/11/627351318/caught-in-the-extended-stay-motel-trap.

3. In his classic essay on how vernacular landscapes are designed to catch the eye of the passing motorist, J. B. Jackson noted that the highway strip is a place "where modesty has no place." See "Other-Directed Houses," *Landscapes: Selected Writings of J. B. Jackson*, ed. Ervin H. Zube (Boston: University of Massachusetts Press, 1970).

4. See Brian Goldstone, "The New American Homeless," *New Republic*, August 21, 2019, https://newrepublic.com/article/154618/new-american-homeless-housing-insecurity-richest-cities.

5. Scott Pelley, "Hard Times Generation: Homeless Children," *CBS News*, March 6, 2011, https://www.cbsnews.com/video/hard-times-generation-homeless-kids/. The following year, the show produced a follow-up, "Hard Times Generation: Families Living in Cars," June 4, 2012, https://www.cbsnews.com/news/hard-times-generation-families-living-in-cars-04-06-2012/.

6. Ryan Gillespie and Kate Santich, "Osceola Looks at Solutions for Homeless," *Orlando Sentinel*, March 30, 2018, https://www.orlandosentinel.com/news/osceola-county/os-osceola-proposed-crisis-center-20180327-story.html.

7. Department of Housing and Urban Development, *Point-in-Time Count and Housing Inventory Count*, January 2019, https://www.hudexchange.info/programs/hdx/pit-hic/.

8. National Center for Homeless Education, "Education for Homeless Children and Youth: Federal Data Summary 2015–2018" (UNC Greensboro, January 2020), https://nche.ed.gov/wp-content/uploads/2020/01/Federal-Data-Summary-SY-15.16-to-17.18-Published-1.30.2020.pdf.

9. In her 2012 doctoral study of Kissimmee-area motel residents, Stephanie Guittar Gonzalez found a similar split: *This Is Just Temporary: A Study of Extended-Stay Motel Residents in Central Florida* (Orlando: University of Central Florida, 2012), https://api.semanticscholar.org/CorpusID:157577899.

10. See Kenneth Kusmer, *Down and Out, On the Road: The Homeless in American History* (New York: Oxford University Press, 2002).

CHAPTER 2: RELUCTANT LANDLORDS

1. For a systematic survey of motel life, conducted for the US Census Bureau, see Leslie Brownrigg, "People Who Live in Hotels: An Explanatory Overview," *Ethnographic Exploratory Report #23* (Statistical

Research Division, US Census Bureau, May 31, 2006), https://www
.census.gov/srd/papers/pdf/ssm2006-03.pdf. Also see Christopher
Dum's *Exiled in America: Life on the Margins in a Residential Motel* (New
York: Columbia University Press, 2016).

2. Margaret Talbot with photos by Danna Singer, "The People Staying,
and Living, in America's Motels," *New Yorker*, April 2, 2020, https://
www.newyorker.com/culture/photo-booth/the-people-staying-and
-living-in-americas-motels. Elizabeth Lloyd Fladung, "The Hidden
Homeless," http://elizabethlloyd.com/blog/category/uncategorized
/page/3/.

3. "Interview with Melissa Lyttle," *Langly Field Notes* (October 6, 2015),
https://www.langly.co/blogs/interviews/52253124-melissa-lyttle
-motel-families-and-my-florida.

4. Ashley Lee, "The Florida Project: Director Sean Baker Explains How
and Why He Shot That Ending," *Hollywood Reporter*, October 11, 2017,
https://www.hollywoodreporter.com/news/florida-project-ending
-director-sean-baker-explains-meaning-how-he-did-it-1047215.

5. At least one reporter records that the motel has tried to phase out
extended-stay residents, while "grandfathering in" some long-term
locals. Richard Luscombe, "In the Shadow of Disney, Living on the
Margins," *The Guardian*, October 15, 2017, https://www.theguardian
.com/us-news/2017/oct/15/in-the-shadow-of-disney-living-life-on
-the-margins.

6. Pawan Dhingra, *Life behind the Lobby: Indian American Motel Owners and
the American Dream* (Palo Alto, CA: Stanford University Press, 2012).

7. Tunku Varadarajan, "A Patel Motel Cartel?," *New York Times*, July 4,
1999, https://www.nytimes.com/1999/07/04/magazine/a-patel-motel
-cartel.html.

8. A lioness named Nala escaped from the zoo in 1997 and ran wild for
two days before it was sedated and caught.

9. According to data provided by the Osceola County Property Apprais-
er's office.

10. Gabrielle Russon and Marco Santana, "New International Drive Attractions Compete More with Disney, Universal for Tourist Time," *Orlando
Sentinel*, December 27, 2018, https://www.orlandosentinel.com/business
/tourism/os-bz-idrive-themepark-competition-20181218-story.html.

11. Florida Statute 509, https://www.flsenate.gov/Laws/Statutes/2018
/0509.013.

12. Sarah Clarke, "Hotel Sues Osceola Sheriff over Unwanted Guests,"

Orlando Sentinel, March 18, 2014, https://www.orlandosentinel.com /business/os-xpm-2014-03-18-os-hotels-sue-osceola-sheriff-20140318 -story.html.

13. Some of the weeklies whom I interviewed cited this rule in order to set themselves apart from the "truly homeless." One of my Sandpiper neighbors told me that the renewal of his stay every month made him feel like a regular tenant, with some stability and security. "Homeless folks are more nomadic," he commented. "They blow with the wind." But another one had quite the opposite response. As he put it, "The fact I have to move out of my room and then back in whenever they tell me makes me feel I am homeless, and maybe I am."

14. Eviction Lab, "Eviction: Intersection of Poverty, Inequality, and Housing," Princeton University, https://www.un.org/development/desa /dspd/wp-content/uploads/sites/22/2019/05/GROMIS_Ashley _Paper.pdf.

15. Matthew Desmond's book *Evicted: Poverty and Profit in the American City* (New York: Crown Books, 2016) records that some renters initiate evictions through nonpayment in order to use that month's rent check to secure another place.

16. In April 2020, California launched the $100 million Project Roomkey to house as many as fifteen thousand homeless persons in vacant hotel rooms rented through FEMA. It was phased out after six months, having failed to house more than a third. Lawsuits from NIMBY neighbors proliferated, and there were allegations that the program misjudged its clients' needs. Evan Symon, "Project Roomkey to Wrap Up Hotel Stays for Homeless in California," *California Globe*, September 24, 2020, https://californiaglobe.com/section-2/project-roomkey-to-wrap-up -hotel-stays-for-homeless-in-california/. The state's successor, Project Homekey, was focused on buying up mostly vacant motel properties, rather than leasing the rooms.

17. Jessica Silver-Greenberg and Amy Julia Harris, "'They Just Dumped Him Like Trash': Nursing Homes Evict Vulnerable Residents," *New York Times*, June 21, 2020, https://www.nytimes.com/2020/06/21 /business/nursing-homes-evictions-discharges-coronavirus.html.

18. Some elders believed that a mission for the homeless on 192 would be a corrective for Celebration's reputation as well-to-do and aloof. Angie Etman, a key member of the women's ministry, acknowledged that "it might help take away the stigma of Celebration, that we are a community that only helps themselves and isn't really out there enough." Over

the first six years, the church funneled almost $1.5 million to Hope, along with a steady stream of volunteers and supplies donated from its congregation.

19. The phrase and its implications for poverty relief were popularized for Christian audiences by Steve Corbett and Brian Fikkert, *When Helping Hurts: Alleviating Poverty without Hurting the Poor . . . and Yourself* (Chicago: Moody Publishers, 2009).

20. The Housing First model was developed by Sam Tsemberis, at Pathways to Housing in New York, in the early 1990s, and then research by Dennis Culhane provided evidence of its success: Dennis P. Culhane, Stephen Metraux, and Trevor Hadley, "Public Service Reductions Associated with Placement of Homeless Persons with Severe Mental Illness in Supportive Housing," *Housing Policy Debate* 13, no. 1 (Fannie Mae Foundation, 2002), https://shnny.org/uploads/The_Culhane_Report.pdf. For a full-length overview, see Deborah Padgett, Benjamin Henwood, and Sam Tsemberis, *Housing First: Ending Homelessness, Transforming Systems, and Changing Lives* (New York: Oxford University Press, 2015).

21. Mary Downey, "Community Hope Center to Buy Hotel to Create Affordable Housing," *Orlando Business Journal*, September 17, 2020, https://www.bizjournals.com/orlando/news/2020/09/17/community-hope-center-buy-hotel-affordable-housing.html.

22. The humanitarian crisis also sorely tested the Hope Center philosophy of encouraging self-sufficiency. Responding to the most urgent need of food insecurity, the center stepped up to run one of the county's many food distribution operations, serving several hundred families a week.

CHAPTER 3: DOPESICK AND HOMESICK

1. John Temple focuses on the most infamous Florida pill mill, American Pain, based in Palm Beach County, in *American Pain: How a Young Felon and His Ring of Doctors Unleashed America's Deadliest Drug Epidemic* (New York: Lyons Press, 2015).

2. Aric Chokey and Skyler Swisher, "5.6 Billion Opioid Pills Flooded the State," *South Florida Sun Sentinel*, July 27, 2019, https://www.sun-sentinel.com/news/florida/fl-ne-opioids-flood-florida-data-20190726-3gltamcwojbltehe45aj73fyoy-story.html.

3. See Beth Macy's account of the opioid crisis, *Dopesick: Dealers, Doctors, and the Drug Company That Addicted America* (New York: Little, Brown, 2018).

4. Julia Ochoa, "Florida Fails to Open Methadone Clinics in Opioid Crisis," *WJCT News*, January 24, 2019, https://news.wjct.org/post/florida-fails-open-methadone-clinics-opioid-crisis.

CHAPTER 4: FORTY-ACRE WOOD

1. Julie Hunter et al., *Welcome Home: The Rise of Tent Cities*, Allard K. Lowenstein International Human Rights Clinic at Yale Law School and the National Law Center on Homelessness and Poverty, March 2014, https://nlchp.org/wp-content/uploads/2018/10/WelcomeHome_TentCities.pdf.

2. Adam Liptak, "Supreme Court Won't Revive Law Barring Homeless People from Sleeping Outdoors," *New York Times*, December 16, 2019, https://www.nytimes.com/2019/12/16/us/supreme-court-idaho-homeless-sleeping.html.

3. Andrew Heben, *Tent City Urbanism: From Self-Organized Camps to Tiny House Villages* (Eugene, OR: Village Collaborative, 2014).

4. Liz Navratil, "Minneapolis Mayor Frey Issues Order to Help Create 'Indoor Village' for Homeless," *Star Tribune*, October 30, 2020, https://www.startribune.com/frey-moves-to-speed-up-indoor-village-for-homeless/572916211/.

5. Michael Cooper, "Life in the Woods: North Carolina's Growing Homeless Tent Camps," *Scalawag Magazine*, November 6, 2019, https://scalawagmagazine.org/2019/11/hickory-nc-homelessness/.

6. Margot Kushel, "Why There Are So Many Unsheltered Homeless People on the West Coast," *The Conversation*, June 14, 2018, https://theconversation.com/why-there-are-so-many-unsheltered-homeless-people-on-the-west-coast-96767.

7. "CoC Homeless Populations and Subpopulations Reports," *HUD Exchange* (2019), https://www.hudexchange.info/programs/coc/coc-homeless-populations-and-subpopulations-reports/?filter_Year=2019.

8. Nineteenth-century Floridians' view of the Seminoles was shaped by Minnie Moore-Willson, whose bestselling book *The Seminoles of Florida* (1896) was the first full-length work dealing with their post-removal history. Like Charles Coe's *Red Patriots* (1898), it advanced a reform-minded agenda taken up by Friends of the Florida Seminoles, based in Kissimmee. Pressure from the Friends helped to win the setting aside of the Brighton reservation, just north of Lake Okeechobee, for the Cow Creek Seminoles.

9. Editorial, "Picks for Top Command Staff Dashing High Hopes for Osceola's First Hispanic Sheriff," *Orlando Sentinel*, January 25, 2021, https://www.orlandosentinel.com/opinion/editorials/os-op-marcos-lopez-oscoela-sheriff-hiring-20210125-w3jdabn32ndtjnvrqmqtg4apqe-story.html.

10. In their study of Orlando's homeless, James Wright and Amy Donley warn against taking such comments at face value, especially given the prevalence of mental illness. They write: "A common feature of untreated bipolar disorder is to believe in the manic phase that nothing is wrong and to believe in the depressive phase that nothing can be done to help. The chronic mental illness so evident and widespread in this population often leads to a fatalism that is easily mistaken for a carefree, nonchalant, or even happy disposition." *Poor and Homeless in the Sunshine State: Down and Out in Theme Park Nation* (New York: Routledge, 2017), p. 167.

11. According to Hilary Malson and Gary Blasi, "forcing people to relocate into sanctioned settlements transforms them from forms of shelter into forms of incarceration." See their historically informed study of urban encampments, *For the Crisis Yet to Come: Temporary Settlements in the Era of Evictions*, UCLA Luskin Institute on Inequality and Democracy, 2020, https://escholarship.org/uc/item/3tk6p1rk.

12. Laura Kinsler, "Dominium Eyes Kissimmee Site for Affordable Senior Housing," *GrowthSpotter*, July 2, 2020, https://www.growthspotter.com/news/residential-property-developments/senior-living/gs-news-dominium-kissimmee-20200702-6eprbcdqnjbkjp2iqrvhsfkdiq-story.html.

13. Kate Santich, "Cost of Homelessness in Central Florida? $31K per Person," *Orlando Sentinel*, May 21, 2014, https://www.orlandosentinel.com/news/os-xpm-2014-05-21-os-cost-of-homelessness-orlando-20140521-story.html.

14. Orlando Housing First Initiative, *Housing the First 100* (Corporation for Supportive Housing, 2016), https://www.csh.org/wp-content/uploads/2016/09/Orlando-Frequent-User-Initiative-ProfileFINAL.pdf.

CHAPTER 5: THE DISNEY PRICE

1. Moore-Willson, *History of Osceola County*; and Alma Hetherington, *River of the Long Water* (1980), as cited by Jim Robison in *Kissimmee:*

Gateway to the Kissimmee River Valley (Kissimmee: Osceola County Historical Society, 2003), pp. 17–18.

2. Charles Hudson provides a more authoritative account of the journey in *Knights of Spain, Warriors of the Sun: Hernando de Soto and the South's Ancient Chiefdoms* (Athens: University of Georgia Press, 1997). Also see Michael Gannon, ed., *The New History of Florida* (Gainesville: University Press of Florida, 1996).

3. Tim Ingham, "What the Music Business Can Learn from Disney+'s Subscriber Success," *Rolling Stone,* April 13, 2020, https://www.rollingstone.com/pro/features/disney-plus-music-business-lessons-981880/.

4. For a Disney World vacation, at the low end, $5,000 will cover an off-season six-day package, at a "value" resort with a mid-tier dining package.

5. Tarik Dogru et al., "Employee Earnings Growth in the Leisure and Hospitality Industry," *Tourism Management* 74 (October 2019): 1–11.

6. One 2019 study estimated a 3,000 percent rise in admission prices since Disney World opened. Clarissa Moon, "Study Finds Cost of Admission at Disney World Has Increased 3,014% over the Past 60 Years," *Orlando Sentinel*, July 22, 2019, https://www.orlandoweekly.com/Blogs/archives/2019/07/22/study-finds-cost-of-admission-at-disney-world-has-increased-3014-over-the-past-60-years.

7. According to Bill Zanetti, a founding member of the University of Central Florida's Entertainment Management Advisory Board, cited in John Gregory, "How Expensive Can Disney World Tickets Get? Not Even Disney Knows," *Orlando Rising*, January 13, 2019, https://orlando-rising.com/how-expensive-can-disney-world-tickets-get-not-even-disney-knows/.

8. Richard E. Foglesong tells the story best in *Married to the Mouse: Walt Disney World and Orlando* (New Haven, CT. Yale University Press, 2001).

9. The 2011 study was a reprise of an earlier 1967 estimate, commissioned at a time when the company was trying to sell its Florida project to the state legislature. That earlier report suggested that the theme park would "generate a measurable addition in excess of $6.6 billion in new wealth." Economics Research Associates, *Economic Impact of Disney World on Florida* (Los Angeles and Washington, DC, January 20, 1967).

10. According to the report, Disney World vacationers spent an estimated $1.7 billion at off-site businesses, and the company purchased $900 million in goods and services from local vendors. When "indirect and induced" impacts from Disney's operations were factored in, the

cumulative economic impact of $6.3 billion swelled to $18.2 billion and approximately 161,000 jobs. Jason Garcia, "Disney Says It Generates $18.2 Billion Annual Ripple Effect in Florida," *Orlando Sentinel*, April 13, 2011, https://www.orlandosentinel.com/os-xpm-2011-04-13-os-disney-economic-impact-20110413-story.html.

11. Chabeli Carrazana, "Laborland," *Orlando Sentinel*, December 5, 2019, https://www.orlandosentinel.com/business/tourism/laborland/os-bz-tourism-industry-disney-wages-20191205-46u5ykiro5cx3n25qronziiify-story.html.

12. Jason Garcia, "Big Businesses Cut Their Florida Taxes by Using Income-Shifting Strategies," *Orlando Sentinel*, November 14, 2019, https://www.orlandosentinel.com/politics/os-ne-florida-corporate-tax-avoidance-dr-pepper-20191114-y2ltzlx5jvhklpmka7hw6vzqai-story.html.

13. Jason Garcia, "Disney Triples Offshore Profits, Saving on U.S. Taxes," *Orlando Sentinel*, December 9, 2013, https://www.orlandosentinel.com/business/os-xpm-2013-12-09-os-disney-offshore-profits-taxes-20131206-story.html.

14. Jason Garcia, "Walt Disney World's Political Spending," *Florida Trend*, July 26, 2019, https://www.floridatrend.com/article/27473/walt-disney-worlds-political-spending?page=1. The company has a long record of backing Disney-friendly elected officials and hobbling those who threaten its tax-averse stance. See Gabrielle Russon, "Disney World Is Suing over Its Property Taxes—Again," *Orlando Sentinel*, June 12, 2020, https://www.orlandosentinel.com/business/tourism/os-bz-disney-rick-singh-20200612-6hiunjd6hjef3c7si5imzjte3e-story.html. It also takes advantage of the state's agricultural tax break to preserve rural land from urban sprawl. Often called the "two-cow tax break" because of the low bar it sets for landowners seeking an exception, the law is widely abused by developers and corporations like Disney. Jason Garcia, "Ca$h Cow: Tavistock, Disney and Others Save Millions from Tax Break Meant to Help Farmers," *Orlando Sentinel*, February 19, 2021, https://www.orlandosentinel.com/news/os-prem-ne-florida-farming-property-tax-break-20210217-xngxwwbc4vakjlrbcq5sfltdcq-htmlstory.html.

15. Peter Dreier et al., *Working for the Mouse: A Survey of Disneyland Employees* (Occidental College Urban & Environmental Policy Institute and the Economic Roundtable, February 2018), https://economicrt.org/publication/disneyland/.

16. Jennifer Medina, "By Day, a Sunny Smile for Disney Visitors. By Night, an Uneasy Sleep in a Car," *New York Times*, February 27, 2018,

https://www.nytimes.com/2018/02/27/us/disneyland-employees -wages.html; Paulina Velasco, "Cinderella Is Homeless, Ariel 'Can't Afford to Live on Land': Disney Under Fire for Pay," *The Guardian*, July 17, 2017, https://www.theguardian.com/us-news/2017/jul/17 /disneyland-low-wages-anaheim-orange-county-homelessness.

17. Bernie Sanders, "Disneyland Workers Face Ruthless Exploitation. Their Fight Is Our Fight," *The Guardian*, June 7, 2018, https://www .theguardian.com/commentisfree/2018/jun/07/disneyland-workers -living-wage-disney-inequality.

18. Gabrielle Russon, "Disney World Workers Endure Tourists Who Scream, Punch and Even Grope Them," *Orlando Sentinel*, September 23, 2019, https://www.orlandosentinel.com/business/os-bz-disney-employees -abuse-20190923-zy7o3lka3fhmhfeohjicftx74a-story.html.

19. Arlie Russell Hochschild, *The Managed Heart: Commercialization of Human Feeling* (Berkeley: University of California Press, 1983).

20. Brooke Erin Duffy, *(Not) Getting Paid to Do What You Love: Gender, Social Media, and Aspirational Work* (New Haven, CT: Yale University Press, 2017).

21. The solidarity was bicoastal. The California resort unions won a $15 agreement at Disneyland in late July 2018, which put pressure on Disney World management to concede over the next month.

22. Cristina Caron, "Walt Disney World Workers Reach Deal for $15 Minimum Wage by 2021," *New York Times*, August 15, 2018, https://www .nytimes.com/2018/08/25/business/disney-world-minimum-wage -union.html.

23. National Low Income Housing Coalition, "Out of Reach 2020: Florida," https://reports.nlihc.org/oor/florida/.

24. Richard Bilbao, "Breaking: Disney to Furlough Workers at Walt Disney World, Disneyland Resort," *Orlando Business Journal*, April 2, 2020, https://www.bizjournals.com/orlando/news/2020/04/02/breaking -disney-to-furlough-workers-at-walt-disney.html.

25. Caroline Glenn, "Unemployment in Metro Orlando Jumps to 22.6% in May," *Orlando Sentinel*, June 19, 2020, https://www.orlandosentinel .com/coronavirus/jobs-economy/os-bz-coronavirus-florida-orlando -may-unemployment-20200619-2eseklimmjatrcjtiflli34yl4-story.html.

26. Patricia Mazzei and Sabrina Tavernise, "'Florida Is a Terrible State to Be an Unemployed Person,'" *New York Times*, April 23, 2020, https://www .nytimes.com/2020/04/23/us/florida-coronavirus-unemployment .html; and Jim De Fede, "Gov. Ron DeSantis Acknowledges State's

Unemployment System Was Built with 'Pointless Roadblocks' to Pay Out 'Least Number of Claims,'" *CBS Miami*, August 4, 2020, https://miami.cbslocal.com/2020/08/04/exclusive-governor-ron-desantis-acknowledges-florida-unemployment-system-designed-frustrate/.

27. Concerned Cast Members, "Protect Our Magic Makers: Don't Open Theme Parks until It's Safe" (July 2020), https://sign.moveon.org/petitions/protect-our-magic-makers-don-t-open-theme-parks-until-it-s-safe.

28. Gabrielle Russon and Stephen Lemongello, "More Disney World Layoffs Revealed," *Orlando Sentinel*, October 9, 2020, https://www.orlandosentinel.com/business/tourism/os-bz-disney-union-layoffs-part-time-20201007-m5rochxtq5gmpphip3kwdzclce-story.html.

29. Laura Kinsler, "Lender, County Foreclosing on Kissimmee Motels Where Power Was Shut Off," *GrowthSpotter*, June 5, 2020, https://www.growthspotter.com/news/osceola-county-developments/gs-news-lake-cecile-motels-20200605-k4e3n6hd3fgs3o27qpbiy65hay-story.html.

30. Greg Jaffe, "A Pandemic, A Motel without Power, and a Potentially Terrifying Glimpse of Orlando's Future," *Washington Post*, September 10, 2020, https://www.washingtonpost.com/graphics/2020/national/kissimmee-star-motel/.

31. Kate Santich, "Families Rescued from Decrepit Kissimmee Motel," *Orlando Sentinel*, September 16, 2020, https://www.orlandosentinel.com/news/os-ne-star-motel-families-rescued-will-motels-house-homeless-20200916-s6jdlo3efnf33n4p6ewclrtnt4-story.html.

32. Gina Heeb, "Rent in Queens Fell after Amazon Backed Out of Plans to Build Its HQ2 There," *Business Insider*, March 15, 2019, https://markets.businessinsider.com/news/stocks/amazon-hq2-pulls-out-of-new-york-queens-rents-fall-2019-3-1028034011.

33. Alana Semuels, "How Amazon Helped Kill a Seattle Tax on Business," *The Atlantic*, June 13, 2018, https://www.theatlantic.com/technology/archive/2018/06/how-amazon-helped-kill-a-seattle-tax-on-business/562736/.

34. Edward Ongweso Jr., "Silicon Valley Owes Us $100 Billion in Taxes (At Least)," *Vice*, December 3, 2019, https://www.vice.com/en_us/article/59n7e8/silicon-valley-owes-us-dollar100-billion-in-taxes-at-least.

35. After Amazon unsuccessfully backed its own candidates to the tune of $1.5 million in the fall 2019 elections, the city council finally passed a modified head tax on corporations with payrolls of more than $7

million and employees with salaries above $150,000. Higher tax rates applied to even larger companies like Amazon.

36. Conor Dougherty argues that in California specifically, the lack of affordable housing has many historical causes, including a tradition of anti-tax legislation and strong anti-density sentiment. Dougherty, *Golden Gates: Fighting for Housing in America* (New York: Penguin Press, 2020).

37. The only employee housing directly offered by the company is for those enrolled in the Disney College Program. A campground for these student workers—called Snow White Village—operated just off Route 192 (at Seven Dwarfs Lane and Princess Lane) from 1981 through the 1990s before the current apartment housing was built at Little Lake Bryan, in Lake Buena Vista.

38. Faye Fiore, "Disney's Florida Critics Warn of a Greedy Monster," *LA Times*, February 20, 1990, https://www.latimes.com/archives/la-xpm-1990-02-20-mn-1122-story.html.

39. Sarah Tully, "Affordable-Housing Debate Grows for Disney Employees," *Orange County Register*, April 22, 2007, https://www.ocregister.com/2007/04/22/april-22-affordable-housing-debate-grows-for-disney-employees/.

40. Michael Sainato, "When Working in Disney World Means Being Stuck Living in a Cheap Motel," *Vice*, June 1, 2018, https://www.vice.com/en_us/article/xwma3q/when-working-in-disney-world-means-being-stuck-living-in-a-cheap-motel; and Jeff Collins, "Disney Donates $5 Million to Help Fund Housing for Orange County's Homeless," *Orange County Register*, March 5, 2019, https://www.ocregister.com/2019/03/05/disney-donates-5-million-to-help-fund-housing-for-orange-countys-homeless/.

41. Andrew Edgecliffe-Johnson, "Abigail Disney: 'I'm Choosing to Be a Traitor to My Class,'" *Financial Times*, July 5, 2019, https://www.ft.com/content/b2a8b2ea-9c16-11e9-9c06-a4640c9feebb.

42. National Labor Committee, "The U.S. in Haiti: How to Get Rich on 11¢ an Hour" (New York, 1996); and Andrew Ross, ed., *No Sweat: Fashion, Free Trade, and the Rights of Garment Workers* (New York: Verso, 1997). Subsequent exposés by Students and Scholars Against Corporate Misconduct (SACOM), China Labor Watch, and the Institute for Global Labor Rights focused on facilities in mainland China producing Disney garments, toys, and children's books. See SACOM, *Looking for Mickey Mouse's Conscience—A Survey of the Working Conditions of*

Disney's Supplier Factories in China (Hong Kong: SACOM, 2005); and SACOM and Stop Toying Around, *Exploitation of Toy Factory Workers at the Bottom of the Global Supply Chain* (Hong Kong: SACOM, 2009). In almost every case of reported labor abuse, the company has denied responsibility, claiming that the problems lay with subcontractors.

43. But this arrangement typically gave the employer far too much control over employees' lives (as would have been the case in the ur-EPCOT company town). So, too, the temptation to capture their wages at the company store proved irresistible. See Margaret Crawford, *Building the Worker's Paradise: The Design of American Company Towns* (New York: Verso, 1995).

44. William Feuer, "Jeff Bezos' Day One Fund Gives $98.5 Million to 32 Groups Helping the Homeless," CNBC, November 21, 2019, https://www.cnbc.com/2019/11/21/bezos-day-one-fund-gives-98point5-million-to-groups-helping-the-homeless.html.

CHAPTER 6: WALL STREET COMES TO TOWN

1. According to Richard Foglesong, the housing assistance funds benefited only seventy-seven people and only seven of them were low-income: *Married to the Mouse: Walt Disney World and Orlando*, p. 162.

2. The Celebration Foundation, funded through a transfer fee on home sales, also does some outreach beyond the "bubble." Several years ago, it launched a program to help familiarize high school children with the county's Valencia College, and it provides some scholarships for students.

3. When I returned to town in 1999 to give a book talk about *The Celebration Chronicles*, I suggested to residents that Celebration had the opportunity to be a good neighbor in Osceola County in a way that Disney has never been. But if they used their many resources only to strengthen their community inside the "bubble," as they had begun to call it, then that opportunity would be wasted. See Andrew Ross, "Can You Go Home Again to Celebration?," *Orlando Weekly*, October 7, 1999, https://www.orlandoweekly.com/orlando/can-you-go-home-again-to-celebration/Content?oid=2263089.

4. Two of the architects in town have served a term on planning boards, but otherwise, in twenty-four years, there have only been two runs for elected office, both for seats on the school board and both unsuccessful; the most recent candidate, backed by Republicans who favored

charter schools, amassed a campaign fund that dwarfed his opponent's, but he chose, arrogantly and disastrously, not to debate her.

5. Sarah Treuhaft et al., *When Investors Buy Up the Neighborhood: Preventing Investor Ownership from Causing Neighborhood Decline*, Northwest Area Foundation, PolicyLink, and Family Housing Fund (St. Paul, Oakland, and Minneapolis, 2010), https://www.fhfund.org/wp-content /uploads/2019/07/WHENINVESTORSBUYUPTHENEIGHBOR HOOD.pdf. On the takeover of mobile home parks, see the report by Private Equity Stakeholder Project, MHAction, and Americans for Financial Reform, *Private Equity Giants Converge on Manufactured Homes* (February 2019), https://mhaction.org/wp-content/uploads/2019/02 /PrivateEquityGiantsFinal.pdf.

6. But the purchase of a mixed-use entity also brings with it the potential for conflicts between owner-occupants, investor owners, commercial business owners, and institutional investors, each of whom have different interests and values.

7. Lauren Coleman-Lochner and Eliza Ronalds-Hannon, "Everything Is Private Equity Now," *Bloomberg News*, October 8, 2019, https:// www.bloomberg.com/news/features/2019-10-03/how-private-equity -works-and-took-over-everything; and Eileen Appelbaum and Rosemary L. Batt, *Private Equity at Work: When Wall Street Manages Main Street* (New York: Russell Sage, 2014).

8. Mike Elk, "Private Equity's Latest Scheme: Closing Urban Hospitals and Selling Off the Real Estate," *American Prospect*, July 11, 2019, https://prospect.org/health/private-equity-s-latest-scheme-closing -urban-hospitals-selling-real-estate/.

9. Rana Foroohar, "Why Big Investors Are Buying Up American Trailer Parks," *Financial Times*, February 7, 2020, https://www.ft.com/content /3c87eb24-47a8-11ea-aee2-9ddbdc86190d.

10. According to Negrin's profile in "The 50 Most Influential Turkish Americans," *Turk of America* 13, no. 40 (April 8, 2014), https://issuu .com/turkofamerica/docs/ilovepdf.com/65.

11. In large part because of the risk to brand exposure from such stories, Disney is highly unlikely to try its hand at another Celebration. In its only other residential venture to date, the company allowed Four Seasons to carve out Golden Oak, an ultra-luxury enclave of three hundred residences nestled inside its property line but de-annexed from Reedy Creek. The Golden Oak homeowners association is more like a country club, while the concierge services on offer and exclusive

privileges at the theme parks round out its CEO lifestyle profile, quite distinct from the community-oriented, mixed-income blueprint for Celebration.

12. Laura Kusisto, "Leaks and Mold Are Ruining the Disney Magic in Celebration, Florida," *Wall Street Journal,* November 15, 2016, https://www.wsj.com/articles/leaks-and-mold-are-ruining-the-Disney-magic-in-celebration-florida-1479249246.

13. In September 2005, Negrin was able to raise an additional $72 million from investors to open a private equity fund with Amtrust Bank for real estate acquisitions across the country. Four years later, after the market turndown, the Amtrust fund handed back $24 million to investors. "Lexin Fund Returns Capital to LPs," *Hedge Fund Alert* (September 23, 2009).

14. "New Higher Majority Requirement for Condominium Deconversions in Chicago: Here's What You Need to Know," *National Law Review,* October 16, 2019, https://www.natlawreview.com/article/new-higher-majority-requirement-condominium-deconversions-chicago-here-s-what-you.

15. While working for LaSalle Investment Management in the early 1990s, Negrin (who spoke to me briefly on the phone but turned down requests for a longer interview) told me he had some contact with Disney, advising officials on the price points for homes. It was his entry, he claimed, to the world of Celebration. At that time, he was creating joint-venture equity partnerships between LaSalle and the federal government's Resolution Trust Corporation (RTC), set up to dispose of bankrupt properties inherited from insolvent savings and loan associations. Selected parcels transferred into a land fund were able to generate long-term cash flows for the RTC and the joint equity partner as their value recovered. The fiscal operating model that Negrin adopted for Celebration's town center was close, in spirit at least, to the formula he worked on at La Salle for ensuring steady income streams and borrowing more money by collateralizing the asset.

16. Maya Abood et al., *Wall Street Landlords Turn the American Dream into a Nightmare* (Americans for Financial Reform, ACCE Institute, and Public Advocates, January 17, 2018), pp. 25–26, http://ourfinancialsecurity.org/2018/01/afr-report-wall-street-and-single-family-rentals/.

17. Kathleen Howley, "Disney-Built Town in Florida Rocked by Deaths, Foreclosures," *Seattle Times,* December 17, 2010, https://www

.seattletimes.com/business/real-estate/Disney-built-town-in-florida
-rocked-by-deaths-foreclosures/.

18. Negrin's purchase of Mirasol, another apartment complex in Celebration, set a Central Florida record price of $402,000 per unit, but a full
half were unsold by the time of the crash. Greenwich Capital ended
up foreclosing on almost $55 million of the loan principal, along with
$5.7 million of interest, and suing Negrin for unpaid real estate taxes.
Greenwich Capital Fin. Prods., Inc. v. Negrin, 2009 NY Slip Op 51890(U)
[24 Misc 3d 1245(A)]. Decided on September 1, 2009, Supreme Court,
New York County, https://law.justia.com/cases/new-york/other
-courts/2009/2009-51890.html. Enders Place, an acquisition in Orlando's Baldwin Park, another New Urbanist community, built on the site
of the former US Naval Training Center, was auctioned off in April
2009 after Negrin defaulted on his $46 million debt to the lender, HSH
Nordbank.

19. One of Opalka's videos, demonstrating rooftop damage and set to the
Drifters' carefree song "Up on the Roof," can be viewed at https://
youtu.be/0mcZdX6Wjac.

20. Michelle Conlin, "Spider, Sewage, and a Flurry of Fees—the Other
Side of Renting a House from Wall Street," *Reuters*, July 27, 2018,
https://www.reuters.com/investigates/special-report/usa-housing
-invitation/.

21. Kelly began posting a blog (*Rescuing Celebration: Disney's Ideal Town Is
Falling Down*) that traded on her mordant wit: "I have begun my holi-
day decorations, this year using a 'Shabby Chic' theme as I am repurposing some of Lexin's disintegrated roof tarps—pieces of which have
been deposited all over Town Center thanks to Time, the Florida Sun
and Prevailing Breezes." The blog was copiously illustrated with stark
visual evidence of the physical damage sustained by condo residents.
The blog is at https://cookiekellyblog.com/2016/12/14/1490/.

22. Kusisto, "Leaks and Mold Are Ruining the Disney Magic."

23. As an unincorporated part of Osceola County, with no municipal government of its own, Celebration's internal affairs are deliberated by a
bewildering cluster of these association boards, referred to by everyone as the "alphabet soup." In addition to CROA, the Celebration Residential Homeowners Association, there is CNOA, the Celebration
Non-Residential Owners Association, representing the commercial
owners; CCDD, the Celebration Community Development District,
which owns and maintains the common area infrastructure; ECDD,

the Enterprise Community Development District, which owns and maintains strictly commercial areas; CJC, the Celebration Joint Committee, which comprises reps from Disney, CROA, and CNOA and operates Town Hall; and CCMC, the managing agent retained by CJC to provide Town Hall services.

24. The company will not relinquish control of all Celebration governance boards until 90 percent of the land is sold, and even then, the founding documents reserve its right to "disapprove of any action, policy, or program" of the other associations.

25. When Michael Eisner returned to Celebration for the twentieth anniversary in 2016, he is said to have privately expressed dismay at the dilapidated state of Town Center buildings and, in particular, at the shuttered and decaying condition of the downtown movie theater.

26. After twenty-five years, and despite the wealth and talents of its residents, there are only a few genuinely homegrown initiatives on the town's landscape. Ironically, the one independent project that rose to meet, or even exceed, the standards set by Disney was steered by Kelly herself, and it was never built. In the mid-2000s, with the proceeds of her realty sales, she purchased the last five-acre lot in the Aldo Rossi–designed office park out on Celebration's commercial corridor and set about planning the greenest building in the state. Working with Rossi's protégé, Morris Adjmi, a crew of engineers, and her son's development expertise, she crafted the blueprint for a 160,000-square-foot, six-story office condominium, called The Conservatory at Celebration Place. Nominated for building of the year awards, it was the first building in Florida to be pre-certified as LEED Platinum–rated by the US Green Building Council, and one of the first private office buildings anywhere to achieve that topmost rating. Fully loaded with energy-efficient components, the Conservatory included a signature "green roof," with solar arrays, designed to cool the building and collect rainwater for use in toilets and irrigation. If Kelly had not pushed hard for the greenest engineering available, the units would all have been presold by the time of the financial crash. Her investment was wiped out, and she even had to sell the land back to Disney to settle the debts. In the course of the Great Recession, the company relaxed its rigorous land-use restrictions and allowed fast-food chains to set up shop on the site. Instead of the high-minded Conservatory, which would have been Celebration's most innovative technological showpiece, it now hosts a food court comprising Five Guys, Panera, Appleby's, and Pei Wei.

27. US Census Bureau, *2018 Rental Housing Finance Survey*, https://www .census.gov/programs-surveys/rhfs.html.
28. Adam Travis, "The Organization of Neglect: Limited Liability Companies and Housing Disinvestment," *American Sociological Review* 84, 1 (January 2019): 142–70.
29. "States and Real Estate Private Equity Firms Questioned for Compliance with Human Rights," United Nations Human Rights Office of the High Commissioner (March 26, 2019), https://www.ohchr.org/EN /NewsEvents/Pages/DisplayNews.aspx?NewsID=24404&LangID=E.

CHAPTER 7: YOUR HOME CAN BE A HOTEL

1. Because Osceola's tax collector does not enforce the requirement to register and pay the business license tax, the records that show 30,000 licensed short-term rental units in the county (in 2019, Osceola overall had 162,161 housing units) fall far short of the estimate of 50,000 from the tourist agency Experience Kissimmee.
2. In 2018, 11.2 percent of the total 127 million tourists who came to Florida stayed in a vacation home, and the total economic contribution of the industry amounted to $27.4 billion. Notably, only 38 percent of the owners who hosted them resided in the US. Robertico Croes et al., *Estimating the Economic Impact of Vacation Home Rentals in Florida*, Dick Pope Sr. Institute for Tourism Studies (Orlando: University of Central Florida, 2019).
3. Grand View Research, "Vacation Rental Market Size, Share & Trends Analysis Report by Accommodation Type (Home, Apartments, Resort/Condominium), by Booking Mode (Online, Offline), by Region, and Segment Forecasts, 2020–2027," May 2020, https://www .grandviewresearch.com/industry-analysis/vacation-rental-market.
4. The foreign capital invested in Florida real estate is predominantly from Brazil, Canada, UK, Argentina, and Venezuela, while the major foreign buyers of New York real estate are from Europe, Asia, Russia, and the Middle East. In 2016, foreign buyers of Florida property accounted for 21 percent of the residential dollar volume of sales, while the national average is 10 percent. Of these buyers, 72 percent paid in cash. National Association of Realtors, *2017 Profile of International Residential Real Estate Activity in Florida*, Florida Realtors (October 2017), https://www.nar.realtor/sites/default/files/documents/2017-Profile-of-International-Activity-in-US-Residential-Real-Estate.pdf.

5. Derek Thompson, "Why Manhattan's Skyscrapers Are Empty," *The Atlantic*, January 16, 2020, https://www.theatlantic.com/ideas/archive/2020/01/american-housing-has-gone-insane/605005/.

6. Charlie Reed, "Marketing Madness: Osceola Vacation Rental Homes among Most Popular in the State," *Osceola News-Gazette*, July 26, 2019, https://ufdc.ufl.edu/UF00028318/01517.

7. Tiffani Sherman, "Reunion's Biggest Vacation Home Hits the Market for $9.75M," *GrowthSpotter*, October 17, 2019, https://www.growthspotter.com/news/notable-home-sales/gs-news-isole-villa--20191017-q7qibl6jo5ggtazf5wxo2m6r7u-story.html.

8. Dustin Mauser-Claassen et al., "Osceola County Passes Increased School Impact Fees for Most Residential Construction," *Mondaq*, March 14, 2018, https://www.mondaq.com/unitedstates/Real-Estate-and-Construction/682714/Osceola-County-Passes-Increased-School-Impact-Fees-For-Most-Residential-Construction.

9. Dick Pope Sr. Institute for Tourism Studies, "Disclosing the Economic Impact of the Vacation Home Industry on Osceola County," prepared for Experience Kissimmee (Orlando: University of Central Florida, 2016), https://www.experiencekissimmee.com/sites/default/files/Vacation_Home_Impact_Study.pdf.

10. Thorben Wieditz, "Addressing Toronto's Housing Crisis?," *Fairbnb*, January 9, 2019, https://fairbnb.ca/2019/01/09/addressing-torontos-housing-crisis/.

11. According to a 2017 study, the increase in Airbnb listings nationally accounted for about one-fifth of rent growth and about one-seventh of housing price growth. Kyle Barron, Edward Kung, and Davide Proserpio, "The Effect of Home-Sharing on House Prices and Rents: Evidence from Airbnb," Social Science Research Network, July 25, 2017, https://papers.ssrn.com/sol3/papers.cfm?abstract_id=3006832.

12. Tripp Mickle and Preetika Rana, "'A Bargain with the Devil'—Bill Comes Due for Overextended Airbnb Hosts," *Wall Street Journal*, April 28, 2020, https://www.wsj.com/articles/a-bargain-with-the-devilbill-comes-due-for-overextended-airbnb-hosts-11588083336.

13. The controversial impact of these new landlords is most visible in urban neighborhoods, where Airbnb has the greatest booking density, but they are not exclusive to cities. In Florida, Osceola County is second only to the more urban Miami-Dade County in the number of Airbnb guests and revenue. It is also the site of the first "Niido Powered by Airbnb," the company's line of branded apartment complexes,

which allow renters to make income (shared with the company) by leasing out their unit on Airbnb for up to 180 days per year. Niido is Airbnb's effort to move into the market created by multiunit owners of rental properties, who are essentially running small-scale lodging companies on an absentee basis.

14. Josh Bivens, "The Economic Costs and Benefits of Airbnb," Economic Policy Institute, January 30, 2019, https://www.epi.org /publication/the-economic-costs-and-benefits-of-airbnb-no-reason -for-local-policymakers-to-let-airbnb-bypass-tax-or-regulatory -obligations/.

15. David Wachsmuth et al., "The High Cost of Short-Term Rentals in New York City," School of Urban Planning, McGill University, January 30, 2018, https://www.mcgill.ca/newsroom/files/newsroom/channels /attach/airbnb-report.pdf.

16. Diana Olick, "Build-to-Rent Housing Market Explodes as Investors Rush In," *CNBC*, June 26, 2019, https://www.cnbc.com/2019 /06/26/suddenly-the-build-to-rent-single-family-housing-market-is -exploding.html.

17. Kyle Foster, "Central Florida's First Build-for-Rent Subdivision Heading to Four Corners," *GrowthSpotter*, April 3, 2020, https://www .growthspotter.com/news/polk-county-developments/gs-news-stellar -championsgate-20200403-mjdobd6zpzez7gk56tpvu57onu-story.html. Not long after, American Homes 4 Rent, the nation's largest build-for-rent operator, followed suit, extending its empire into Osceola County itself. Laura Kinsler, "Build-for-Rent Developer Pays $5.77M for Former St. Cloud Airfield Site," *GrowthSpotter*, October 20, 2020, https://www .growthspotter.com/news/osceola-county-developments/gs-news -rental-homes-20201020-g4ha5dgpcfaudaqtedstl2uhzy-story.html.

18. Occupancy data for all Florida tourist properties can be found at "COVID-19 FL Tourism Impacts," Visit Florida, https://www .visitflorida.org/resources/crisis-preparation/covid-19-resources-and -information-for-businesses/covid-19-fl-tourism-impacts/.

19. Ken Storey, "Route 192 in Kissimmee Is About to Get a Dubai-Style Resort," *Orlando Weekly*, April 4, 2016, https://www.orlandoweekly .com/Blogs/archives/2016/04/04/route-192-in-kissimmee-is-about -to-get-a-dubai-style-resort. The pandemic recession put paid to the most ambitious version of the site plan; the towers were dropped and retail scaled back to reflect grimmer economic forecasts. But the corridor's inventory of mega-projects got an upgrade with the announcement of

development plans for the three-thousand-unit Grand Medina, North America's first Muslim-friendly resort and Osceola's first five-star property. Laura Kinsler, "Canadian Developer Prepping for Construction on Huge W192 Resort District," *GrowthSpotter*, December 30, 2020, https:// www.growthspotter.com/news/osceola-county-developments/gs-news -everest-update-20201231-qzumtgcptjf3fgetirvzvric6m-story.html.

20. West 192 Economic Advisory Board, *Final Report* (Kissimmee, January 23, 2012), https://www.west192.org/Home/ShowDocument?id=34.

21. Sara K. Clarke, "Region's Other Tourist Strip Struggling to Recover from Downturns, Decay," *Orlando Sentinel*, May 4, 2013, https://www .orlandosentinel.com/news/osceola-county/os-kissimmee-tourism -192-development-20130503-story.html.

22. Sam Roberts, "Homes Dark and Lifeless, Kept by Out-of-Towners," *New York Times*, July 6, 2011, https://www.nytimes.com/2011/07/07 /nyregion/more-apartments-are-empty-yet-rented-or-owned-census -finds.html.

23. Nor is it easy to distinguish between pieds-à-terre, investor properties, and short-term rentals. Nathan Tempey, "Lights Out: New York City's Ghost Apartments Multiply," *Brick Underground*, March 14, 2018, https://www.brickunderground.com/rent/pied-a-terre-airbnb -affordable-housing-crisis-nyc.

CHAPTER 8: THE BATTLE OF SPLIT OAK

1. Todd Litman, "Analysis of Public Policies That Unintentionally Encourage and Subsidize Urban Sprawl," *New Climate Economy and LSE Cities* (working paper, June 22, 2015), https://newclimateeconomy.net /sites/default/files/public-policies-encourage-sprawl-nce-report.pdf. According to the study, sprawl development "imposes more than $400 billion in external costs and $625 billion in internal costs annually in the U.S." These costs include significant increases in per capita land development and transport, expenditures on public infrastructure and service, as well as reduced agricultural and ecological productivity and public fitness and health.

2. In South Florida, even the Everglades are under threat from expansion of Miami's Urban Development Boundary. See Chloe Levine, "Miami-Dade: Do Not Move the UDB," *Harvard Political Review*, December 9, 2019, http://harvardpolitics.companylogogenerator.com/united-states /miami-dade-udb/.

3. At the meeting, Rachel Deming, director of Barry University's Environmental and Earth Law Clinic, explained that the parkway extension may be a violation of a 1998 amendment to Florida's constitution (passed with more than 70 percent of the vote) that clearly prohibits the "disposal" of conservation lands.

4. Kevin Spear, "Saving Split Oak Forest: A Bruising Environmental Battle on the Ballot," *Orlando Sentinel*, October 19, 2020, https://www .orlandosentinel.com/news/environment/os-ne-split-oak-saving-or -destroying-20201016-g43frbodabbsrmg3zxc6vq77v4-htmlstory.html.

5. Cited in Claire Provost, "From Book to Boom: How the Mormons Plan a City for 500,000 in Florida," *The Guardian*, January 30, 2017, https:// www.theguardian.com/cities/2017/jan/30/from-book-to-boom-how -the-mormons-plan-a-city-for-500000-in-florida.

6. According to Gary Mormino, the church did, however, consider selling the ranch in 1968, for $84 million. Mormino, *Land of Sunshine, State of Dreams: A Social History of Modern Florida* (Gainesville: University Press of Florida, 2005), p. 192.

7. Courtesy reviews were solicited by the DCA from Florida Fish and Wildlife Conservation Commission, 1000 Friends of Florida, South Florida Water Management District, Florida Department of Transportation, St. Johns River Water Management District, Everglades Law Center, and Florida's Department of Environmental Protection, among others.

8. Renewed Citizen Objections to Adoption, Osceola County 10–2ER CPA09–0009 Northeast Conceptual Master Plan, filed by Ralf Brookes, August 25, 2010, http://www.ralfbrookesattorney.com/images/Renewed _Objections_to_Adoption_NE_Master_Plan_Osceola_County.pdf.

9. State of Florida, Department of Community Affairs, "Statement of Intent to Find Comprehensive Plan Amendments Not in Compliance," Northeast District Conceptual Master Plan, October 6, 2010, https:// www.doah.state.fl.us/DocDoc/2010/009856/10009856_10252010 _02362436_130.pdf.

10. The DCA's request for remedial amendments to the plan included some wide-ranging conservation measures and a radical reduction of the scope of the UGB expansion. A subsequent legal proceeding produced a negotiated settlement between the DCA, Osceola County, the developer Tavistock, and the LDS's Suburban Land Reserve. Pointedly, the environmental petitioners refused to go along with the settlement process.

11. Before the DCA was abolished, local governments were limited to two amendments per year, but now there are no restrictions. Charlie Reed, "Commission Changes Comprehensive Growth Plan at Tavistock's Request," *Osceola News-Gazette*, December 15, 2018, https://whatsuposceola.com/commission-changes-comprehensive-growth-plan-at-tavistocks-request/.

12. That number, obtained from Susan Caswell, at the county's Department of Community Development, does not include transportation rights of way, and it excludes the North Ranch's 70,192 acres (of which 45,625 acres are developable).

13. Scott's fateful 2011 Community Planning Act largely withdrew state oversight of local land-use plans, leaving understaffed (and more easily bought) local government officials to make decisive rulings on developers' applications. In addition, the governor's omnibus bill—a wet dream for developers statewide—expedited all reviews by the Department of Environmental Protection and eliminated the all-important concurrency requirement, which had required developers to ensure that schools, roads, and other infrastructure were in place before their projects were completed.

14. The land was bought from the St. Joe Company, hitherto Florida's largest landowner. In 1997, St. Joe recruited Peter Rummell, chair of Walt Disney Imagineering and president of the Disney Development Company, which created Celebration, to develop New Urbanist communities (Watercolor, Southwood, Watersound, Windmark Beach, Breakfast Point, Camp Creek, and Wild Heron) in the Panhandle.

15. The ecologists faulted the plan for drawing on data from twenty-year-old, non–peer reviewed surveys that lacked input from on-site fieldwork on habitats and ecosystems. Their peer review also found that the plan neglected the core habitats of focal species, like the scrub jay, and that some natural communities, like scrubland and old-growth longleaf pine flatwoods, were also neglected, even though they are important habitats for many imperiled species. Under the plan, other conservation areas would be orphaned in the form of unconnected islands, which have much less ecological value. Jay Exum, Richard Hilsenbeck, and Reed Noss, *Peer Review of the Environmental Plan, North Ranch Sector* (Osceola County Commission, April 2015), https://www.osceola.org/core/fileparse.php/2731/urlt/042015_North-Ranch-Sector-Plan-Peer-Review-Report.pdf.

16. Deseret officials solicited a response from Breedlove, Dennis, and Associates (BDA), their own environmental consultants, who took issue not only with the tone but also the accuracy of some aspects of the peer report. In turn, Exum, Hilsenbeck, and Noss expressed "disappointment in the low quality of the BDA critique." "Rather than being a thoughtful rebuttal of our work," they wrote, "it is filled with erroneous and misleading statements, which if taken seriously, would undermine conservation of the regionally significant natural resources of the North Ranch." The BDA criticisms and the response by the Peer Review Team, "Response to BDA Critique (05/11/15) of Peer Review of the North Ranch Environmental Plan" (June 8, 2015), were both shared with the author by Jay Exum.

17. Lee told me that he had suggested that the planners concentrate development in one large city instead of a network of smaller urban nodes. But he found that the LDS officials "were still at a point in their reasoning when the traditional home on a quarter or half-acre lot with a big green lawn was seen as the product appealing to the majority of buyers, and so they were unwilling to break away from that perspective."

18. Stephen Lemongello, "Osceola Vote Sets Course for Major Transformation of Central Florida," *Orlando Sentinel*, September 26, 2015, https://www.orlandosentinel.com/news/breaking-news/os-osceola-deseret-ranch-future-plan-20150926-story.html.

19. Jimmy Tobias, "DEFANGED: Money and Politics Could Doom the Florida Panther," *The Intercept*, January 24, 2021, https://theintercept.com/2021/01/24/florida-panther-collier-engangered-species-act/.

20. According to the final version, North Ranch can break ground after "substantial progress has been made to achieve the job creation objectives" of the urban and employment centers in Northeast District/ Sunbridge. But there are no clear yardsticks in the plan for calculating "the amount, velocity, and character of the jobs created" other than vague references to the "jobs/housing ratio" and "the likelihood of further success in job creation," or to "economic connections" that will "further the County's economic development goals." *North Ranch Long-Term Master Plan/Sector Plan* (transmittal draft) (Osceola County Board of Commissioners, September 29, 2015), https://www.osceola.org/core/fileparse.php/2731/urlt/021516_NorthRanchSectorPlanAdoption.pdf.

21. The East Central Florida Corridor Task Force included recommendations for three multimodal corridors in its final report, *Recommendations*

for Connecting Established and Emerging Economic Centers in Brevard, Orange, and Osceola Counties, December 1, 2014, https://spacecoasttpo.com/wp -content/uploads/2014/11/ECFCTF_Report-Draft_102314.pdf.

22. Fish and Wildlife Research Institute, *Closing the Gaps in Florida's Wildlife Habitat Conservation System* (Tallahassee: Florida Fish and Wildlife Conservation Commission, 1994), https://conservationcorridor.org /cpb/Cox_et_al_1994.pdf.

23. The North Ranch sector plan approval process, including summaries of public hearings, is documented by the county at https://www .osceola.org/agencies-departments/strategic-initiatives/north-ranch -sector-plan.stml.

24. In 1991, Gordon B. Hinckley, then LDS president, stated that "we have felt that good farms, over a long period, represent a safe investment where the assets of the Church may be preserved and enhanced, while at the same time they are available as an agricultural resource to feed people should there come a time of need," in "The State of the Church," *Ensign*, May 1991, p. 54, https://www.churchofjesuschrist .org/study/general-conference/1991/04/the-state-of-the-church?lang =eng.

25. Claire Provost, "Building Zion: The Controversial Plan for a Mormon-Inspired City in Vermont," *The Guardian*, January 31, 2017, https://www .theguardian.com/cities/2017/jan/31/building-zion-controversial -plan-mormon-inspired-city-vermont.

26. Kelly Patton Thompson, "River Report Raises Water Quality Red Flags," *St. Johns Riverkeeper* (September 2019), https://www.stjohnsriverkeeper .org/river-report-raises-water-quality-red-flags-elevated-levels-of -pollution-and-saltwater-intrusion-cause-for-alarm.

27. See Mario Alejandro Ariza, *Disposable City: Miami's Future on the Shores of Climate Catastrophe* (New York: Bold Type Books, 2020); Jeff Goodell, *The Water Will Come: Rising Seas, Sinking Cities and the Remaking of the Civilized World* (New York: Little, Brown, 2017); and Elizabeth Rush, *Rising: Dispatches from the New American Shore* (New York: Milkweed, 2018).

28. Jesse Keenan, Thomas Hill, and Anurag Gumber, "Climate Gentrification: From Theory to Empiricism in Miami-Dade County, Florida," *Environmental Research Letters* 13, no. 5 (April 2018), https://iopscience .iop.org/article/10.1088/1748-9326/aabb32/pdf.

29. Southeast Florida Regional Climate Change Compact Sea Level Rise Work Group, *Unified Sea Level Rise Projection Southeast Florida*

(February 2020), https://southeastfloridaclimatecompact.org/wp
-content/uploads/2020/04/Sea-Level-Rise-Projection-Guidance
-Report_FINAL_02212020.pdf.

30. Mathew E. Hauer, "Migration Induced by Sea-Level Rise Could Reshape
the US Population Landscape," *Nature Climate Change* 7 (2017): 321–25.

31. Southern Poverty Law Center and Americans for Immigrant Justice,
*Prison by Any Other Name: A Report on South Florida's Detention Cen-
ters* (2019), https://www.splcenter.org/sites/default/files/cjr_fla
_detention_report-final_1.pdf.

32. The term "eco-apartheid" was popularized by Van Jones. See my application of it to Metro Phoenix in Andrew Ross, *Bird on Fire: Lessons from
the World's Least Sustainable City* (New York: Oxford University Press,
2012).

33. Marcos Santana, "Osceola County Takes a Peek at Potential NeoCity
Plans," *Orlando Sentinel*, July 10, 2017, https://www.orlandosentinel
.com/business/os-bz-kissimmee-sensor-research-campus-20170710
-story.html.

34. Colin Wolf and Monivette Cordeiro, "Orlando's Failed Bid for Amazon's
HQ2 Involved Millions in Tax Incentives, Free Land and a New High
School," *Orlando Weekly*, January 25, 2018, https://www.orlandoweekly
.com/Blogs/archives/2018/01/25/orlandos-failed-bid-for-amazons
-hq2-involved-millions-in-tax-incentives-free-land-and-a-new-high
-school.

35. Annie Martin, "UCF Seeks to Cut Ties with Struggling Manufacturing Facility BRIDG," *Orlando Sentinel*, February 20, 2020, https://www
.orlandosentinel.com/news/education/os-ne-ucf-bridg-20200220
-v2gjn4rjf5btbjgglprzniycqu-story.html; and Annie Martin, "Osceola
OKs Semiconductor Company to Take Over BRIDG from UCF,"
Orlando Sentinel, January 25, 2021, https://www.orlandosentinel
.com/news/education/os-ne-osceola-skywater-bridg-20210125
-65bxktwxmvebtd5vsckp5qkd5q-story.html.

36. Just before the pandemic, the county's courting of corporations in South
Korea appeared to pay off when the electronics giant LG announced
its interest in building a twenty-five-acre "smart town center" in
NeoCity. But that still leaves most of the five-hundred-acre site to fill.
Laura Kinsler, "Osceola Consultant Says LG's $800M Smart City Is a
Go," *GrowthSpotter*, February 6, 2020, https://www.growthspotter
.com/news/osceola-county-developments/gs-news-lg-neocity-report
-20200206-vglicxbc35hovaolc3wgryfkuq-story.html.

37. In 2017, phase one of Tavistock's master plan for Sunbridge had to be amended when Osceola officials concluded that its ratio of commercial to industrial land use was too high, and therefore likely to yield yet another concentration of retail or service-sector jobs. "We don't want to see more low-wage employment," declared Kerry Godwin, the county's director of planning. Sunbridge, he pointed out, "was set up to reverse that trend and create high-wage employment." Laura Kinsler, "Osceola Staff Wants Major Changes to Tavistock Sunbridge Plan," *GrowthSpotter*, May 19, 2017, https://www.growthspotter.com/projects/gs-osceola-staff-wants-major-changes-to-tavistock-sunbridge-plan-20170518-story.html.

38. In June 2021, Tavistock came back to the county with a request to amend the Northeast District Plan. Citing the impact of the coronavirus, the developer petitioned to reduce the plan's allotment for industrial and commercial space, and to increase the acreage permitted for retirement communities. Such a change would undermine the rationale of high-wage job creation that had driven the county's approval of the plan. Nadeen Yanes, "Osceola County Developer Wants to Change Plans to Huge 30,000-Home Development," *Click Orlando*, June 21, 2021, https://www.clickorlando.com/news/local/2021/06/21/osceola-county-developer-wants-to-change-plans-to-huge-30000-home-development/.

39. Osceola County, *Strategies for a Sustainable Future* (2017), http://osceola.solodev.net/core/fileparse.php/2731/urlt/111317_Osceola-CO-Strategies-For-A-Sustainable-Future-Final-Report_171026.pdf.

40. Kevin Spear, "Controversial Split Oak Forest Toll Road Likely Delayed until 2034," *Orlando Sentinel*, May 28, 2020, https://www.orlandosentinel.com/news/transportation/os-ne-cfx-split-oak-forest-parkway-20200528-a32y4hjznbavvavq43cz3hdnjq-story.html.

41. The commissioners' nontransparent actions prompted lawsuits from concerned citizens. Scott Powers, "Leader of Orange County's Split Oak Election to Osceola County's Opponents: 'Get Ready,'" *Florida Politics*, August 26, 2020, https://floridapolitics.com/archives/362158-leader-of-orange-countys-split-oak-election-to-osceola-countys-opponents-get-ready.

42. See Gary Mormino's excellent chapter on "The Beach," in *Land of Sunshine, State of Dreams*, pp. 301–67.

43. Dan Sweeney, "Florida Has Spent More Than $100 Million Pouring More Sand onto Beaches in the Past Three Years," *South Florida Sun Sentinel*, June 8, 2018, https://www.sun-sentinel.com/news/sound-off-south-florida/fl-reg-beach-renourishment-20180608-story.html.

44. Lizette Alvarez, "Where Sand Is Gold, the Reserves Are Running Dry," *New York Times*, August 24, 2013, https://www.nytimes.com/2013/08/25/us/where-sand-is-gold-the-coffers-are-running-dry-in-florida.html; and Maria Bakkalapulo, "'Sand Wars': The Battle to Replenish Florida's Beaches amid Climate Crisis," *The Guardian*, October 25, 2019, https://www.theguardian.com/us-news/2019/oct/25/surfside-florida-beaches-climate-crisis-sea-levels.

45. Kevin Derby, "Rubio Brings Back Proposal to Import Foreign Sand for Beach Renourishment," *Sunshine State News*, September 14, 2019, http://www.sunshinestatenews.com/story/marco-rubio-brings-back-proposal-import-foreign-sand-renourish-beaches.

CONCLUSION: HOMES FOR ALL

1. Jack Witthaus, "As Banks Shy Away, Private Equity Steps In to Fund More Orlando Real Estate Deals," *Orlando Business Journal*, September 23, 2020, https://www.bizjournals.com/orlando/news/2020/09/23/orlando-commercial-projects-fewer-bank-loans.html.

2. Emily Benfer et al., "The COVID-19 Eviction Crisis," Aspen Institute, August 7, 2020, https://www.aspeninstitute.org/blog-posts/the-covid-19-eviction-crisis-an-estimated-30-40-million-people-in-america-are-at-risk/.

3. Not untypically, Florida proved to be a worst-case scenario because state law requires tenants facing eviction to pay the rent they owe into the court registry just to get a hearing for their case. If the tenants can't come up with the funds within five days, landlords are entitled to an immediate default judgment for removal of the tenant.

4. Gretchen Morgenson, "Large Corporate Landlords Have Filed 10,000 Eviction Actions in Five States since September," *NBC News*, October 26, 2020, https://www.nbcnews.com/business/personal-finance/large-corporate-landlords-have-filed-10–000-eviction-actions-five-n1244711.

5. In January 2021, California took a big step in providing relief to low-income tenants by offering to pay landlords 80 percent of pandemic back rent. "COVID-19 Tenant Relief Act (CTRA)," California Apartment Association (January 29, 2021), https://caanet.org/ctra/.

6. Rob Warnock, "Rent Debt & Racial Inequality in 2021," *Apartment List*, January 14, 2021, https://www.apartmentlist.com/research/rent-debt-2021.

7. During the first year of the pandemic, rents softened and declined considerably in several high-price coastal cities, though with little evidence of a collapse, while, in midsized Sunbelt metro regions, rent growth

accelerated. Chris Salviati, Igor Popov, and Rob Warnock, "National Rent Report," *Apartment List*, February 25, 2021, https://www.apartmentlist .com/research/national-rent-data. With low inventory nationwide (and Central Florida's housing supply at a fifteen-year low), housing prices jumped when closings restarted, raising the bar even higher for first-time buyers, while pandemic flight from metro cores boosted the prospect of a new spurt in single-family rentals.

8. In *The Housing Question* (1872), Friedrich Engels argued that, since the capitalist system was the *cause* of the "housing crisis" for working people, capitalism could not be expected to solve it.

9. The United States signed the UN's International Covenant on Economic, Social and Cultural Rights (1966), which recognizes a right to adequate housing, but it has never been ratified by Congress. On the right to housing, see Working Group on Housing, *The Right to Housing: A Blueprint for Housing the Nation* (Washington, DC: Institute for Policy Studies, 1989); Rachel G. Bratt, Michael E. Stone, and Chester Hartman, *A Right to Housing: Foundations for a New Social Agenda* (Philadelphia: Temple University Press, 2006); and David Madden and Peter Marcuse, *In Defense of Housing: The Politics of Crisis* (London: Verso, 2016).

10. The Housing Justice National Platform (https://www.housingjustice platform.org/) was endorsed by dozens of movement groups and organizations, including the Alliance for Housing Justice, Action Center for Race and the Economy, Center for Popular Democracy, People's Action, Right to the City Alliance, Homes for All, and MH Action. For an overview of the issues, see Homes for All and Right to the City Alliance, *Communities over Commodities: People-Driven Alternatives to an Unjust Housing System* (March 2018). Regionally, the Florida Housing Justice Alliance includes Miami Workers Center, Community Justice Project, Organize Florida, MHAction, SEIU FL, New Florida Majority, Family Action Network Movement, Struggle for Miami's Affordable and Sustainable Housing (SMASH), and Catalyst Miami.

11. See Jennifer Schuetz, "Cost, Crowding, or Commuting? Housing Stress on the Middle Class" (Washington, DC: Brookings Institution, May 7, 2019), https://www.brookings.edu/research/cost-crowding -or-commuting-housing-stress-on-the-middle-class/.

12. Kate Santich and Adelaide Chen, "Fastest-Growing Metro in the Nation? The Villages," *Orlando Sentinel*, April 18, 2019, https://www .orlandosentinel.com/news/os-ne-the-villages-fastest-growing-us -metro-20190417-story.html.

13. Amee Chew and Sarah Truehaft, *Our Homes, Our Future: How Rent Control Can Build Stable, Healthy Communities* (Center for Popular Democracy, Right to the City Alliance, and Policy Link, February 2019), https://populardemocracy.org/sites/default/files/OurHomesOurFuture_Web-fin.pdf.

14. According to Florida's preemptive version, relaxations of the rent control ban are only permitted in order "to eliminate an existing housing emergency which is so grave as to constitute a serious menace to the general public." Seizing on the evidence that COVID-19 was indeed proving to be a "serious menace," Organize Florida lobbied commissioners in Orange County and Osceola County to declare an emergency and place a rent freeze proposition on the 2020 ballot. Sounding the alarm about "market distortion" from government action, lobbyists from Orlando Regional Realtor Association and the Apartment Association of Greater Orlando leaned hard on Orange County commissioners to block the proposition. Osceola, as ever, proved to be an even heavier lift. Only one commissioner, Peggy Choudhry, showed any interest, and so the organizers' initiative went nowhere. Stephen Hudak and Caroline Glenn, "Affordable Housing Company to Raise Rent, Just as Orange County Shoots Down Rent Freeze," *Orlando Sentinel*, June 23, 2020, https://www.orlandosentinel.com/coronavirus/jobs-economy/os-ne-company-raises-rent-bonilla-proposes-freeze-20200623-r7dod5qtnzcdffak74vb6sta74-story.html.

15. See Dennis Keating and Peter Marcuse, "The Permanent Housing Crisis: The Failures of Conservatism and the Limits of Liberalism," in Bratt et al., *A Right to Housing*, pp. 139–62. Even Section 8 housing vouchers, which allow recipients to rent anywhere, are a boon to private landlords, who are prone to overcharging voucher holders for rent. More than 2.2 million of these vouchers are provided to ELI (Extremely Low Income) families as part of the largest federal program of assistance to renters, but they still reach only 22 percent of those eligible. Ryan Cooper and Peter Gowan, "How to Solve the Housing Problem," *Jacobin*, Spring 2019, https://jacobinmag.com/2019/06/how-to-solve-the-housing-problem/.

16. See Vicki Been, Ingrid Gould Ellen, and Katherine O'Regan, "Supply Skepticism: Housing Supply and Affordability" (NYU Furman Center, August 2018), https://furmancenter.org/research/publication/supply-skepticismnbsp-housing-supply-and-affordability.

17. Dan Parolek and Arthur C. Nelson, *Missing Middle Housing: Thinking*

Big and Building Small to Respond to Today's Housing Crisis (Washington, DC: Island Press, 2020).

18. Emily Badger and Quoctrung Bui, "Cities Start to Question an American Ideal: A House with a Yard on Every Lot," *New York Times*, June 18, 2019, https://www.nytimes.com/interactive/2019/06/18/upshot /cities-across-america-question-single-family-zoning.html.

19. Yonah Freemark, "Upzoning Chicago: Impacts of a Zoning Reform on Property Values and Housing Construction," *Urban Affairs Review* (2019); and Andrés Rodríguez-Pose and Michael Storper, "Housing, Urban Growth and Inequalities: The Limits to Deregulation and Upzoning in Reducing Economic and Spatial Inequality," *Urban Studies* 57, no. 2 (February 2020): 223–48. For a rebuttal of the latter, see Michael Manville, Michael Lens, and Paavo Monkkonen, "Zoning and Affordability: A Reply to Storper and Rodríguez-Pose," *Urban Studies* 57, no. 11 (August 2020).

20. Stefanos Chen, "The People vs. Big Development," *New York Times*, February 7, 2020, https://www.nytimes.com/2020/02/07/realestate /the-people-vs-big-development.html. In California, similar concerns about gentrification contributed to the failure in 2020 of a legislative measure (SB 50) aimed at increasing density around transit corridors. Liam Dillon and Taryn Luna, "California Bill to Dramatically Increase Home Building Fails for the Third Year in a Row," *Los Angeles Times*, January 29, 2020, https://www.latimes.com/california/story/2020-01-29 /high-profile-california-housing-bill-to-allow-mid-rise-apartments -near-transit-falls-short.

21. In November 2019, Minnesota representative Ilhan Omar introduced the Homes for All Act, a New 21st Century Public Housing Vision, which authorizes funding for twelve million new affordable homes over ten years, most of which would take the form of public housing, https://omar.house.gov/media/press-releases/rep-ilhan-omar -introduces-homes-all-act-new-21st-century-public-housing-vision. And in July 2020, an Ocasio-Cortez bill to repeal the Clinton-era Faircloth Amendment (which outlawed the building of any new public housing unless old units were demolished) finally passed in the House. Julia Conley, "Fair Housing Advocates Celebrate Passage of AOC's Repeal of Faircloth Amendment," *Common Dreams*, July 2, 2020, https://www.commondreams.org/news/2020/07/02/fair-housing -advocates-celebrate-passage-aocs-repeal-faircloth-amendment.

22. Gianpaolo Baiocchi and Jacob Carlson, *The Case for a Social Housing*

Development Authority (Urban Democracy Lab, New York University, 2020), https://urbandemos.nyu.edu/wp-content/uploads/2020/11/SHDA-whitepaper-Nov2020.pdf.

23. The task force was set up to implement some of the recommendations made by a tri-county commission, convened in 2016 by Orange County mayor Teresa Jacobs. Despite the abject failure of the local real estate industry to deliver housing at economical prices, the commission was asked to look to the private sector to get the job done. Documentation of the work of the commission, which met over a two-year period, can be found at https://www.orangecountyfl.net/NeighborsHousing/RegionalAffordableHousingInitiative.aspx#.XjeAdzJKjX4.

24. Caroline Glenn, "Orange County OKs Plan to Set Up Affordable Housing Trust Fund, Add 30,000 Places to Live," *Orlando Sentinel*, December 17, 2019, https://www.orlandosentinel.com/business/os-bz-housing-for-all-plan-approved-20191217-t4wpcipxjzfxlnyh2t3saafsye-story.html. In February 2020, just before the pandemic, another $100 million housing impact fund was announced to help finance affordable housing through the new Central Florida Regional Housing Trust. "After studying efforts elsewhere around the nation," leaders of the initiative once again "decided the Central Florida response needed to be driven by the private sector." Kate Santich, "$100 Million Housing Fund Will Target Central Florida Affordability Crisis," *Orlando Sentinel*, February 4, 2020, https://www.orlandosentinel.com/news/breaking-news/os-ne-new-affordable-housing-impact-fund-central-florida-2020 0204-2lkxpmugnzb27odhycr7wji6tu-story.html.

25. Indeed, from 2007 onward, Tallahassee's lawmakers consistently raided the Sadowski Housing Trust Fund, set up in 1992 to collect fees from real estate sales to assist with affordable housing development. The GOP's annual custom of sweeping these funds—depriving Florida's counties of an estimated $3 billion of assistance—looked to have ended in 2020, when the state legislature finally agreed to resume the payments, but Governor DeSantis reclaimed the entire $225 million in his pandemic budget. Steven Lemongello et al., "Gov. DeSantis Slashes $1 billion from State Budget amid Coronavirus Outbreak," *Orlando Sentinel*, June 29, 2020, https://www.orlandosentinel.com/politics/os-ne-desantis-budget-vetoes-20200629-gz3qge6rczerzpcgmukb3esquu-story.html#nws=true.

26. The number of extremely low-income households had dropped from 70,000 in 2017 to about 58,400 in 2018, the year used for data for the

2020 rankings. Ryan Lynch, "No Longer the Worst," *Orlando Business Journal*, March 12, 2020, https://www.bizjournals.com/orlando/news /2020/03/12/no-longer-the-worst-local-affordable-housing.html.

27. An even bigger push came in the 2018 amendments to the county's Comprehensive Plan, which introduced four new land-use designations—Neighborhood Center, Community Center, Urban Center, and Employment Center—each with its own form-based codes for regulating building types and determining the mix of residential and commercial units. As a way to reduce the steep cost of commuting, commercial development, for example, will not be permitted outside of the Urban or Employment Centers. It is hoped that high-density clustering in these centers, especially the urban ones, will yield less expensive housing and transportation. Within the county's Urban Growth Boundary, developers are allowed to build higher and denser—up to twenty-five units per acre, and fifty on the 192 corridor itself. Osceola County Comprehensive Plan 2040, https://library .municode.com/fl/osceola_county/codes/comprehensive_plan.

28. Currently, affordable housing developers can draw on programs such as the State Apartment Incentive Loan (SAIL), State Housing Incentives Partnership (SHIP), Multifamily Mortgage Revenue Bonds, Elderly Housing Community Loan, and the Predevelopment Loan Program.

29. In the year before the pandemic, developers had finally begun to buy up motel properties or adjacent parcels and were looking to piece together financing for conversions. Laura Kinsler, "South Florida Investor Looking to Convert Two Kissimmee Hotels into Workforce Housing," *GrowthSpotter*, July 9, 2019, https://www.growthspotter.com /news/osceola-county-developments/gs-news-lionsgate-kissimmee -20190709-drtl6vqpovfvthrqkhxqx227rm-story.html; Laura Kinsler, "More W192 Hotels Looking to Convert to Workforce Housing," *GrowthSpotter*, February 21, 2020, https://www.growthspotter.com /news/osceola-county-developments/gs-news-motel-conversions -20200221-tcmy3ogrqbandoqtrtwkjvq3aq-story.html; and Jack Witthaus, "Another Hotel near Disney to Morph into Apartments," *Orlando Business Journal*, February 5, 2020, https://www.bizjournals.com/orlando /news/paid-content/small-business-survey/2019/another-hotel-near -disney-to-morph-into-apartments.html. Not all the conversion plans are for affordable housing, however. In 2020, the school board rejected a developer's request to lower impact fees for a conversion that would offer upscale apartments.

30. During the pandemic, authors of a UCLA study argued that Los Angeles should convert the property use of low-occupancy hotels to affordable housing by using eminent domain. Ananya Roy, Gary Blasi, Jonny Coleman, and Elana Eden, *Hotel California: Housing the Crisis* (Los Angeles: UCLA Luskin Institute on Inequality and Democracy, July 9, 2020), https://challengeinequality.luskin.ucla.edu/2020/07/09/hotel-california/. Subsequently, the city council earmarked $105 million from the state's Project Homekey to buy up ten motel properties. "LA Will Buy Mostly-Vacant Motels for Project Homekey," *The Real Deal*, October 23, 2020, https://therealdeal.com/la/2020/10/23/la-will-buy-mostly-vacant-motels-for-project-homekey/.

31. A similar idea for vacant Airbnbs was adopted in Lisbon. See Feargus O'Sullivan, "Lisbon Has a Plan to Reclaim Housing from Airbnb," *Bloomberg CityLab*, July 8, 2020, https://www.bloomberg.com/news/articles/2020-07-08/lisbon-s-plan-to-reclaim-vacation-rentals-for-housing.

32. Matthew Desmond, "The Tenants Who Evicted Their Landlord," *New York Times*, October 13, 2020, https://www.nytimes.com/2020/10/13/magazine/rental-housing-crisis-minneapolis.html.

33. Peter Calthorpe and Joe DiStefano, "Revolutionizing Transit and Solving the Silicon Valley Housing Crisis," Urban Footprint, August 17, 2018, https://urbanfootprint.com/revolutionizing-transit-while-solving-the-housing-crisis/.

34. Harry Truman, "Special Message to the Congress upon Signing the Housing and Rent Act," June 30, 1947, Harry S. Truman Library and Museum, https://www.trumanlibrary.gov/library/public-papers/131/special-message-congress-upon-signing-housing-and-rent-act.

35. Laura Kusisto, "Investors Are Buying More of the U.S. Housing Market Than Ever Before," *Wall Street Journal*, June 20, 2019, https://www.wsj.com/articles/investors-are-buying-more-of-the-u-s-housing-market-than-ever-before-11561023120.

36. Rana Foroohar, "US Private Equity Moves into Trailer Parks," *Financial Times*, May 29, 2019, https://www.ft.com/content/7addf0c8-77d6-11e9-be7d-6d846537acab.

37. Keeanga-Yamahtta Taylor describes how after the 1968 Fair Housing Act outlawed these discriminatory practices, the "free market" found ways to profit, through "predatory inclusion," from housing segregation, in *Race for Profit: How Banks and the Real Estate Industry Undermined Black Homeownership* (Chapel Hill: University of North Carolina Press, 2019). Books that describe discriminatory government policy from the

1930s include Richard Rothstein, *The Color of Law: A Forgotten History of How Our Government Segregated America* (New York: W. W. Norton, 2017), and Charles Abrams, *Forbidden Neighbors: A Study of Prejudice in Housing* (New York: Harper and Brothers, 1955).

38. Nicholas Dagen Bloom, Fritz Umbach, and Lawrence J. Vale, eds., *Public Housing Myths: Perception, Reality, and Social Policy* (Ithaca, NY: Cornell University Press, 2015).

39. "Housing as a Verb" is collected in John F. C. Turner and Robert Fichte, eds., *Freedom to Build: Dweller Control of the Housing Process* (New York: Macmillan, 1972).

40. John Emmeus Davis, ed., *The Affordable City: Toward a Third Sector Housing Policy* (Philadelphia: Temple University Press, 1994).

41. For example, 60 percent of Viennese still live in government-subsidized buildings, while in the Netherlands, social housing accounts for 32 percent of the total stock and some 75 percent of the rental stock in the country. See Peter Dreier, "Why America Needs More Social Housing," *Prospect*, April 16, 2018, https://prospect.org/infrastructure/america-needs-social-housing/.

ACKNOWLEDGMENTS

My biggest debt is to the residents of Osceola County and environs who took the time to talk with me during the reporting for *Sunbelt Blues*. They are too many to list here, but I will mention those who made a special effort to be available and to offer additional assistance: Cookie Kelly, Laurel Rousseau, Hector Torres and his family, Valerie Anderson, Susan Caswell, Lance and Karin Boyer, Mary Downey, Angie Etman, Raul Salas, Charlie Green, Sharon Harley, Eric Clinton, Jeremy Haicken, Gabby Alcantara-Anderson, Mike Beaver, Peter Sharma, Peggy Choudhry, Karina Veaudry, Robert Holborn, and Gary Graham. Though not in the main narrative, Wendy Brandon was a savvy interlocutor and provider of good cheer in Winter Park.

Gianpaolo Baiocchi gave the manuscript a keen collegial reading when I needed it the most.

I am grateful to the Advanced Research Collaborative at the CUNY Graduate Center, and to its director, Don Robotham, for hosting me while I was writing a draft of the book in the fall of 2019. Tyler Bray once again proved what a remarkable research assistant he is. His keen eye and knowing take on the material were indispensable to the evolution and final form of the book.

Many thanks to Constance Penley, who introduced me to her patch of Central Florida thirty-five years ago, and whose fond encouragement of my own interest in the region over the years has been key.

I'm grateful that I finally had the chance to work with my editor, Sara Bershtel, and to learn firsthand why she is a legend in the publishing world. She asked for a lot, but she was almost always right. Grigory Tovbis, her associate, was just as scrupulous, and made sure the manuscript never veered off the main route.

Thanks to Alice Whitwham and Elyse Cheney for their initial enthusiasm and for Alice's smooth handling of the project when it was still an agent's book proposal.

My partner, Maggie Gray, thoughtfully read parts of the manuscript and, as always, kept me on track. But she contributed much more than that, including a summer spent in Pinellas County that tested her mettle.

INDEX

Note: Page numbers followed by "n" indicate endnotes.

W192 Development Authority, 170
Wall Street, 3–6, 39, 130–33, 142–49,
	202, 211–12
	business of extraction, 133–38
	private equity firms, 6
Wall Street Journal, 133, 142
Walmart, 23, 25, 32, 83, 85, 120
Walt Disney Company, 20–21, 97, 101,
	159, 181
	See also Disney World
Waltrip, Mark, 165
Warnock, Rob, 81
Warren, Brianna, Melissa, and Randy,
	17–18, 25–26
Washington, Cole, 113
Washington, DC, 72
Washington, George, 2
Washington Post, 117
Wawa, 94
welfare housing, 51
	See also housing

West Coast, 19
Western Kentucky, 19
Westgate Vacation Villas, 164–65
West Palm Beach, Florida,
	191
West Virginia, 94
Whyte, Don, 187, 189, 190
Witwatersrand Basin, South Africa, 97
Wodehouse, P. G., 153
Wooden, Dewey, 89
woods dwellers, 74
Wooster, Bertie, 153–54
workforce housing, 51, 172
working-class households, 8
World War II, 205
Wright, James, 226n10
Wyndham, 164
Wyoming, 37

Yamasee, 78
Yuchi, 78

ABOUT THE AUTHOR

ANDREW ROSS is a professor of social and cultural analysis at New York University and a social activist. A contributor to *The New York Times*, *The Guardian*, and *The Nation*, he is the author of many books, including *The Celebration Chronicles*, *Bird on Fire: Lessons from the World's Least Sustainable City*, and *Nice Work If You Can Get It: Life and Labor in Precarious Times*.